JOE HALDEMAN • MARVANO

THE FOREVER WAR

TITAN
COMICS

THE FOREVER
WAR

9781785860898

Published by Titan Comics
A division of Titan Publishing Group Ltd.
144 Southwark St.
London
SE1 0UP

THE FOREVER WAR
Originally published in French as: The Forever War
© 1988 ÉDITIONS DUPUIS / MARVANO / HALDEMAN
English text © 1990 Haldeman

A CIP catalogue record for this title is available from the British Library

First edition: December 2017

10 9 8 7 6 5 4 3 2 1

Printed in China.
Titan Comics.

TITAN COMICS

EDITOR: LIZZIE KAYE
DESIGNER: DONNA ASKEM

Senior Comics Editor: Andrew James
Titan Comics Editorial: Lauren Bowes, Lauren McPhee
Production Assistant: Natalie Bolger
Production Controller: Peter James
Production Supervisior: Maria Pearson
Senior Production Controller: Jackie Flook
Art Director: Oz Browne
Senior Sales Manager: Steve Tothill
Press Officer: Will O'Mullane
Direct Sales & Marketing Manager: Ricky Claydon
Brand Manager: Chris Thompson
Publishing Manager: Darryl Tothill
Publishing Director: Chris Teather
Operations Director: Leigh Baulch
Executive Director: Vivian Cheung
Publisher: Nick Landau

WWW.TITAN-COMICS.COM

Follow us on Twitter @ComicsTitan

Visit us at facebook.com/comicstitan

Titan
COMICS

JOE HALDEMAN • MARVANO

THE FOREVER WAR

WRITER

JOE HALDEMAN

ARTIST

MARVANO

WITH

GAY HALDEMAN

LETTERER

CAT CONNERY

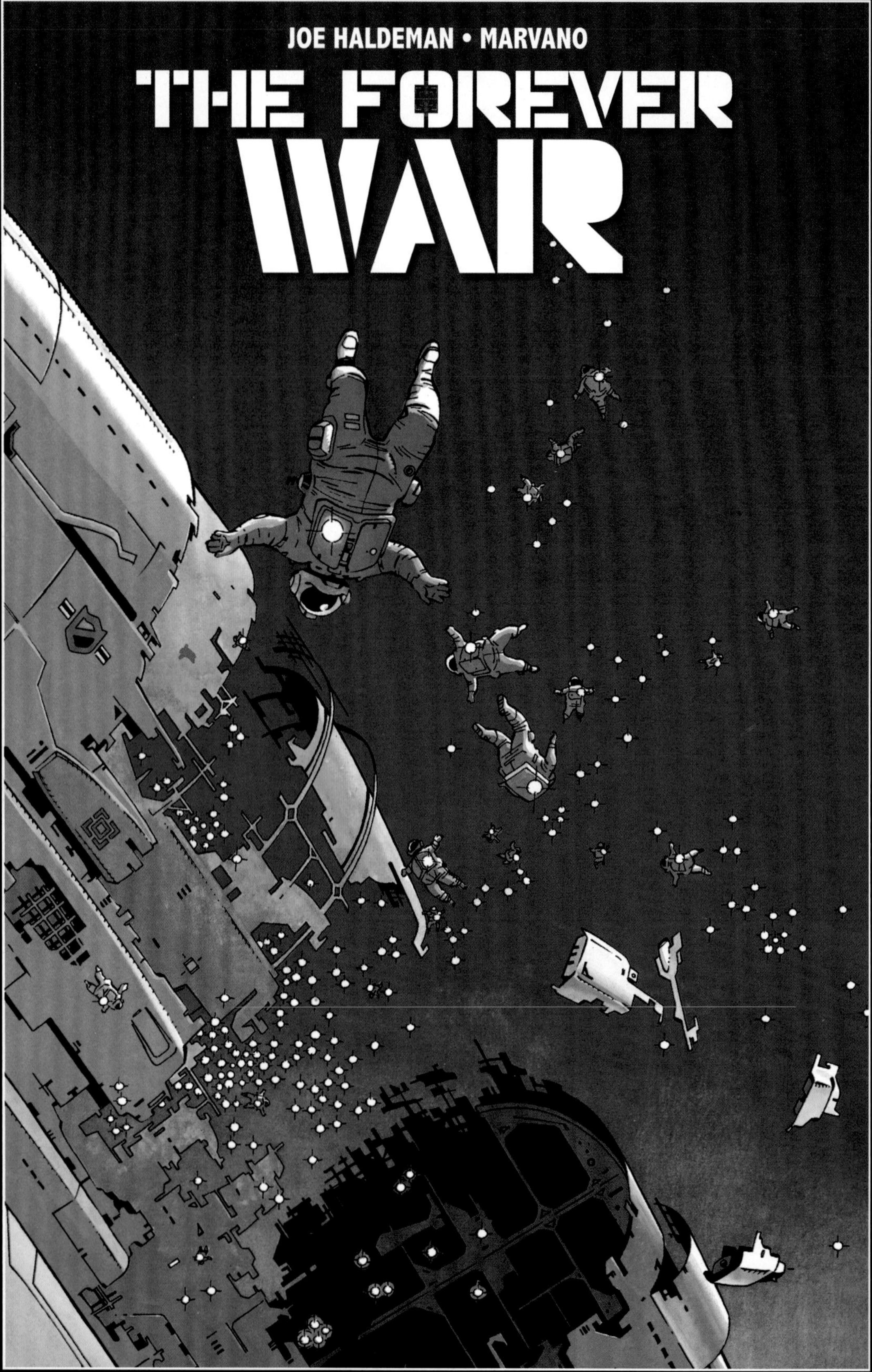
JOE HALDEMAN • MARVANO
THE FOREVER
WAR

ILLSTRATION BY: MARVANO

DEATH STRUCK ON THE THIRD DAY OF OUR INSTRUCTION ON CERBERUS.

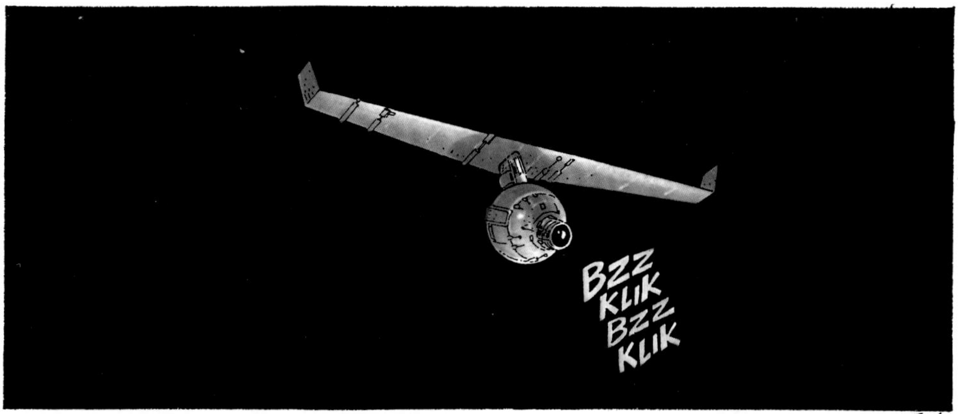
BZZ KLIK BZZ KLIK

WE WERE LEARNING TO DIG THE FROZEN GROUND OF THE GREEN PLANET. BOVANOVITCH HAD JUST SET SOME EXPLOSIVE CHARGES AT THE BOTTOM OF THE CRATER.

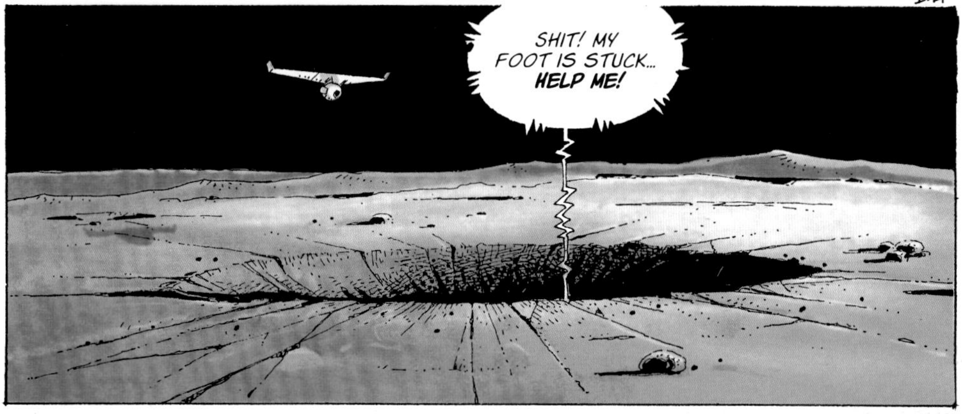
SHIT! MY FOOT IS STUCK... **HELP ME!**

WE COULDN'T HELP HER... NOT WITH A TWENTY MICROTON CHARGE ABOUT TO EXPLODE AT THE BOTTOM OF THAT HOLE. OUR INSTRUCTOR, SERGEANT CORTEZ, DID WHAT HE COULD.

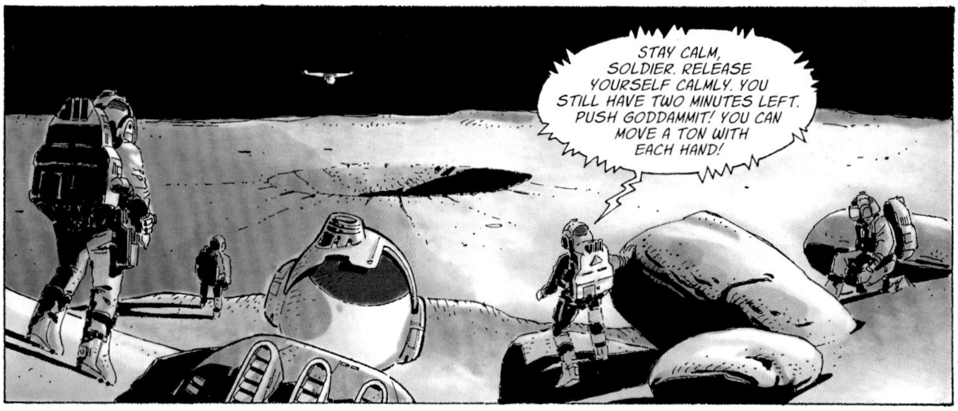
STAY CALM, SOLDIER. RELEASE YOURSELF CALMLY. YOU STILL HAVE TWO MINUTES LEFT. PUSH GODDAMMIT! YOU CAN MOVE A TON WITH EACH HAND!

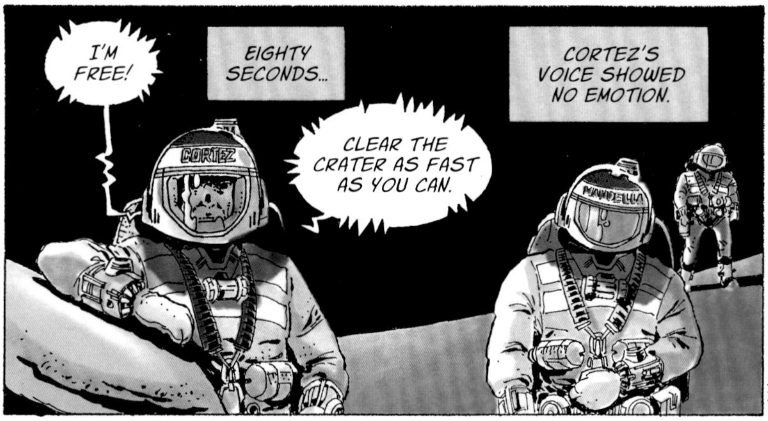
I'M FREE!
EIGHTY SECONDS...
CORTEZ
CLEAR THE CRATER AS FAST AS YOU CAN.
CORTEZ'S VOICE SHOWED NO EMOTION.

HE CALLED BACK THE REMOTE-CONTROLLED CAMERA...WITH IT, WE COULD ANALYZE THE CONSEQUENCES OF THE MISTAKE.

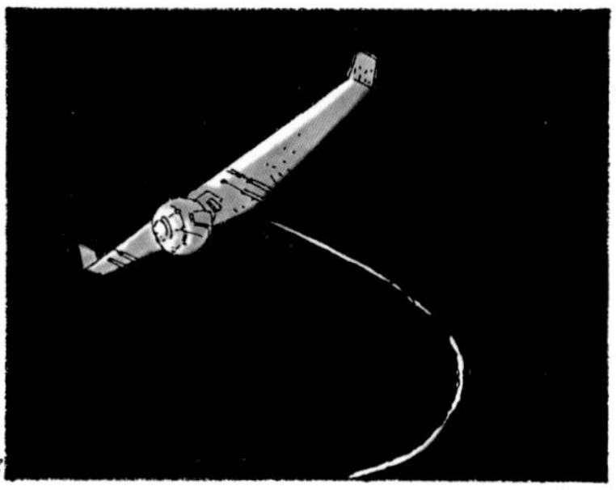

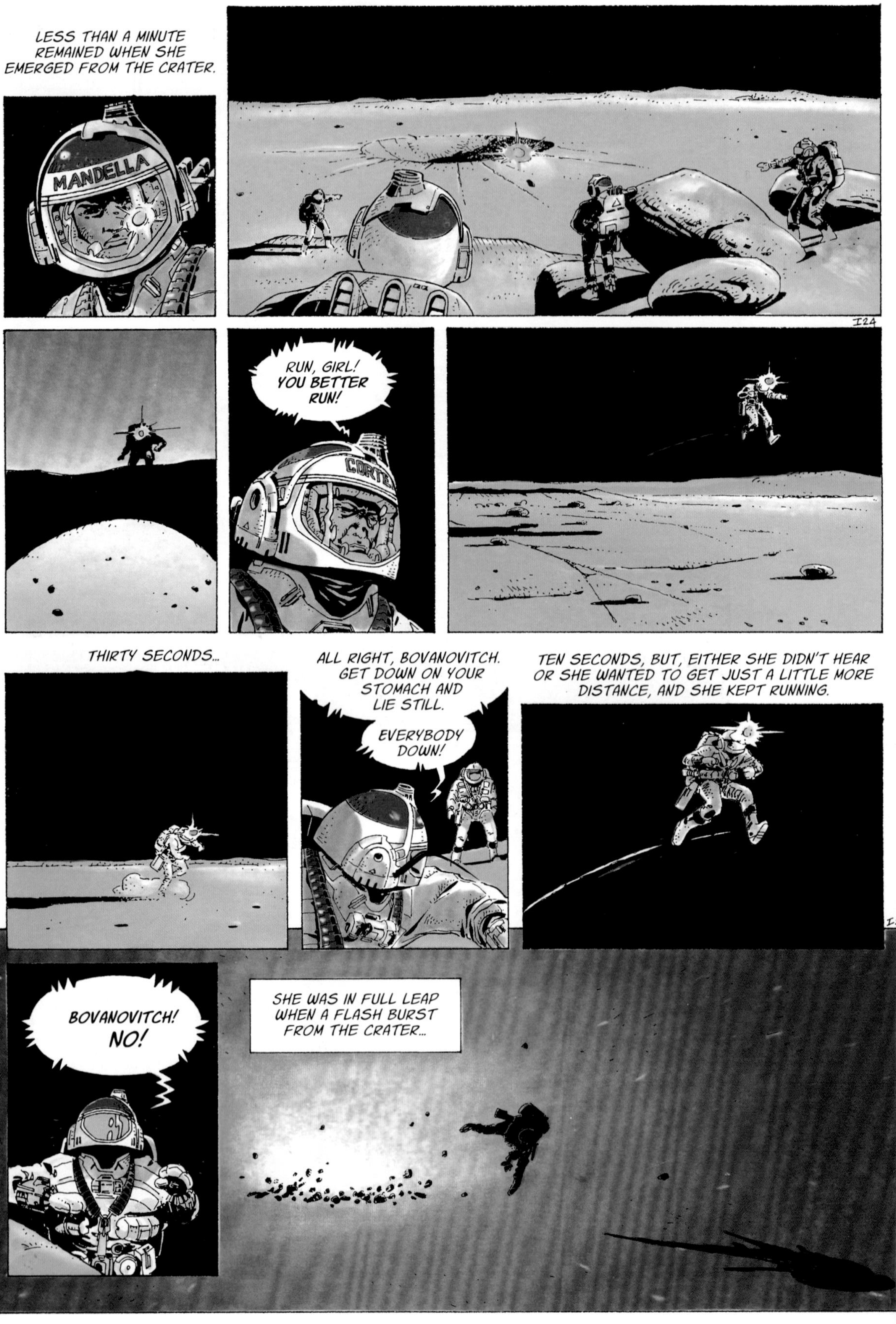
LESS THAN A MINUTE REMAINED WHEN SHE EMERGED FROM THE CRATER.
MANDELLA
RUN, GIRL! YOU BETTER RUN!
CORTE
THIRTY SECONDS...
ALL RIGHT, BOVANOVITCH. GET DOWN ON YOUR STOMACH AND LIE STILL.
EVERYBODY DOWN!
TEN SECONDS, BUT, EITHER SHE DIDN'T HEAR OR SHE WANTED TO GET JUST A LITTLE MORE DISTANCE, AND SHE KEPT RUNNING.
BOVANOVITCH! NO!
SHE WAS IN FULL LEAP WHEN A FLASH BURST FROM THE CRATER...

SOMETHING BIG
HIT HER BELOW
THE NECK.

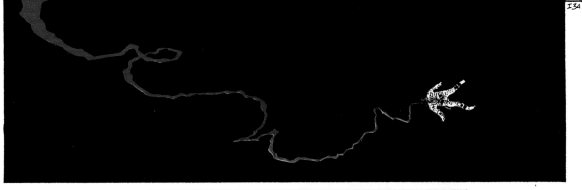

I3A

HER HEADLESS BODY SPUN
OFF END OVER END THROUGH
SPACE, TRAILING A SCARLET
SPIRAL OF FLASH-FROZEN
BLOOD THAT SETTLED
GRACEFULLY TO THE GROUND.

WE FOLLOWED
ITS TRACK: A
TRAIL OF SCARLET
CRYSTALLINE POWDER.
AT THE END OF
THE RED TRACK, WE
GATHERED ROCKS
TO COVER THE POOR
THING THAT WAS
LYING THERE.

I3B

THAT NIGHT
CORTEZ DIDN'T
LECTURE US;
DIDN'T EVEN
SHOW UP
FOR NIGHT-
CHOP. NOBODY
WAS REALLY
HUNGRY...

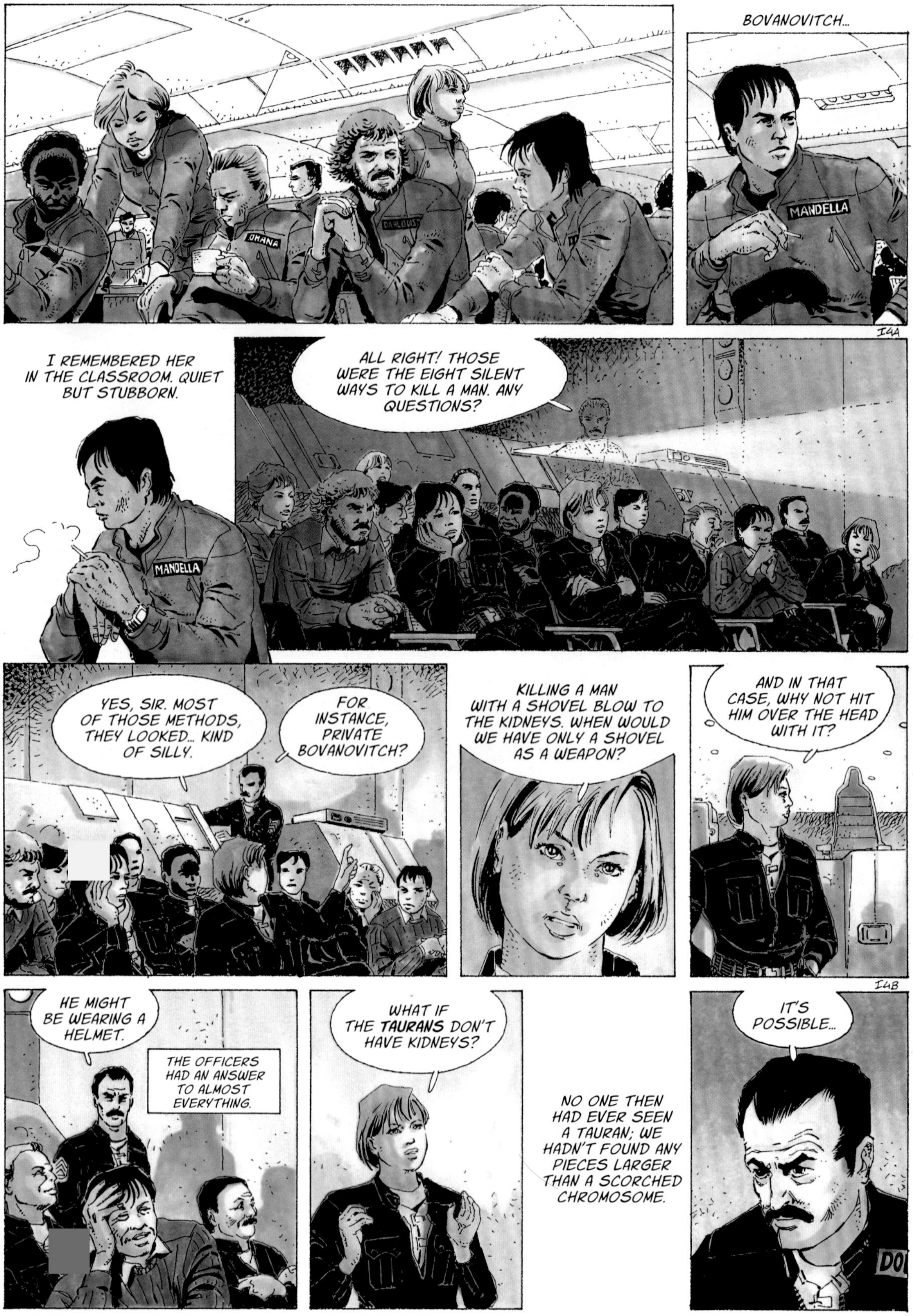
BOVANOVITCH...
MANDELLA
I4A
I REMEMBERED HER IN THE CLASSROOM. QUIET BUT STUBBORN.
MANDELLA
ALL RIGHT! THOSE WERE THE EIGHT SILENT WAYS TO KILL A MAN. ANY QUESTIONS?
YES, SIR. MOST OF THOSE METHODS, THEY LOOKED... KIND OF SILLY.
FOR INSTANCE, PRIVATE BOVANOVITCH?
KILLING A MAN WITH A SHOVEL BLOW TO THE KIDNEYS. WHEN WOULD WE HAVE ONLY A SHOVEL AS A WEAPON?
AND IN THAT CASE, WHY NOT HIT HIM OVER THE HEAD WITH IT?
I4B
HE MIGHT BE WEARING A HELMET.
THE OFFICERS HAD AN ANSWER TO ALMOST EVERYTHING.
WHAT IF THE **TAURANS** DON'T HAVE KIDNEYS?
NO ONE THEN HAD EVER SEEN A TAURAN; WE HADN'T FOUND ANY PIECES LARGER THAN A SCORCHED CHROMOSOME.
IT'S POSSIBLE...

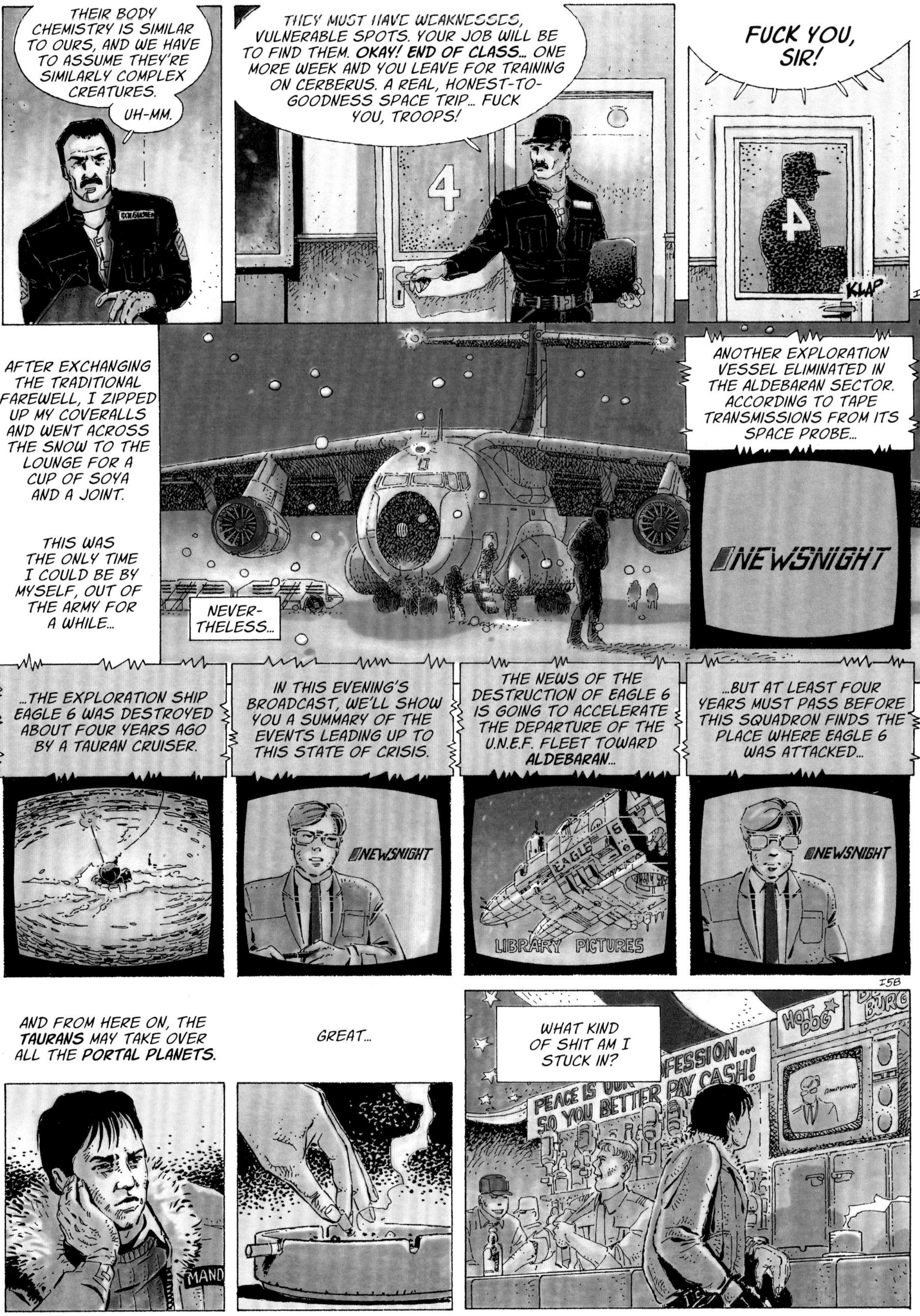
THEIR BODY CHEMISTRY IS SIMILAR TO OURS, AND WE HAVE TO ASSUME THEY'RE SIMILARLY COMPLEX CREATURES.
UH-MM.
THEY MUST HAVE WEAKNESSES, VULNERABLE SPOTS. YOUR JOB WILL BE TO FIND THEM. OKAY! END OF CLASS... ONE MORE WEEK AND YOU LEAVE FOR TRAINING ON CERBERUS. A REAL, HONEST-TO-GOODNESS SPACE TRIP... FUCK YOU, TROOPS!
4
FUCK YOU, SIR!
4
KLAP
AFTER EXCHANGING THE TRADITIONAL FAREWELL, I ZIPPED UP MY COVERALLS AND WENT ACROSS THE SNOW TO THE LOUNGE FOR A CUP OF SOYA AND A JOINT.
THIS WAS THE ONLY TIME I COULD BE BY MYSELF, OUT OF THE ARMY FOR A WHILE...
NEVER-THELESS...
ANOTHER EXPLORATION VESSEL ELIMINATED IN THE ALDEBARAN SECTOR. ACCORDING TO TAPE TRANSMISSIONS FROM ITS SPACE PROBE...
NEWSNIGHT
...THE EXPLORATION SHIP EAGLE 6 WAS DESTROYED ABOUT FOUR YEARS AGO BY A TAURAN CRUISER.
IN THIS EVENING'S BROADCAST, WE'LL SHOW YOU A SUMMARY OF THE EVENTS LEADING UP TO THIS STATE OF CRISIS.
NEWSNIGHT
THE NEWS OF THE DESTRUCTION OF EAGLE 6 IS GOING TO ACCELERATE THE DEPARTURE OF THE U.N.E.F. FLEET TOWARD ALDEBARAN...
EAGLE 6
LIBRARY PICTURES
...BUT AT LEAST FOUR YEARS MUST PASS BEFORE THIS SQUADRON FINDS THE PLACE WHERE EAGLE 6 WAS ATTACKED...
NEWSNIGHT
AND FROM HERE ON, THE TAURANS MAY TAKE OVER ALL THE PORTAL PLANETS.
MAND
GREAT...
WHAT KIND OF SHIT AM I STUCK IN?
HOT DOG
PEACE IS OUR PROFESSION... SO YOU BETTER PAY CASH!

TYPICAL ARMY HALF LOGIC, HAVING US TRAIN IN THE COLD.

SURE, IT WAS GOING TO BE COLD WHERE WE WERE GOING, BUT NOT ICE-COLD OR SNOW-COLD.

A PORTAL PLANET REMAINS WITHIN A DEGREE OR TWO OF ABSOLUTE ZERO.

THE FIRST CHILL YOU FELT, YOU WERE **DEAD**.

THE COLLAPSAR JUMP WAS DISCOVERED IN 1998. IT IS THE ONLY WAY WE KNOW TO TRAVEL FROM STAR TO STAR, USING BLACK HOLES OR COLLAPSARS.

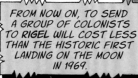

I WAS TEN YEARS OLD AT THAT TIME AND I STILL REMEMBER THAT EVENT. SOME THINGS YOU NEVER FORGET.

THE SPEED OF LIGHT IS ACTUALLY SURPASSED. MATHEMATICIANS HAVE TO REWRITE THE THEORY OF RELATIVITY.

 FROM NOW ON, TO SEND A GROUP OF COLONISTS TO *RIGEL* WILL COST LESS THAN THE HISTORIC FIRST LANDING ON THE MOON IN 1969.

THERE WERE PLENTY OF PEOPLE THE POLITICIANS WOULD LIKE TO SEE CARRY CIVILIZATION TO THE STARS--AS LONG AS THEY WOULD STAY THERE!

THE SPACE VESSELS ARE ACCOMPANIED BY AN AUTOMATIC PROBE THAT FOLLOWS SEVERAL MILLION KILOMETRES BEHIND THEM...

THE PORTAL PLANETS REVOLVE AROUND COLLAPSARS AND SERVE AS RELAY STATIONS FOR THE FARTHEST EXPEDITIONS.

THE PROBE IS PROGRAMMED TO RETURN AUTOMATICALLY IF A PILOT VESSEL IS DESTROYED.

THIS HAPPENED FOR THE FIRST TIME ON DECEMBER 10, 2007. A PROBE FELL IN THE PACIFIC...

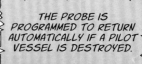

ARTIST'S IMPRESSION

ITS TAPES SIGNALED THAT THE COLUMBIA 4 HAD BEEN INTERCEPTED AND DESTROYED BY A SPACE SHIP...
NEWSNIGHT
...OF EXTRA-TERRESTRIAL ORIGIN. THIS ATTACK HAPPENED NEAR ALDEBARAN, IN THE TAURUS CONSTELLATION.
TAURUS
ALDEBARAN
SINCE THE TERM "ALDEBARANIAN" SOUNDED AWKWARD, THE ENEMIES WERE CALLED TAURANS.
THE ATTACK PROVOKED SHOCK ON EARTH. WE ARE NOT ALONE IN THE UNIVERSE...
NEWSNIGHT
OUR CHILDREN SIMPLY WERE LOOKING FOR OTHER LANDS TO IMPROVE, RIGHT?
QUICKLY, THE GROUNDS DEMANDED A REACTION, AND THE RHETORIC BECAME PASSIONATE...
KILL THE BASTARDS
THIS IS NOT GOD'S WILL
REVENGE
NUKE TAURUS NOW !
TAURANS for children and other
THIS SHIP WAS FULL OF MEN, OF WOMEN AND BABIES. THOSE... BARBARIANS HAD ASSASSINATED THEM! IT WAS A SIN!
THAT'S WHY THE GOVERNMENT DECIDED TO PUT INTO SERVICE SEVERAL SPACE CRUISERS...
FROM THIS TIME ON, THE COLONISTS WERE ESCORTED BY HEAVILY ARMED SHIPS...
THE U.N.E.F. WAS FOUNDED: THE UNITED NATIONS EXPLORATORY FORCE.
EMPHASIS ON "FORCE."
THE GENERAL ASSEMBLY OF THE U.N.E.F. DECIDED TO RECRUIT A CORPS OF ELITE...
WÀÀCK WACK WACK!
WHEW!... THE REST, I KNEW. DAMN IT.
HOT DOG
PEACE IS OUR... SO YOU BETTER PAY

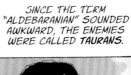

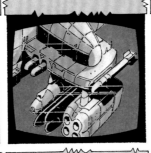

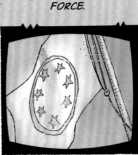

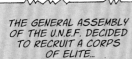

SOME BRIGHT LAD DECIDED THAT WE OUGHT TO FIELD AN ARMY OF FOOT SOLDIERS TO GUARD THE PORTAL PLANETS OF THE NEAREST COLLAPSARS...

THIS WAS THE ELITE CONSCRIPTION ACT OF 2009... AN INTENSIVE SELECTION PROCESS RECRUITED THE MOST ELITE DRAFTEES IN THE HISTORY OF WARFARE...

AND WE WERE IT: FIFTY MEN AND FIFTY WOMEN WITH IQS HIGHER THAN 150 AND BODIES OF UNUSUAL HEALTH AND STRENGTH.

...MINUS ONE... WITH BOVANOVITCH'S DEATH...

SLOGGING ELITELY THROUGH THE MUD AND SLUSH OF CENTRAL MISSOURI... LEARNING HOW, FOR INSTANCE, TO DEFEAT AN ENEMY WITH A BLOW FROM A SHOVEL. NEVER MIND THAT WE DIDN'T KNOW WHETHER IT'S SIX METERS TALL... OR THE SIZE OF AN ANT.

THEN, IT WAS DEPARTURE DAY. I REMEMBER IT AS IF IT WERE YESTERDAY.

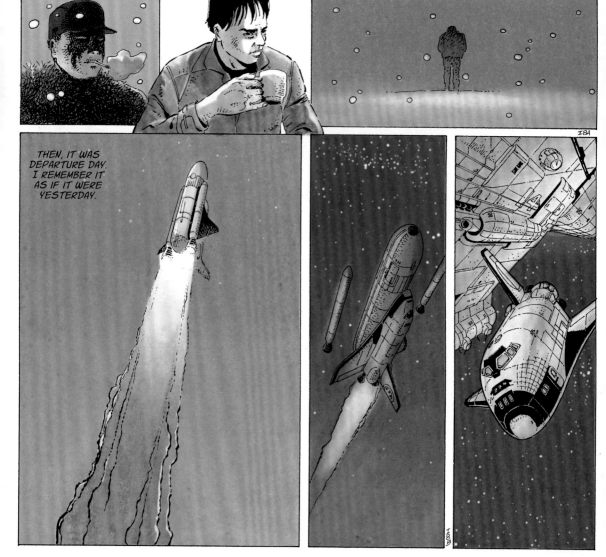

ALTHOUGH LOCATED AT PERIHELION, THE POINT IN ITS ORBIT CLOSEST TO THE SUN, CERBERUS WAS STILL TWICE AS FAR OUT AS PLUTO.

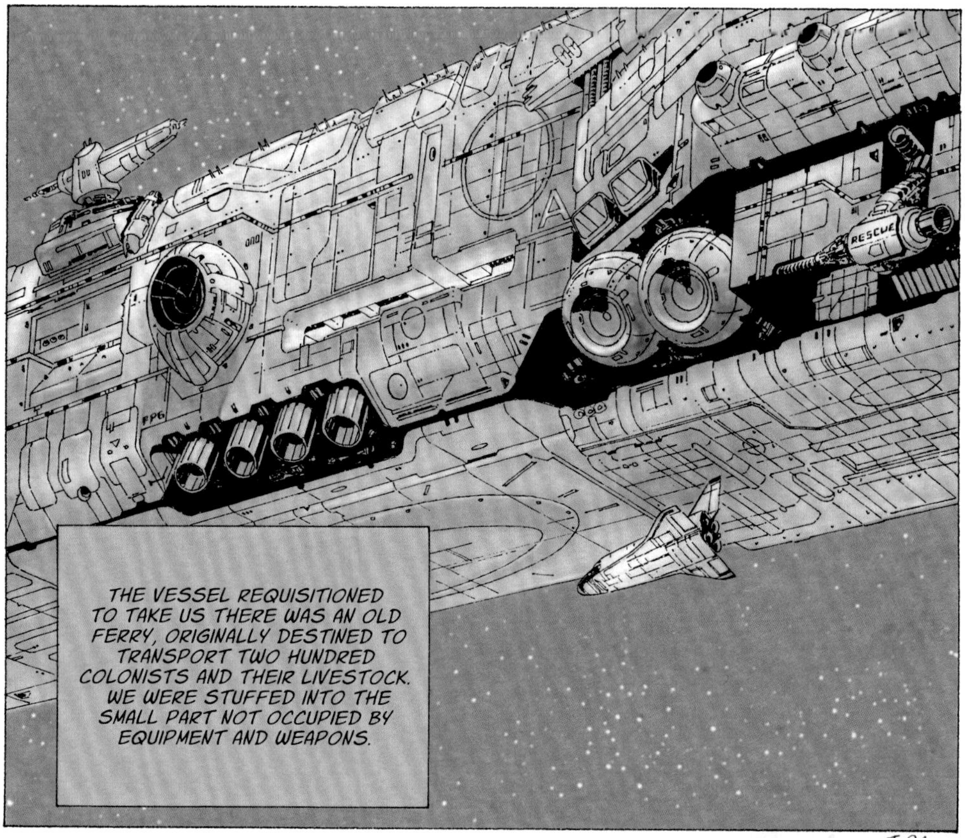
RESCUE
THE VESSEL REQUISITIONED TO TAKE US THERE WAS AN OLD FERRY, ORIGINALLY DESTINED TO TRANSPORT TWO HUNDRED COLONISTS AND THEIR LIVESTOCK. WE WERE STUFFED INTO THE SMALL PART NOT OCCUPIED BY EQUIPMENT AND WEAPONS.

I 9A

THE TRIP TOOK THREE WEEKS, ACCELERATING AT TWO GEES HALFWAY, THEN DECELERATING THE OTHER HALF. OUR TOP SPEED, AS WE ROARED BY THE ORBIT OF PLUTO WAS ABOUT 1/20TH THE SPEED OF LIGHT.

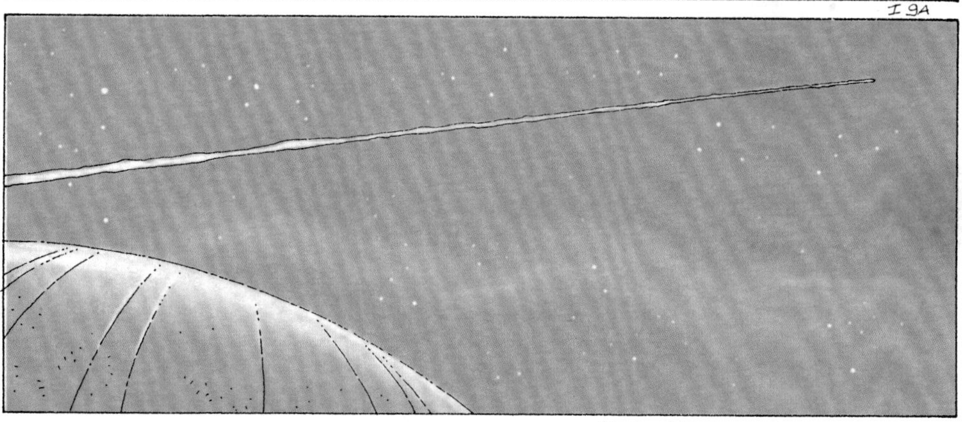

THREE WEEKS OF CARRYING AROUND TWICE AS MUCH WEIGHT AS NORMAL... IT'S NO PICNIC. EXCEPT FOR SOME CAUTIOUS EXERCISES, WE STAYED IN BED DURING THE GREATEST PART OF THE TRIP, FOR...

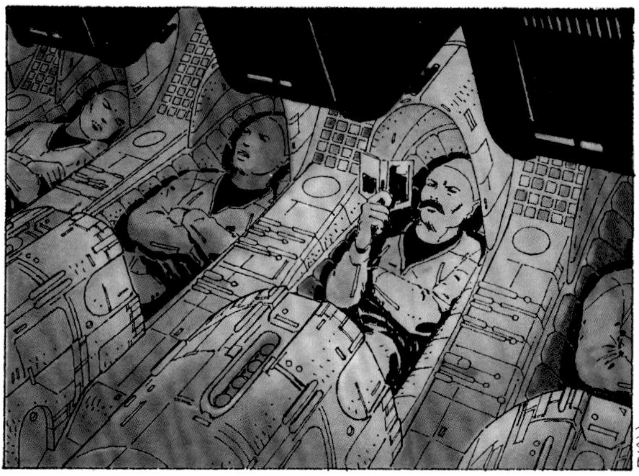
I 9 B

...UNDER THE EFFECT OF ACCELERATION CLUMSINESS WAS PAID BACK WITH SERIOUS FRACTURES AND DISLOCATIONS.

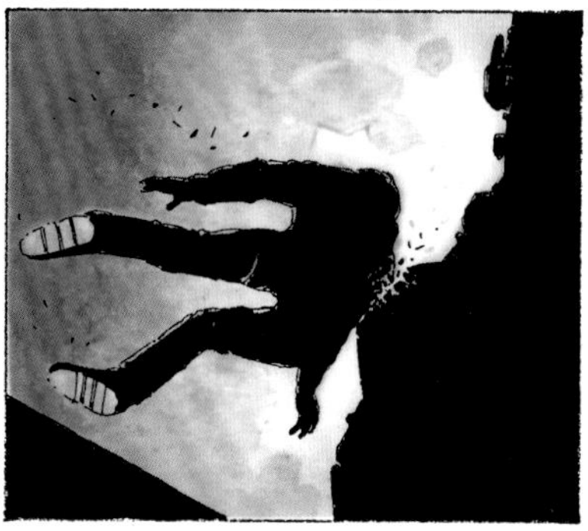

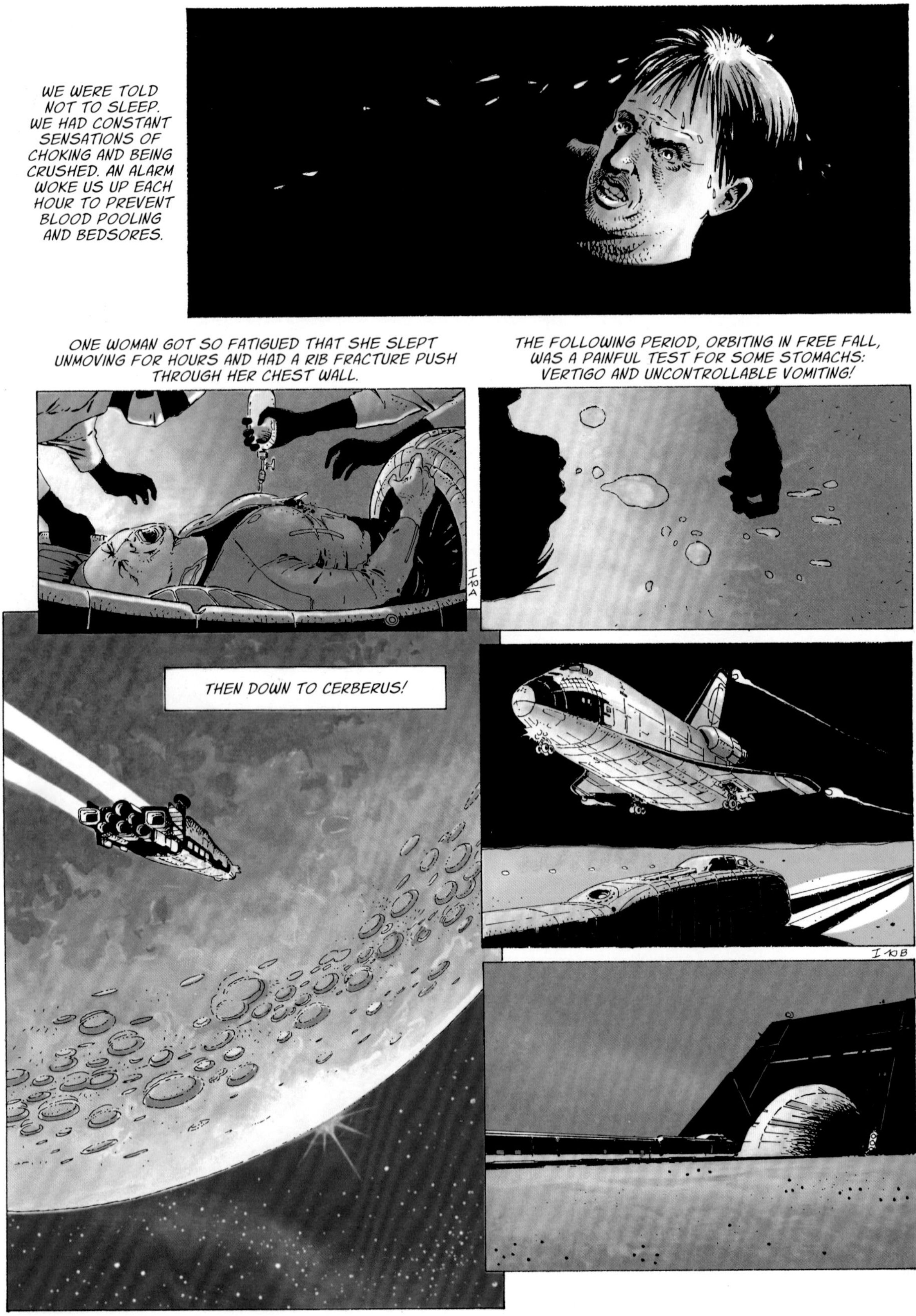
WE WERE TOLD NOT TO SLEEP. WE HAD CONSTANT SENSATIONS OF CHOKING AND BEING CRUSHED. AN ALARM WOKE US UP EACH HOUR TO PREVENT BLOOD POOLING AND BEDSORES.
ONE WOMAN GOT SO FATIGUED THAT SHE SLEPT UNMOVING FOR HOURS AND HAD A RIB FRACTURE PUSH THROUGH HER CHEST WALL.
THE FOLLOWING PERIOD, ORBITING IN FREE FALL, WAS A PAINFUL TEST FOR SOME STOMACHS: VERTIGO AND UNCONTROLLABLE VOMITING!
THEN DOWN TO CERBERUS!

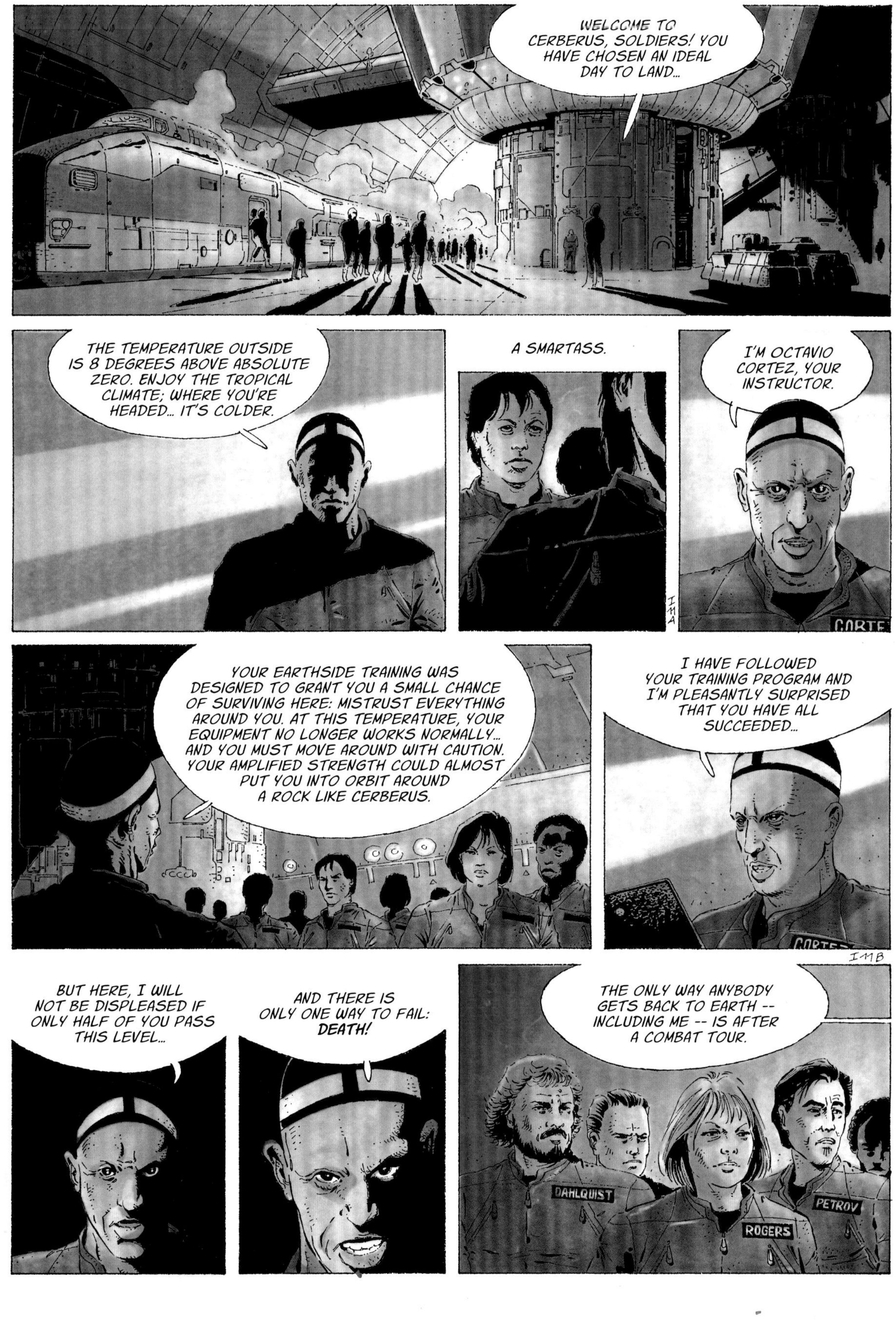
WELCOME TO CERBERUS, SOLDIERS! YOU HAVE CHOSEN AN IDEAL DAY TO LAND...
THE TEMPERATURE OUTSIDE IS 8 DEGREES ABOVE ABSOLUTE ZERO. ENJOY THE TROPICAL CLIMATE; WHERE YOU'RE HEADED... IT'S COLDER.
A SMARTASS.
I'M OCTAVIO CORTEZ, YOUR INSTRUCTOR.
YOUR EARTHSIDE TRAINING WAS DESIGNED TO GRANT YOU A SMALL CHANCE OF SURVIVING HERE: MISTRUST EVERYTHING AROUND YOU. AT THIS TEMPERATURE, YOUR EQUIPMENT NO LONGER WORKS NORMALLY... AND YOU MUST MOVE AROUND WITH CAUTION. YOUR AMPLIFIED STRENGTH COULD ALMOST PUT YOU INTO ORBIT AROUND A ROCK LIKE CERBERUS.
I HAVE FOLLOWED YOUR TRAINING PROGRAM AND I'M PLEASANTLY SURPRISED THAT YOU HAVE ALL SUCCEEDED...
BUT HERE, I WILL NOT BE DISPLEASED IF ONLY HALF OF YOU PASS THIS LEVEL...
AND THERE IS ONLY ONE WAY TO FAIL: DEATH!
THE ONLY WAY ANYBODY GETS BACK TO EARTH -- INCLUDING ME -- IS AFTER A COMBAT TOUR.
DAHLQUIST
ROGERS
PETROV

YOUR INSTRUCTION ENDS IN A MONTH. YOU WILL THEN GO TO THE PORTAL PLANET OF THE COLLAPSAR **STARGATE**, HALF A LIGHT YEAR FROM HERE. IT WILL PROBABLY BE A SIMPLE STOPPING PLACE BEFORE YOU ARE SENT TO A TRULY STRATEGIC SECTOR, WHERE YOU WILL HAVE TO ESTABLISH A BASE AND AWAIT ORDERS.

I 12 A

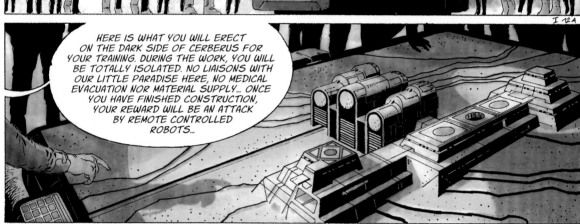

HERE IS WHAT YOU WILL ERECT ON THE DARK SIDE OF CERBERUS FOR YOUR TRAINING. DURING THE WORK, YOU WILL BE TOTALLY ISOLATED. NO LIAISONS WITH OUR LITTLE PARADISE HERE, NO MEDICAL EVACUATION NOR MATERIAL SUPPLY... ONCE YOU HAVE FINISHED CONSTRUCTION, YOUR REWARD WILL BE AN ATTACK BY REMOTE CONTROLLED ROBOTS...

IT WON'T BE A PICNIC, FROM YOUR APTITUDE FOR DEFENDING YOURSELVES WE'LL BE ABLE TO DETERMINE YOUR ULTIMATE CHANCES...

THEY SPENT ALL THAT MONEY TO KILL US DURING TRAINING?

A REMINDER... THIS BASE WAS CONSTRUCTED BY FORTY-FIVE PIONEERS. ONLY TWENTY SURVIVED. I'M GOING TO TRY TO KEEP YOU ALIVE.

MAEJIMA

I 12 B

YOU WILL OBEY ME BLINDLY, FOR THERE IS ONLY ONE PENALTY OUT THERE FOR DISOBEDIENCE...

...THE DEATH PENALTY...

ON THE SPOT!

POTTER

AND I WON'T HAVE TO BE THE EXECUTIONER...

FREE

...CERBERUS WILL BE.

BOVANOVITCH

THAT POINT, WE GOT LOUD AND CLEAR OVER THE NEXT MONTH. A FRACTION OF A SECOND LATE IN ACCOMPLISHING ASSIGNMENTS, AN INSTANT OF PANIC, AND IT WAS THE END...

BOVANOVITCH...

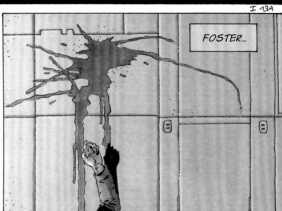

FOSTER...

OHANA...

FREELAND...

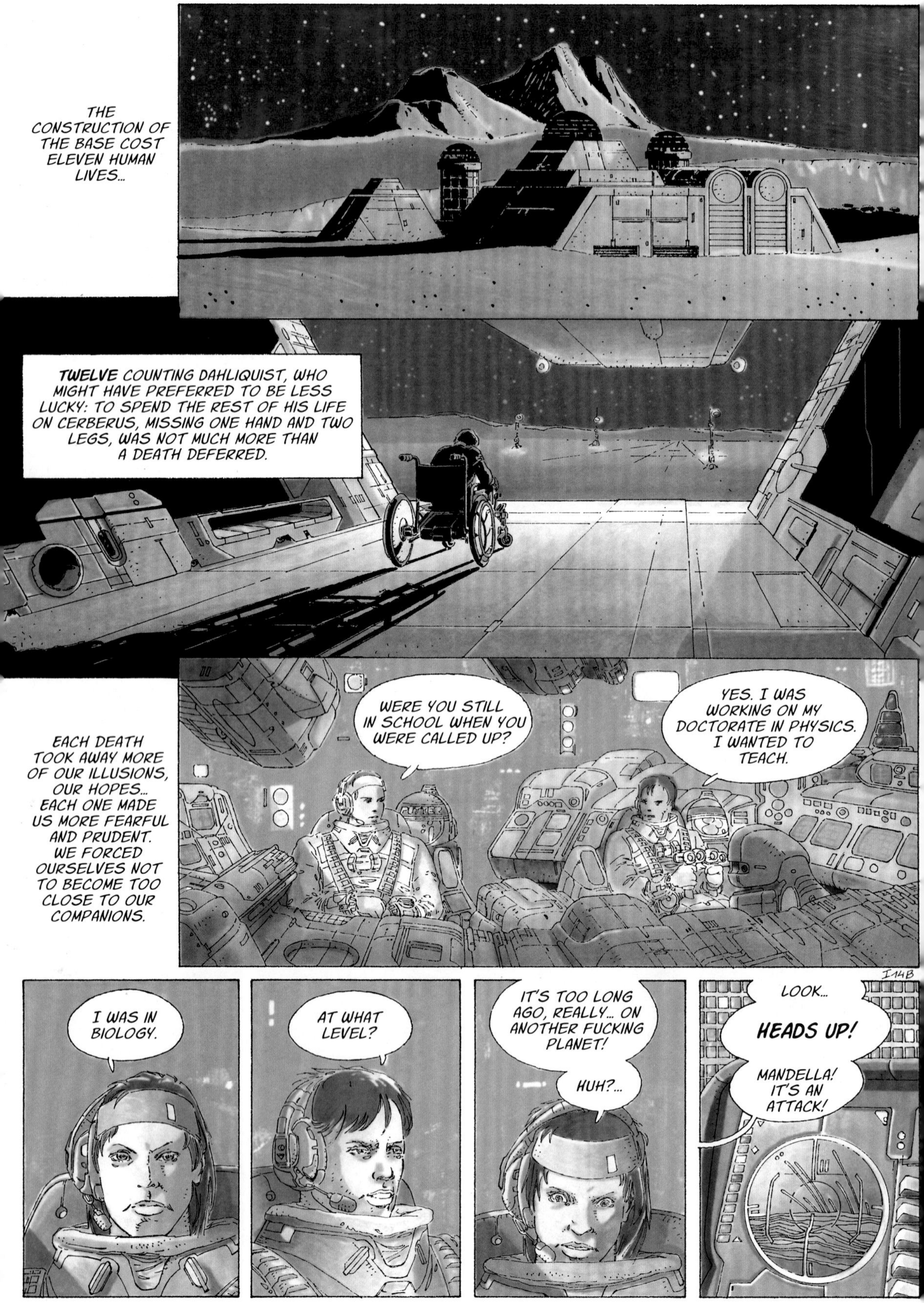

THE CONSTRUCTION OF THE BASE COST ELEVEN HUMAN LIVES...
TWELVE COUNTING DAHLIQUIST, WHO MIGHT HAVE PREFERRED TO BE LESS LUCKY: TO SPEND THE REST OF HIS LIFE ON CERBERUS, MISSING ONE HAND AND TWO LEGS, WAS NOT MUCH MORE THAN A DEATH DEFERRED.
EACH DEATH TOOK AWAY MORE OF OUR ILLUSIONS, OUR HOPES... EACH ONE MADE US MORE FEARFUL AND PRUDENT. WE FORCED OURSELVES NOT TO BECOME TOO CLOSE TO OUR COMPANIONS.
WERE YOU STILL IN SCHOOL WHEN YOU WERE CALLED UP?
YES. I WAS WORKING ON MY DOCTORATE IN PHYSICS. I WANTED TO TEACH.
I WAS IN BIOLOGY.
AT WHAT LEVEL?
IT'S TOO LONG AGO, REALLY... ON ANOTHER FUCKING PLANET!
HUH?...
LOOK...
HEADS UP!
MANDELLA! IT'S AN ATTACK!

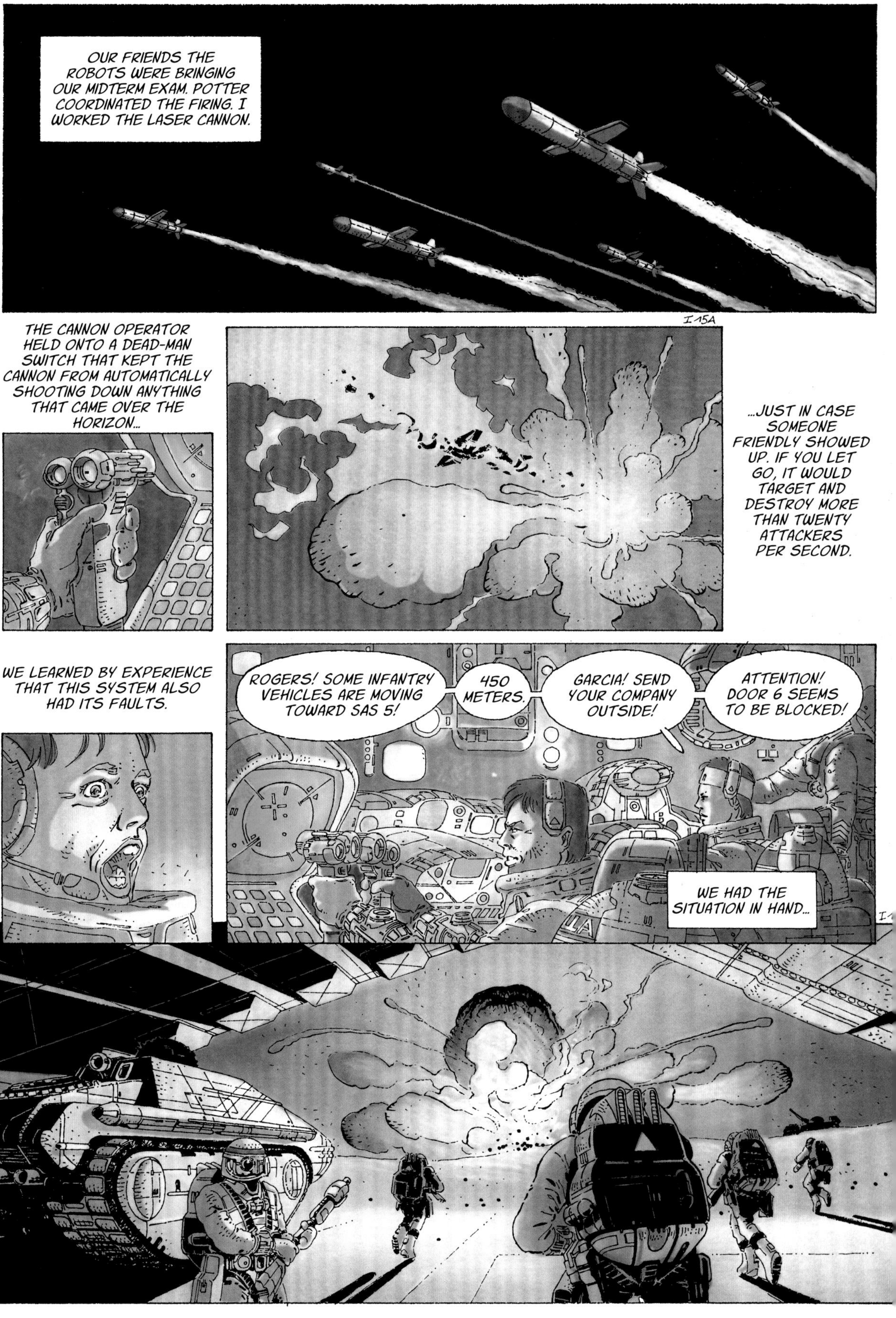
OUR FRIENDS THE ROBOTS WERE BRINGING OUR MIDTERM EXAM. POTTER COORDINATED THE FIRING. I WORKED THE LASER CANNON.
I 15A
THE CANNON OPERATOR HELD ONTO A DEAD-MAN SWITCH THAT KEPT THE CANNON FROM AUTOMATICALLY SHOOTING DOWN ANYTHING THAT CAME OVER THE HORIZON...
...JUST IN CASE SOMEONE FRIENDLY SHOWED UP. IF YOU LET GO, IT WOULD TARGET AND DESTROY MORE THAN TWENTY ATTACKERS PER SECOND.
WE LEARNED BY EXPERIENCE THAT THIS SYSTEM ALSO HAD ITS FAULTS.
ROGERS! SOME INFANTRY VEHICLES ARE MOVING TOWARD SAS 5!
450 METERS.
GARCIA! SEND YOUR COMPANY OUTSIDE!
ATTENTION! DOOR 6 SEEMS TO BE BLOCKED!
WE HAD THE SITUATION IN HAND...

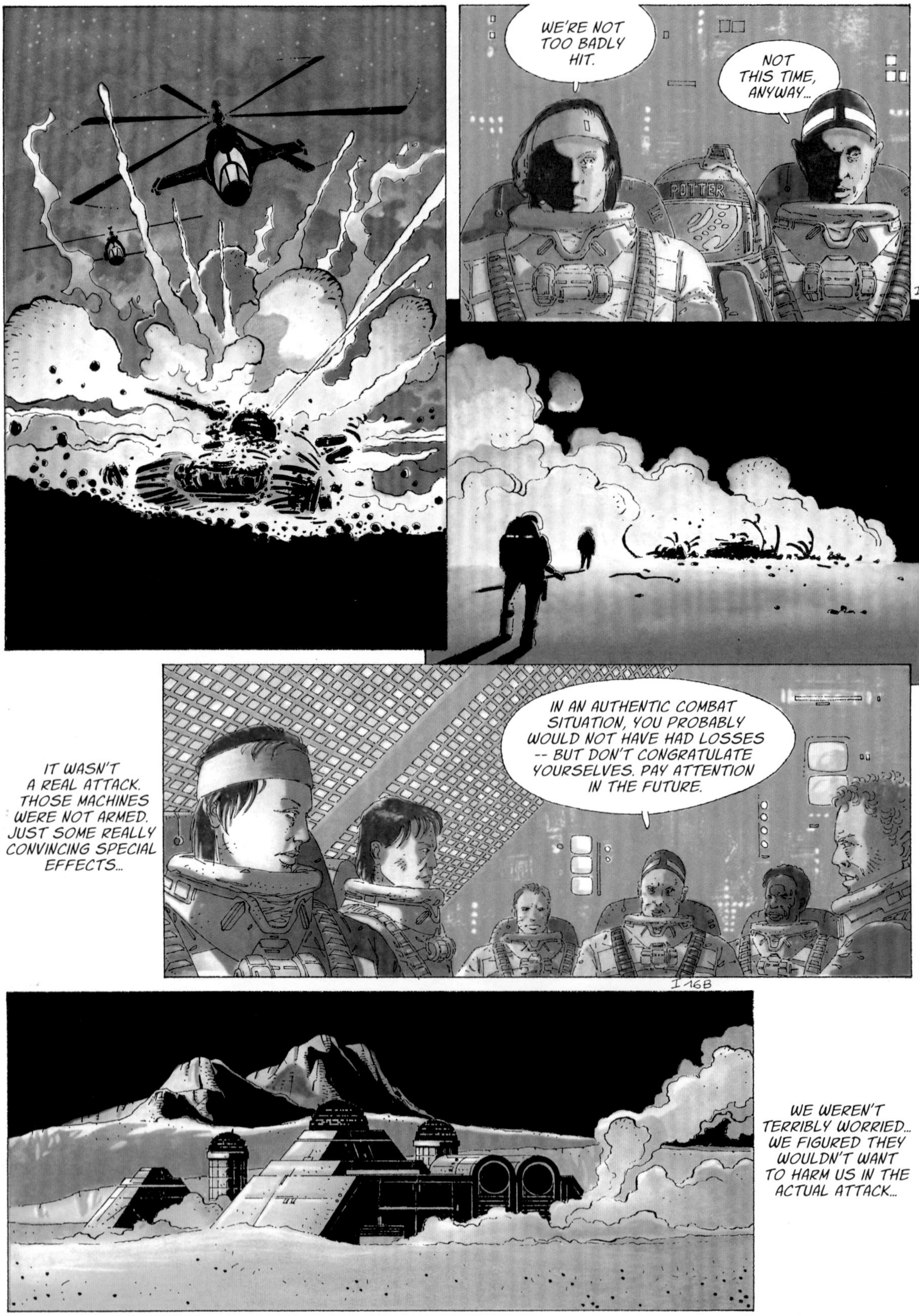
WE'RE NOT TOO BADLY HIT.
NOT THIS TIME, ANYWAY...
POTTER
IT WASN'T A REAL ATTACK. THOSE MACHINES WERE NOT ARMED. JUST SOME REALLY CONVINCING SPECIAL EFFECTS...
IN AN AUTHENTIC COMBAT SITUATION, YOU PROBABLY WOULD NOT HAVE HAD LOSSES -- BUT DON'T CONGRATULATE YOURSELVES. PAY ATTENTION IN THE FUTURE.
WE WEREN'T TERRIBLY WORRIED... WE FIGURED THEY WOULDN'T WANT TO HARM US IN THE ACTUAL ATTACK...

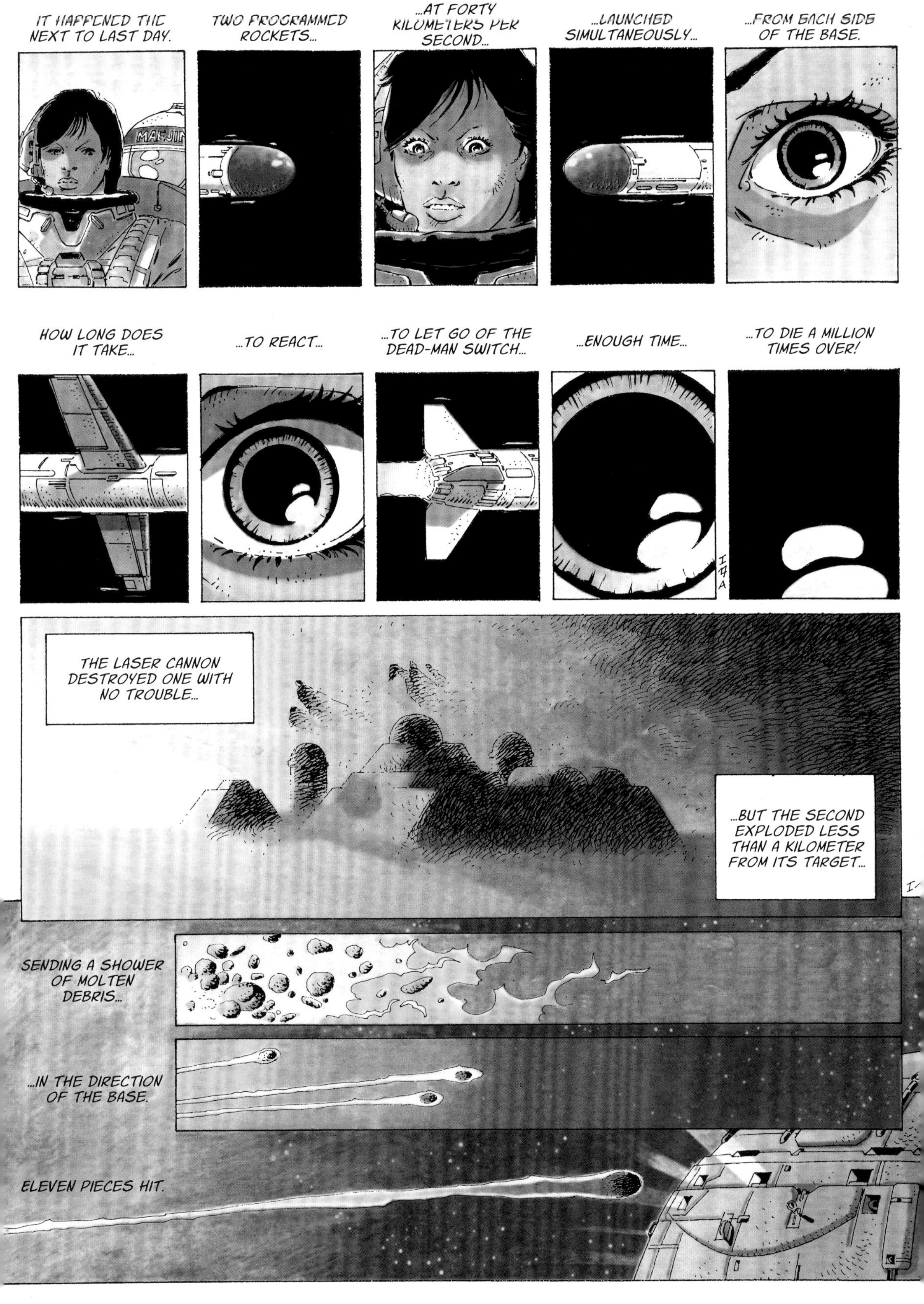
IT HAPPENED THE NEXT TO LAST DAY.
TWO PROGRAMMED ROCKETS...
...AT FORTY KILOMETERS PER SECOND...
...LAUNCHED SIMULTANEOUSLY...
...FROM EACH SIDE OF THE BASE.
MAEJIN
HOW LONG DOES IT TAKE...
...TO REACT...
...TO LET GO OF THE DEAD-MAN SWITCH...
...ENOUGH TIME...
...TO DIE A MILLION TIMES OVER!
THE LASER CANNON DESTROYED ONE WITH NO TROUBLE...
...BUT THE SECOND EXPLODED LESS THAN A KILOMETER FROM ITS TARGET...
SENDING A SHOWER OF MOLTEN DEBRIS...
...IN THE DIRECTION OF THE BASE.
ELEVEN PIECES HIT.

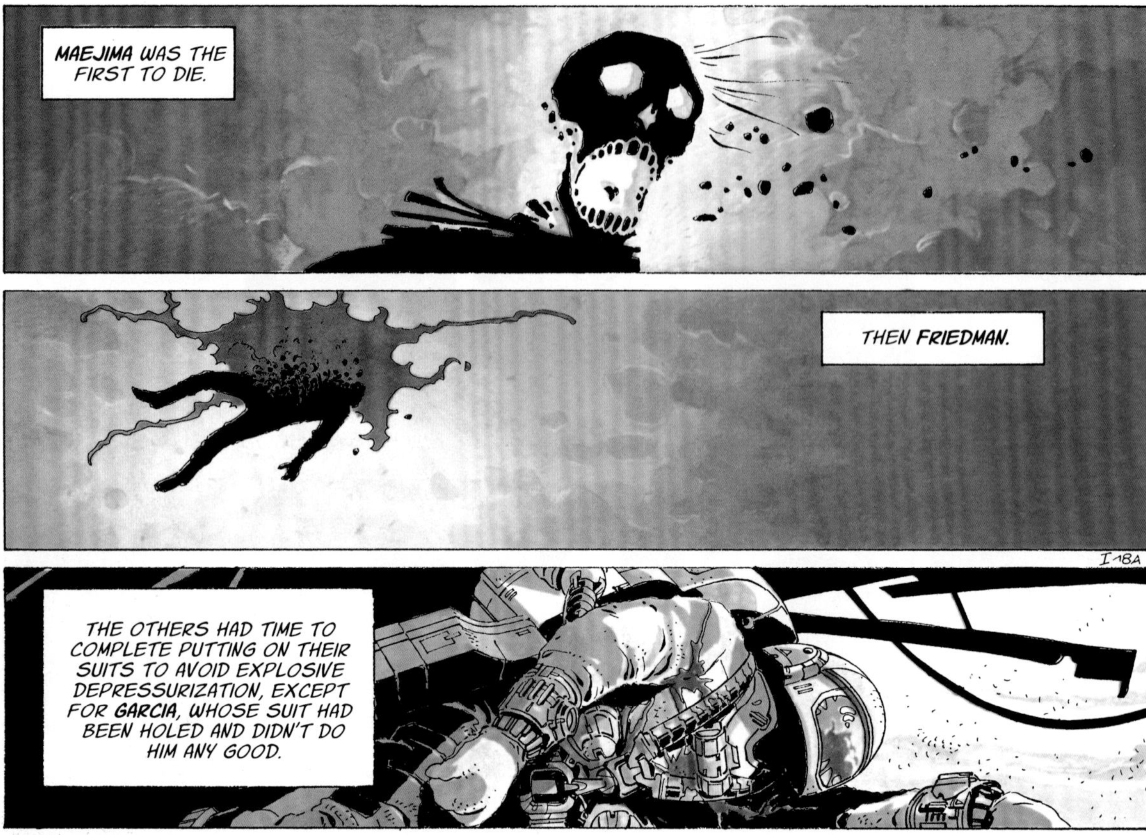
MAEJIMA WAS THE FIRST TO DIE.
THEN FRIEDMAN.
THE OTHERS HAD TIME TO COMPLETE PUTTING ON THEIR SUITS TO AVOID EXPLOSIVE DEPRESSURIZATION, EXCEPT FOR GARCIA, WHOSE SUIT HAD BEEN HOLED AND DIDN'T DO HIM ANY GOOD.

ONE MAN TRIED TO SCRAPE UP WHAT REMAINED OF MAEJIMA.

I HEARD HIM SOBBING AND RETCHING.

CORTEZ LED HIM AWAY AND FINISHED THE JOB. HE DIDN'T ORDER ANYONE TO HELP.

BESIDES, THERE WEREN'T ANY VOLUNTEERS.

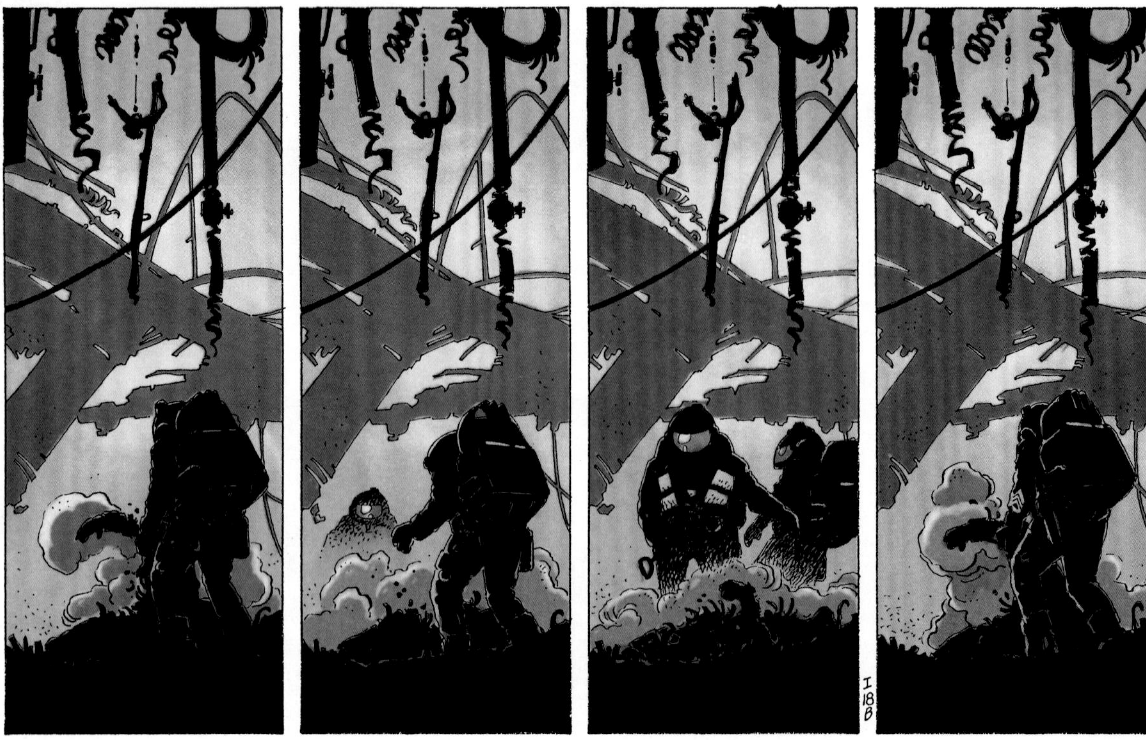

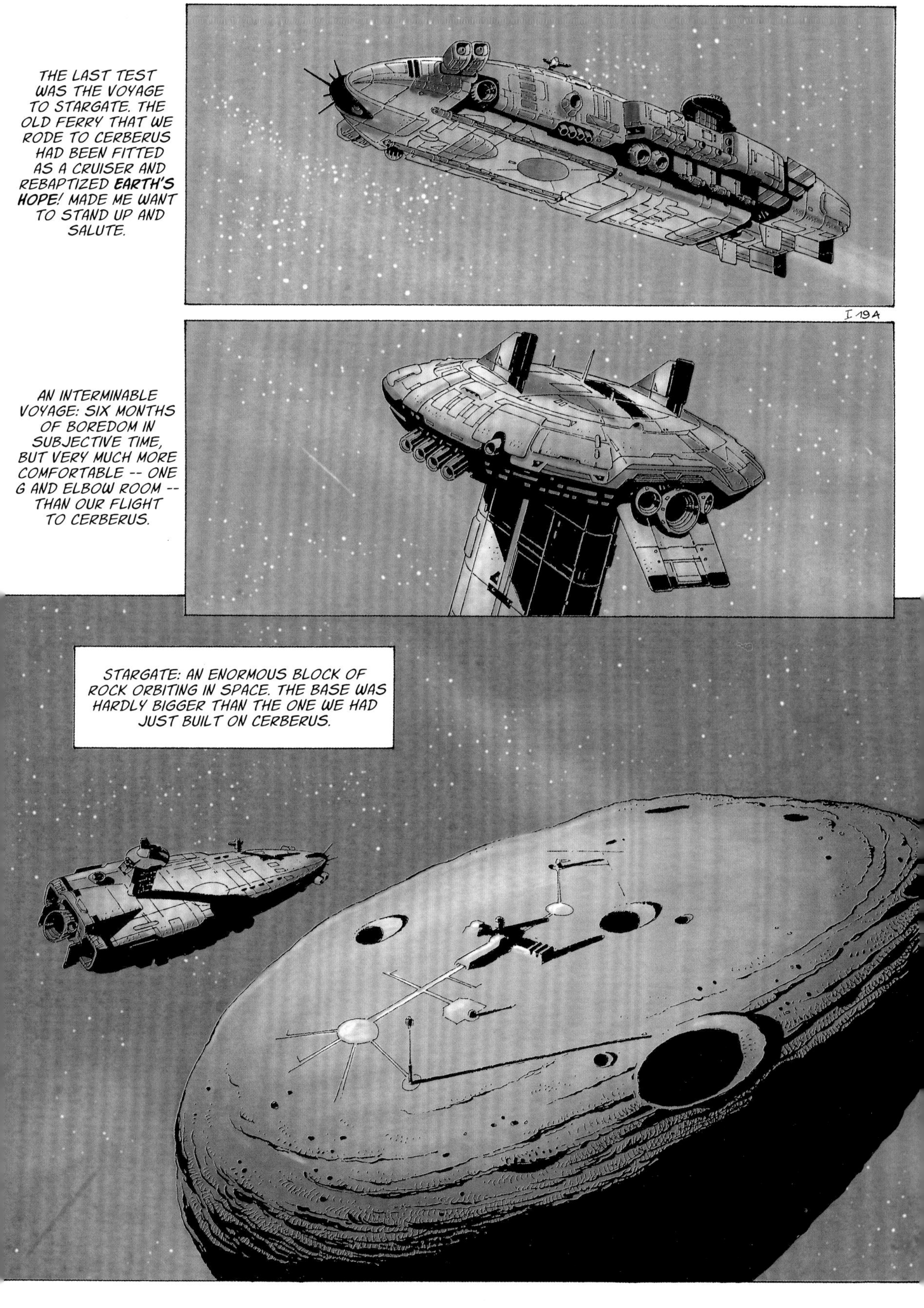
THE LAST TEST WAS THE VOYAGE TO STARGATE. THE OLD FERRY THAT WE RODE TO CERBERUS HAD BEEN FITTED AS A CRUISER AND REBAPTIZED **EARTH'S HOPE!** MADE ME WANT TO STAND UP AND SALUTE.
I 19 A
AN INTERMINABLE VOYAGE: SIX MONTHS OF BOREDOM IN SUBJECTIVE TIME, BUT VERY MUCH MORE COMFORTABLE -- ONE G AND ELBOW ROOM -- THAN OUR FLIGHT TO CERBERUS.
STARGATE: AN ENORMOUS BLOCK OF ROCK ORBITING IN SPACE. THE BASE WAS HARDLY BIGGER THAN THE ONE WE HAD JUST BUILT ON CERBERUS.

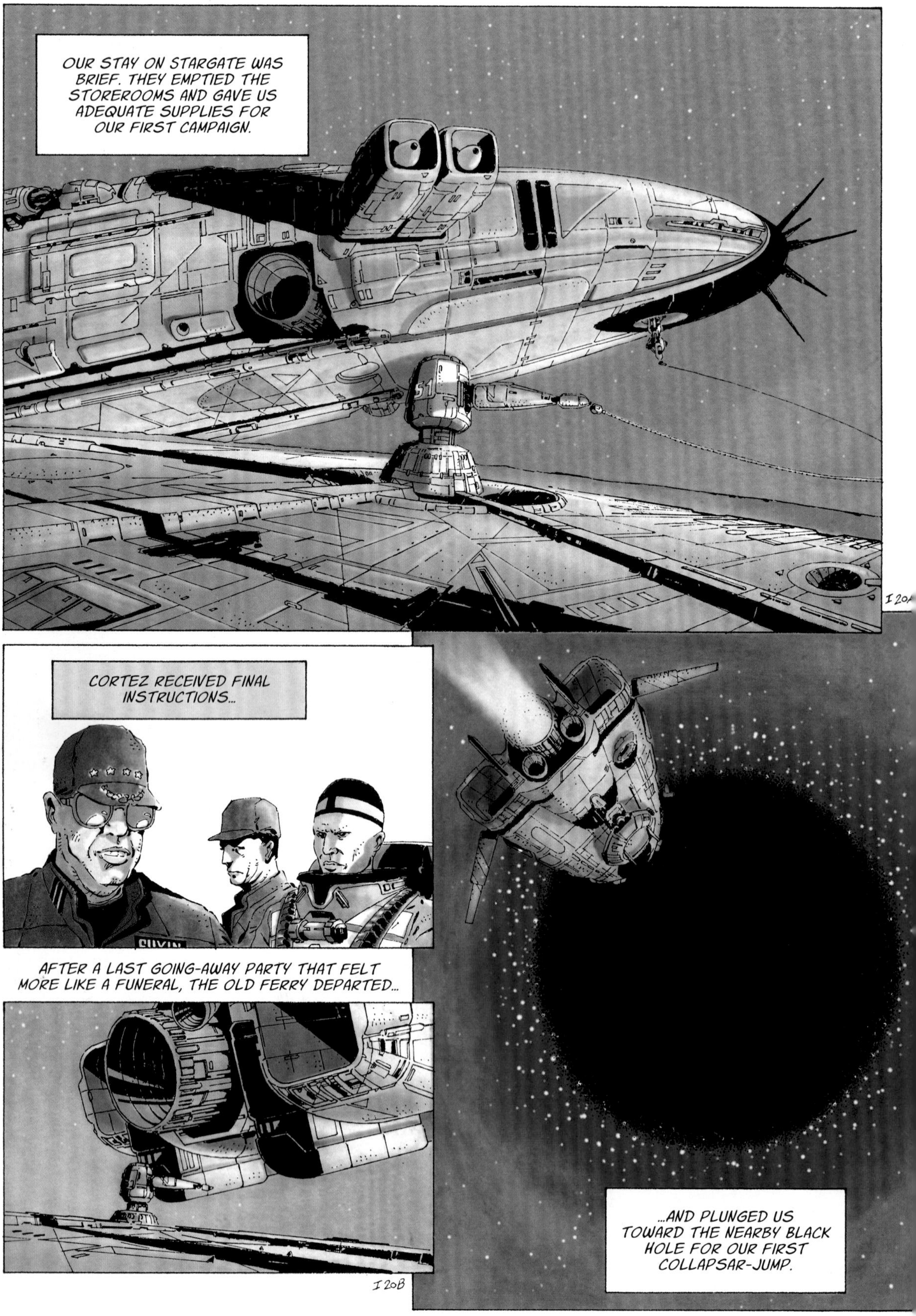
OUR STAY ON STARGATE WAS BRIEF. THEY EMPTIED THE STOREROOMS AND GAVE US ADEQUATE SUPPLIES FOR OUR FIRST CAMPAIGN.
CORTEZ RECEIVED FINAL INSTRUCTIONS...
AFTER A LAST GOING-AWAY PARTY THAT FELT MORE LIKE A FUNERAL, THE OLD FERRY DEPARTED...
...AND PLUNGED US TOWARD THE NEARBY BLACK HOLE FOR OUR FIRST COLLAPSAR-JUMP.

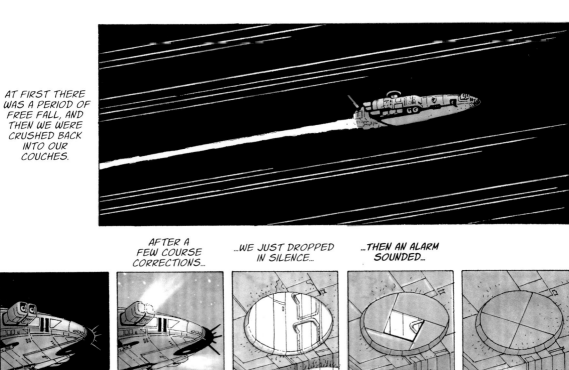

AT FIRST THERE WAS A PERIOD OF FREE FALL, AND THEN WE WERE CRUSHED BACK INTO OUR COUCHES.

AFTER A FEW COURSE CORRECTIONS...

...WE JUST DROPPED IN SILENCE...

...THEN AN ALARM SOUNDED...

WE WERE IN ENEMY TERRITORY.

NICE DAYS OF UNEVENTFUL CRUISING, THEN WE FELT TWO SLIGHT JOLTS...

EIGHT HOURS LATER, WE GOT THE WORD...

ATTENTION CREW! COMMANDER QUINSANA SPEAKING...

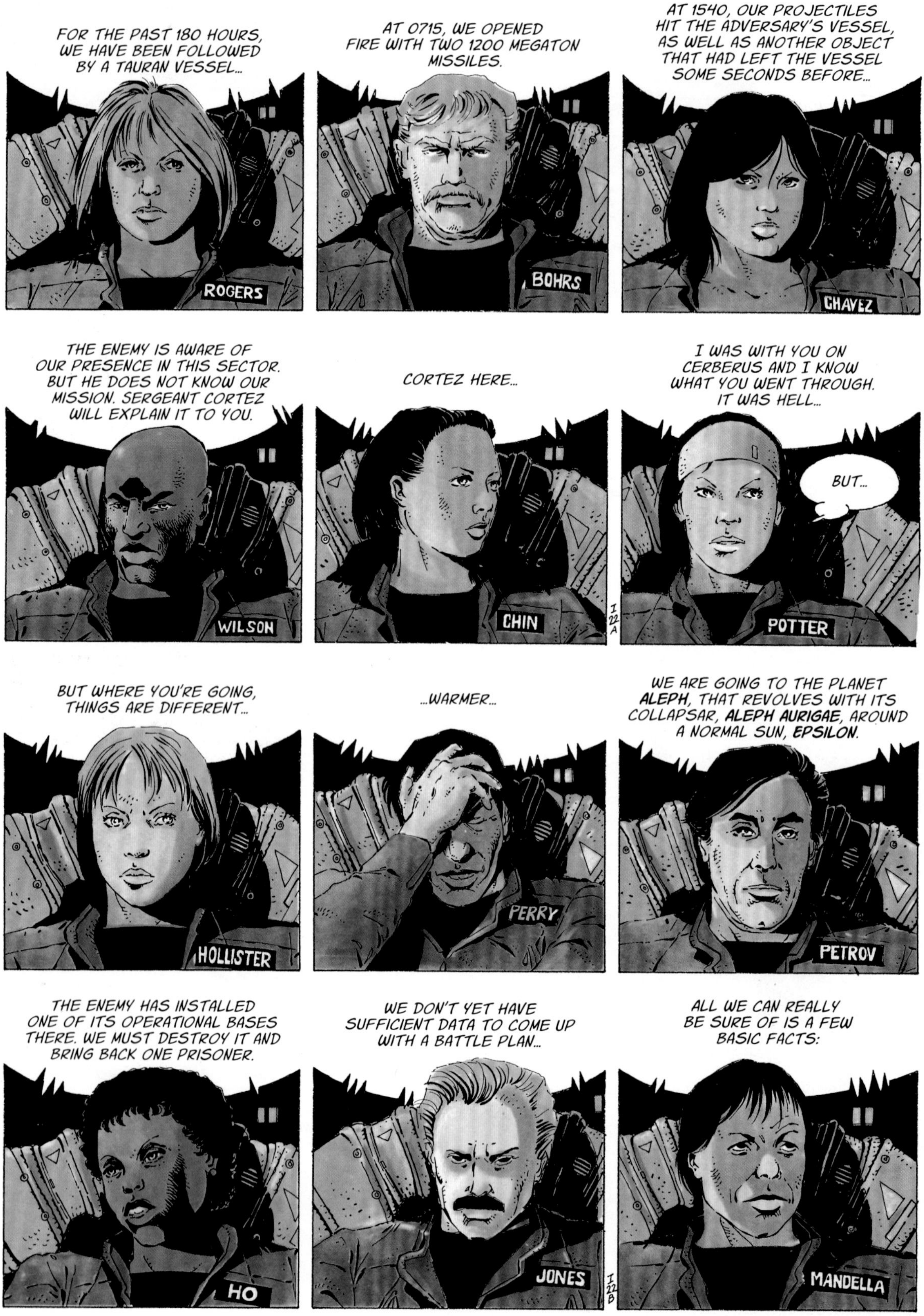
FOR THE PAST 180 HOURS, WE HAVE BEEN FOLLOWED BY A TAURAN VESSEL...
ROGERS
AT 0715, WE OPENED FIRE WITH TWO 1200 MEGATON MISSILES.
BOHRS
AT 1540, OUR PROJECTILES HIT THE ADVERSARY'S VESSEL, AS WELL AS ANOTHER OBJECT THAT HAD LEFT THE VESSEL SOME SECONDS BEFORE...
CHAVEZ
THE ENEMY IS AWARE OF OUR PRESENCE IN THIS SECTOR. BUT HE DOES NOT KNOW OUR MISSION. SERGEANT CORTEZ WILL EXPLAIN IT TO YOU.
WILSON
CORTEZ HERE...
CHIN
I WAS WITH YOU ON CERBERUS AND I KNOW WHAT YOU WENT THROUGH. IT WAS HELL...
BUT...
POTTER
BUT WHERE YOU'RE GOING, THINGS ARE DIFFERENT...
HOLLISTER
...WARMER...
PERRY
WE ARE GOING TO THE PLANET **ALEPH**, THAT REVOLVES WITH ITS COLLAPSAR, **ALEPH AURIGAE**, AROUND A NORMAL SUN, **EPSILON**.
PETROV
THE ENEMY HAS INSTALLED ONE OF ITS OPERATIONAL BASES THERE. WE MUST DESTROY IT AND BRING BACK ONE PRISONER.
HO
WE DON'T YET HAVE SUFFICIENT DATA TO COME UP WITH A BATTLE PLAN...
JONES
ALL WE CAN REALLY BE SURE OF IS A FEW BASIC FACTS:
MANDELLA

"**ALEPH** IS RELATIVELY NEAR ITS SUN. IT'S COVERED WITH WATER, VAPOR CLOUDS, BUT THE TEMPERATURE IS MUCH HIGHER THAN IN THE EQUATORIAL ZONES OF EARTH." WE WERE GOING FROM THE FREEZER INTO THE **OVEN**.

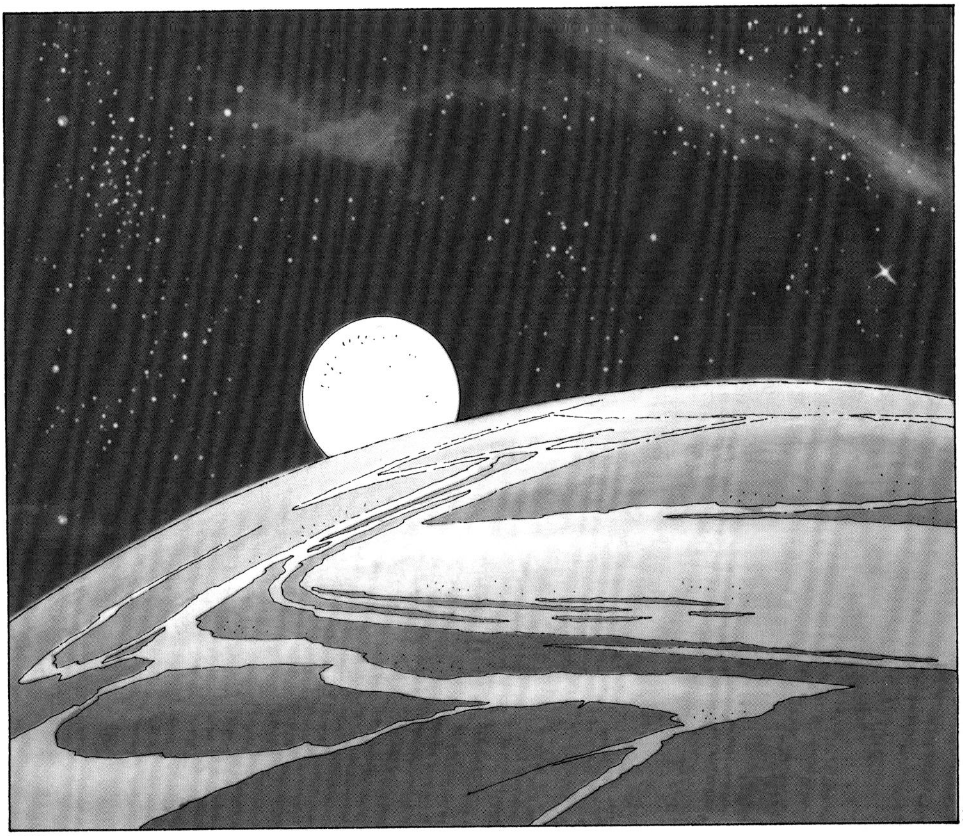

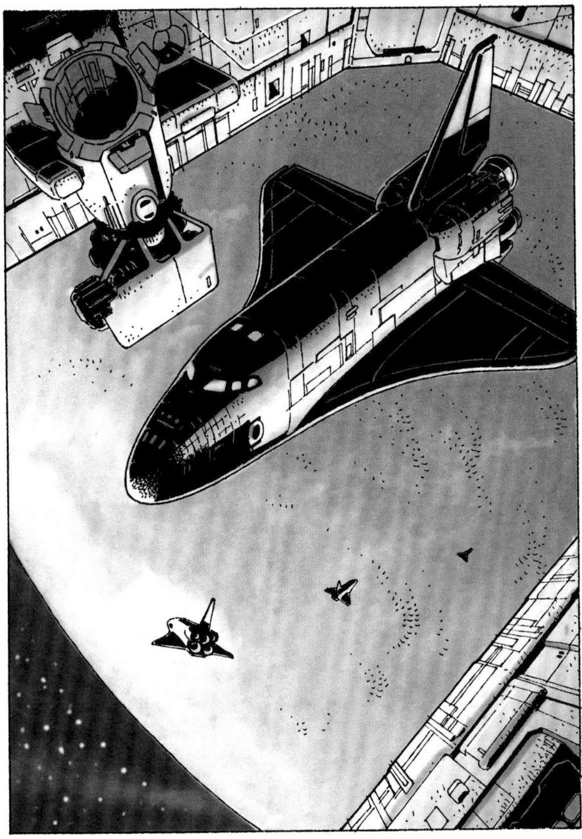

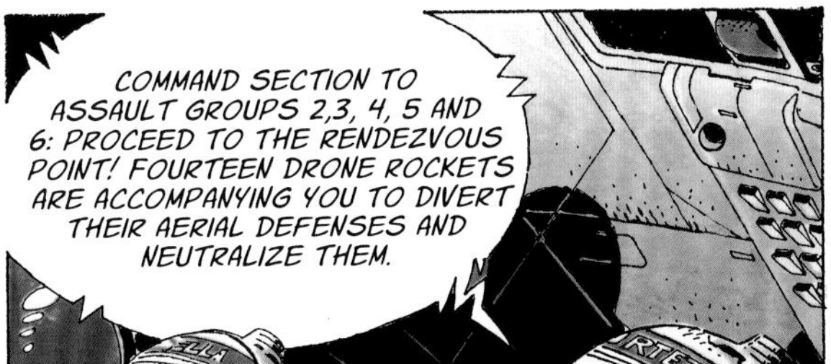
COMMAND SECTION TO ASSAULT GROUPS 2,3, 4, 5 AND 6: PROCEED TO THE RENDEZVOUS POINT! FOURTEEN DRONE ROCKETS ARE ACCOMPANYING YOU TO DIVERT THEIR AERIAL DEFENSES AND NEUTRALIZE THEM.

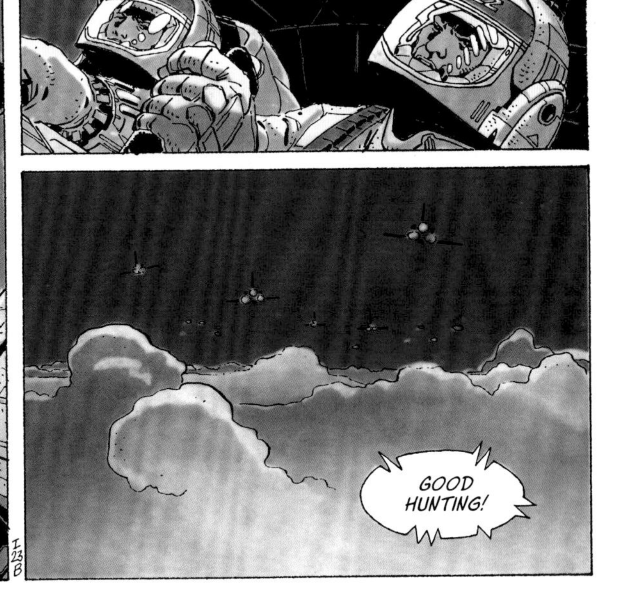
GOOD HUNTING!

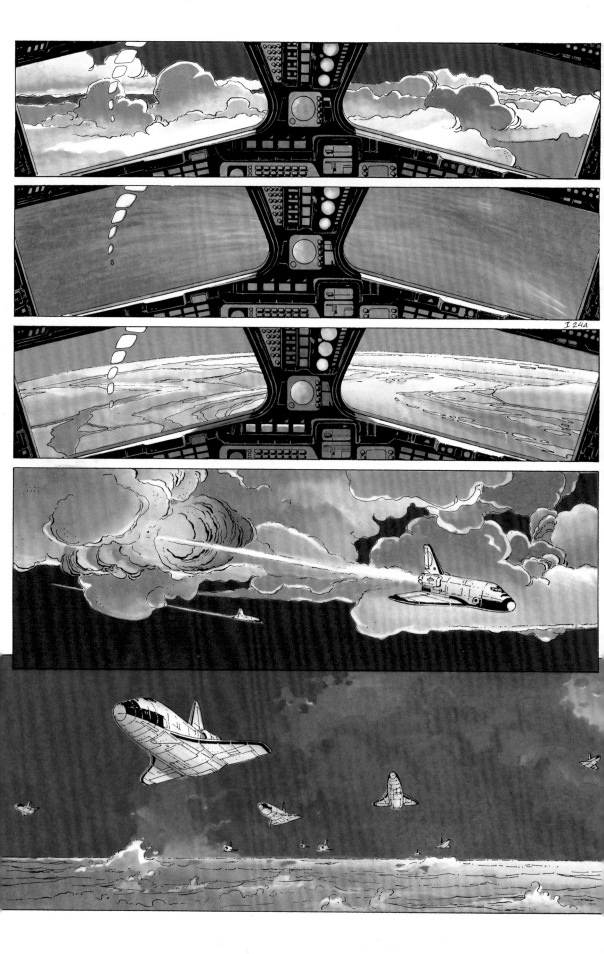

I 24A

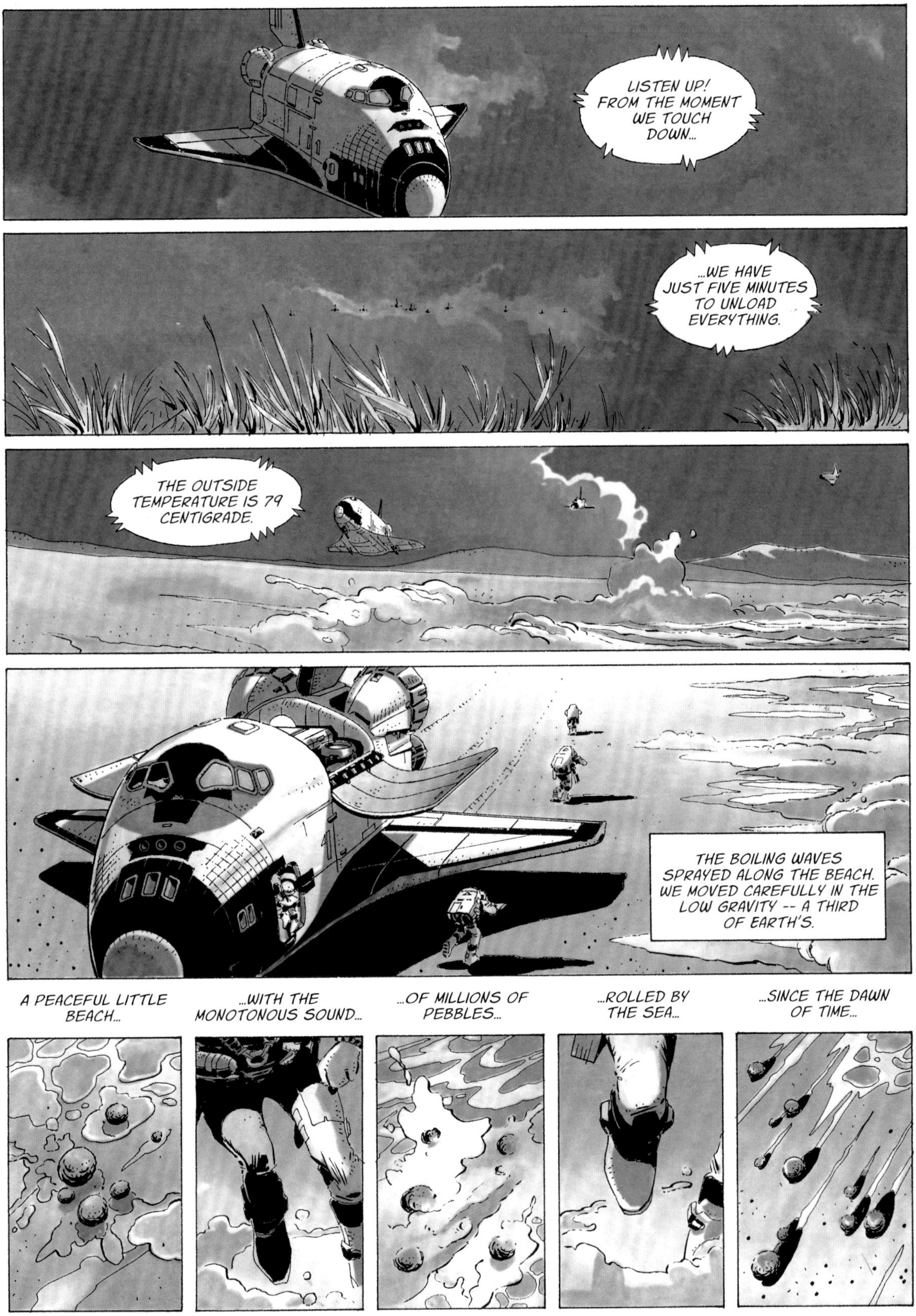
LISTEN UP! FROM THE MOMENT WE TOUCH DOWN...
...WE HAVE JUST FIVE MINUTES TO UNLOAD EVERYTHING.
THE OUTSIDE TEMPERATURE IS 79 CENTIGRADE.
THE BOILING WAVES SPRAYED ALONG THE BEACH. WE MOVED CAREFULLY IN THE LOW GRAVITY -- A THIRD OF EARTH'S.
A PEACEFUL LITTLE BEACH...
...WITH THE MONOTONOUS SOUND...
...OF MILLIONS OF PEBBLES...
...ROLLED BY THE SEA...
...SINCE THE DAWN OF TIME...

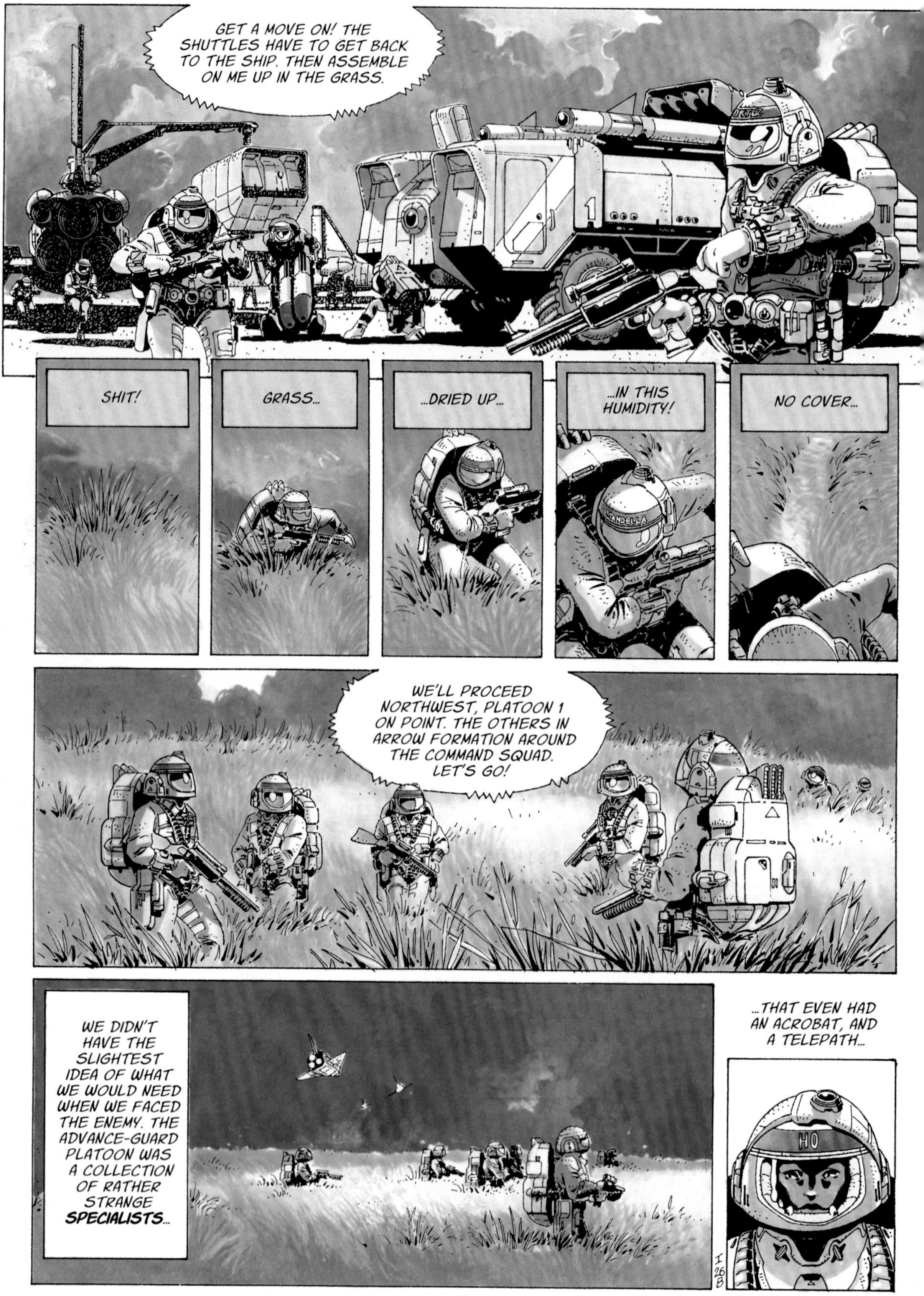
GET A MOVE ON! THE SHUTTLES HAVE TO GET BACK TO THE SHIP. THEN ASSEMBLE ON ME UP IN THE GRASS.
SHIT!
GRASS...
...DRIED UP...
...IN THIS HUMIDITY!
MANDELLA
NO COVER...
WE'LL PROCEED NORTHWEST, PLATOON 1 ON POINT. THE OTHERS IN ARROW FORMATION AROUND THE COMMAND SQUAD. LET'S GO!
WE DIDN'T HAVE THE SLIGHTEST IDEA OF WHAT WE WOULD NEED WHEN WE FACED THE ENEMY. THE ADVANCE-GUARD PLATOON WAS A COLLECTION OF RATHER STRANGE **SPECIALISTS**...
...THAT EVEN HAD AN ACROBAT, AND A TELEPATH...
HO
I 26 B

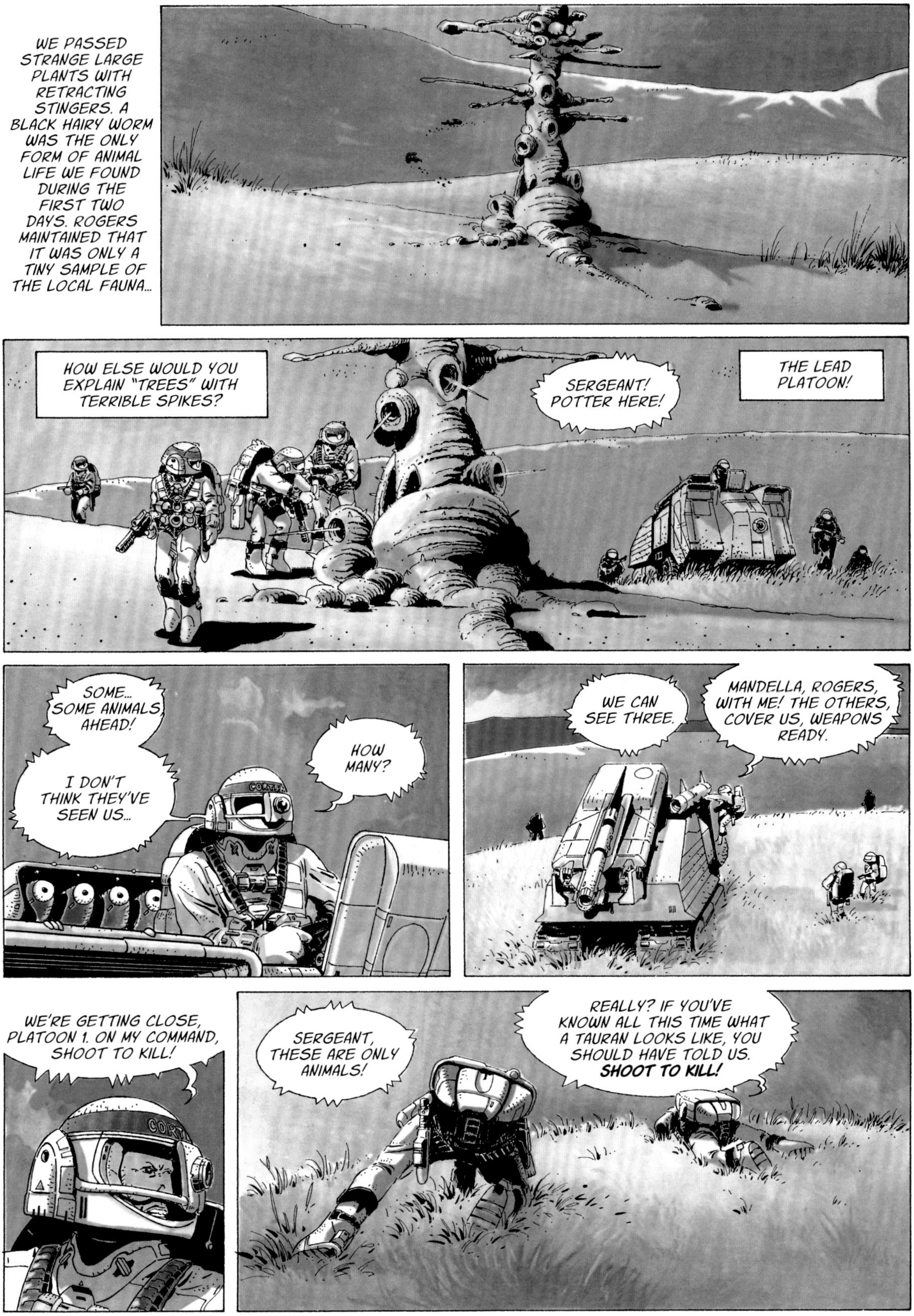
WE PASSED STRANGE LARGE PLANTS WITH RETRACTING STINGERS. A BLACK HAIRY WORM WAS THE ONLY FORM OF ANIMAL LIFE WE FOUND DURING THE FIRST TWO DAYS. ROGERS MAINTAINED THAT IT WAS ONLY A TINY SAMPLE OF THE LOCAL FAUNA...
HOW ELSE WOULD YOU EXPLAIN "TREES" WITH TERRIBLE SPIKES?
SERGEANT! POTTER HERE!
THE LEAD PLATOON!
SOME... SOME ANIMALS AHEAD!
I DON'T THINK THEY'VE SEEN US...
HOW MANY?
WE CAN SEE THREE.
MANDELLA, ROGERS, WITH ME! THE OTHERS, COVER US, WEAPONS READY.
WE'RE GETTING CLOSE, PLATOON 1. ON MY COMMAND, SHOOT TO KILL!
SERGEANT, THESE ARE ONLY ANIMALS!
REALLY? IF YOU'VE KNOWN ALL THIS TIME WHAT A TAURAN LOOKS LIKE, YOU SHOULD HAVE TOLD US. SHOOT TO KILL!

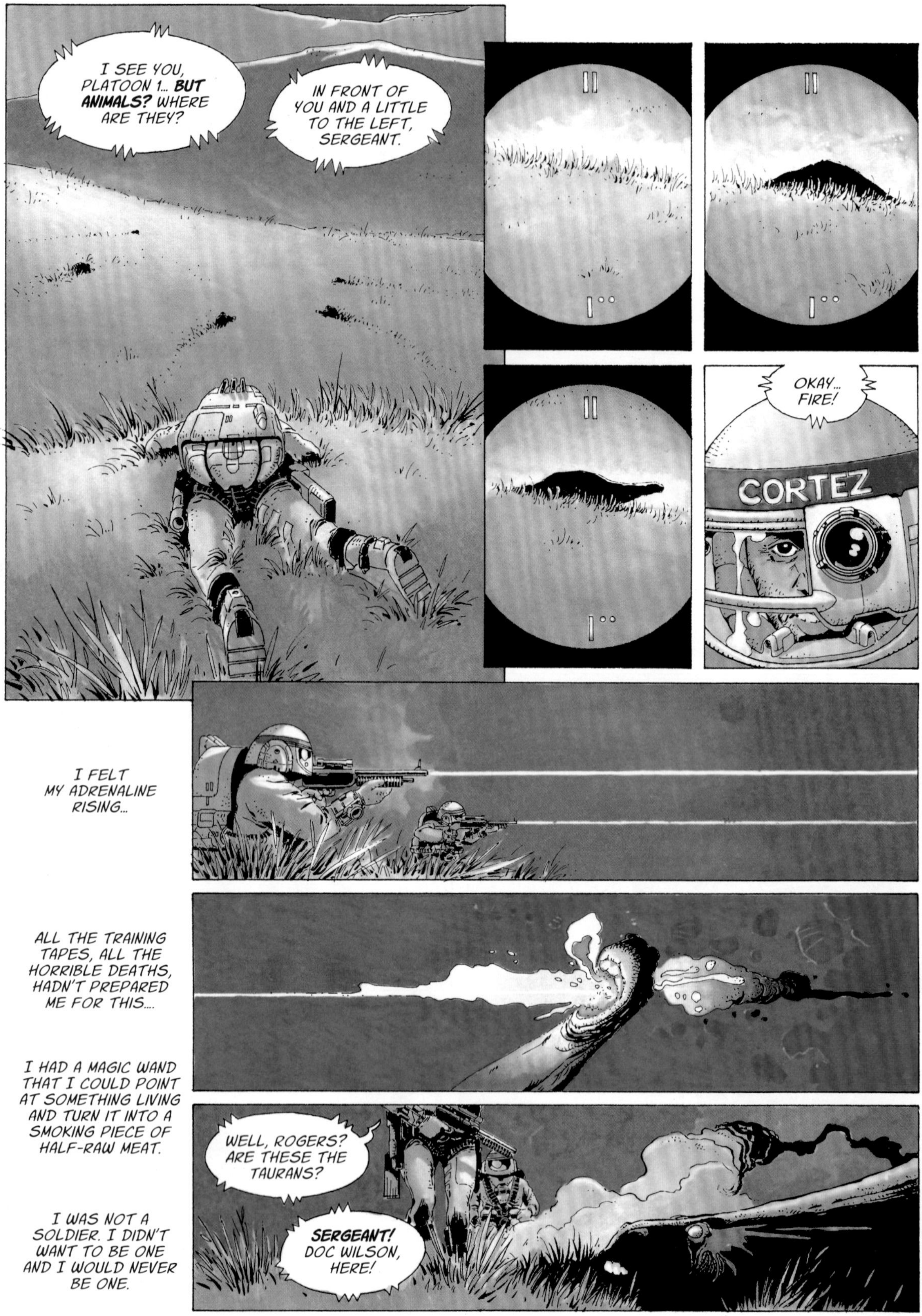
I SEE YOU, PLATOON 1... BUT ANIMALS? WHERE ARE THEY?
IN FRONT OF YOU AND A LITTLE TO THE LEFT, SERGEANT.
OKAY... FIRE!
CORTEZ
I FELT MY ADRENALINE RISING...
ALL THE TRAINING TAPES, ALL THE HORRIBLE DEATHS, HADN'T PREPARED ME FOR THIS....
I HAD A MAGIC WAND THAT I COULD POINT AT SOMETHING LIVING AND TURN IT INTO A SMOKING PIECE OF HALF-RAW MEAT.
WELL, ROGERS? ARE THESE THE TAURANS?
I WAS NOT A SOLDIER. I DIDN'T WANT TO BE ONE AND I WOULD NEVER BE ONE.
SERGEANT! DOC WILSON, HERE!

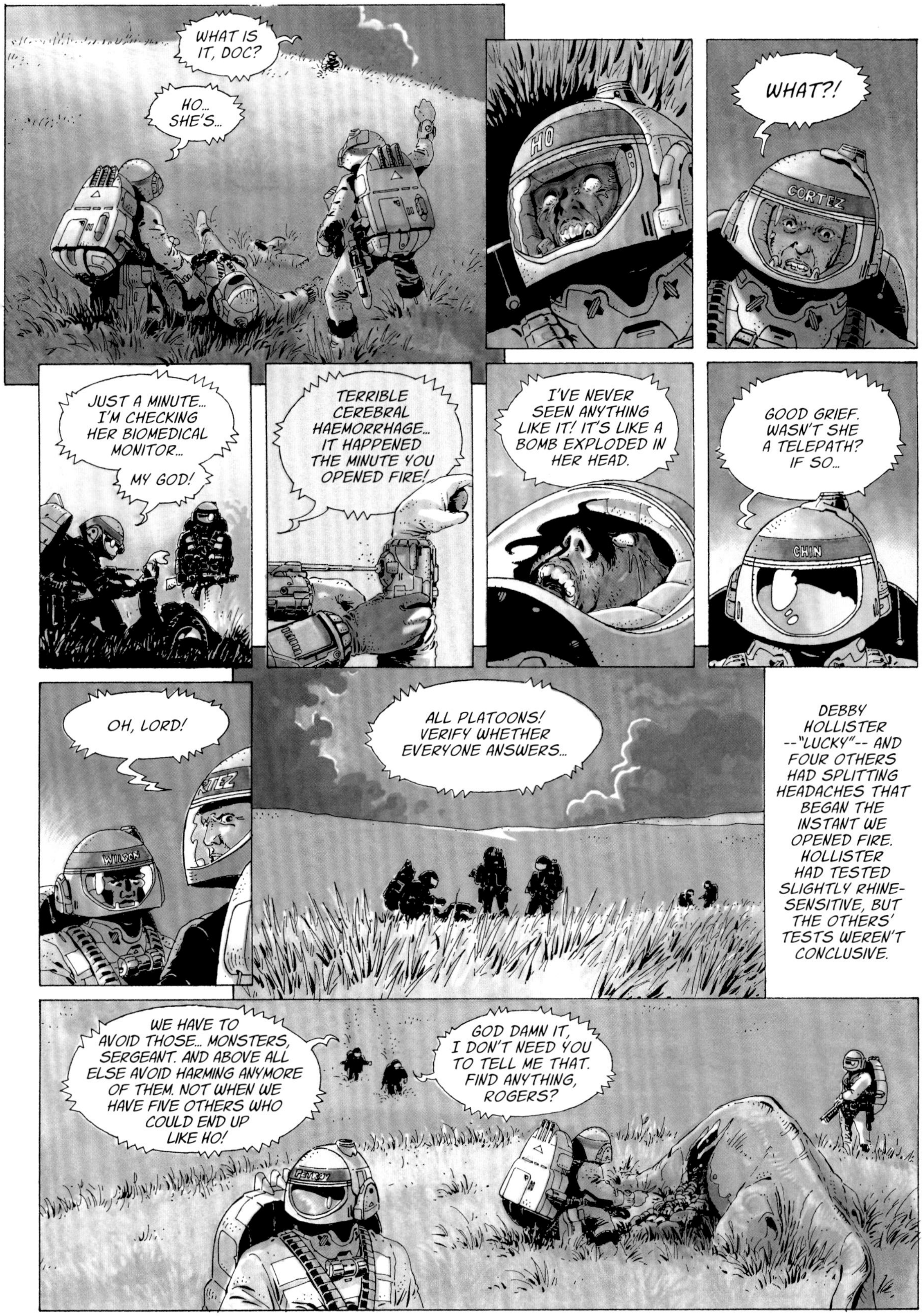
WHAT IS IT, DOC?
HO... SHE'S...
WHAT?!
JUST A MINUTE... I'M CHECKING HER BIOMEDICAL MONITOR...
MY GOD!
TERRIBLE CEREBRAL HAEMORRHAGE... IT HAPPENED THE MINUTE YOU OPENED FIRE!
I'VE NEVER SEEN ANYTHING LIKE IT! IT'S LIKE A BOMB EXPLODED IN HER HEAD.
GOOD GRIEF. WASN'T SHE A TELEPATH? IF SO...
OH, LORD!
ALL PLATOONS! VERIFY WHETHER EVERYONE ANSWERS...
DEBBY HOLLISTER --"LUCKY"-- AND FOUR OTHERS HAD SPLITTING HEADACHES THAT BEGAN THE INSTANT WE OPENED FIRE. HOLLISTER HAD TESTED SLIGHTLY RHINE-SENSITIVE, BUT THE OTHERS' TESTS WEREN'T CONCLUSIVE.
WE HAVE TO AVOID THOSE... MONSTERS, SERGEANT. AND ABOVE ALL ELSE AVOID HARMING ANYMORE OF THEM. NOT WHEN WE HAVE FIVE OTHERS WHO COULD END UP LIKE HO!
GOD DAMN IT, I DON'T NEED YOU TO TELL ME THAT. FIND ANYTHING, ROGERS?

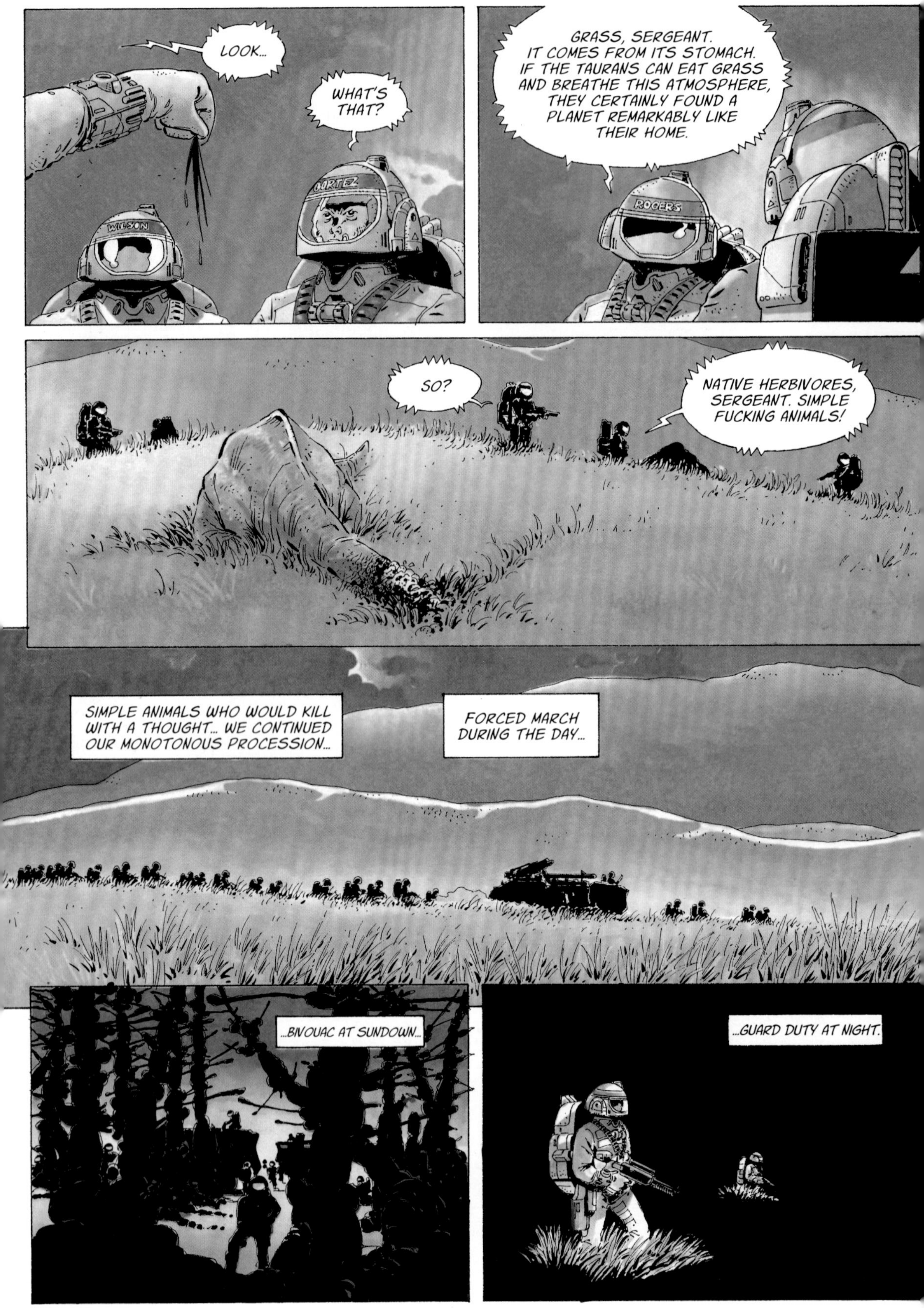
LOOK...
WHAT'S THAT?
GRASS, SERGEANT. IT COMES FROM ITS STOMACH. IF THE TAURANS CAN EAT GRASS AND BREATHE THIS ATMOSPHERE, THEY CERTAINLY FOUND A PLANET REMARKABLY LIKE THEIR HOME.
SO?
NATIVE HERBIVORES, SERGEANT. SIMPLE FUCKING ANIMALS!
SIMPLE ANIMALS WHO WOULD KILL WITH A THOUGHT... WE CONTINUED OUR MONOTONOUS PROCESSION...
FORCED MARCH DURING THE DAY...
...BIVOUAC AT SUNDOWN...
...GUARD DUTY AT NIGHT.

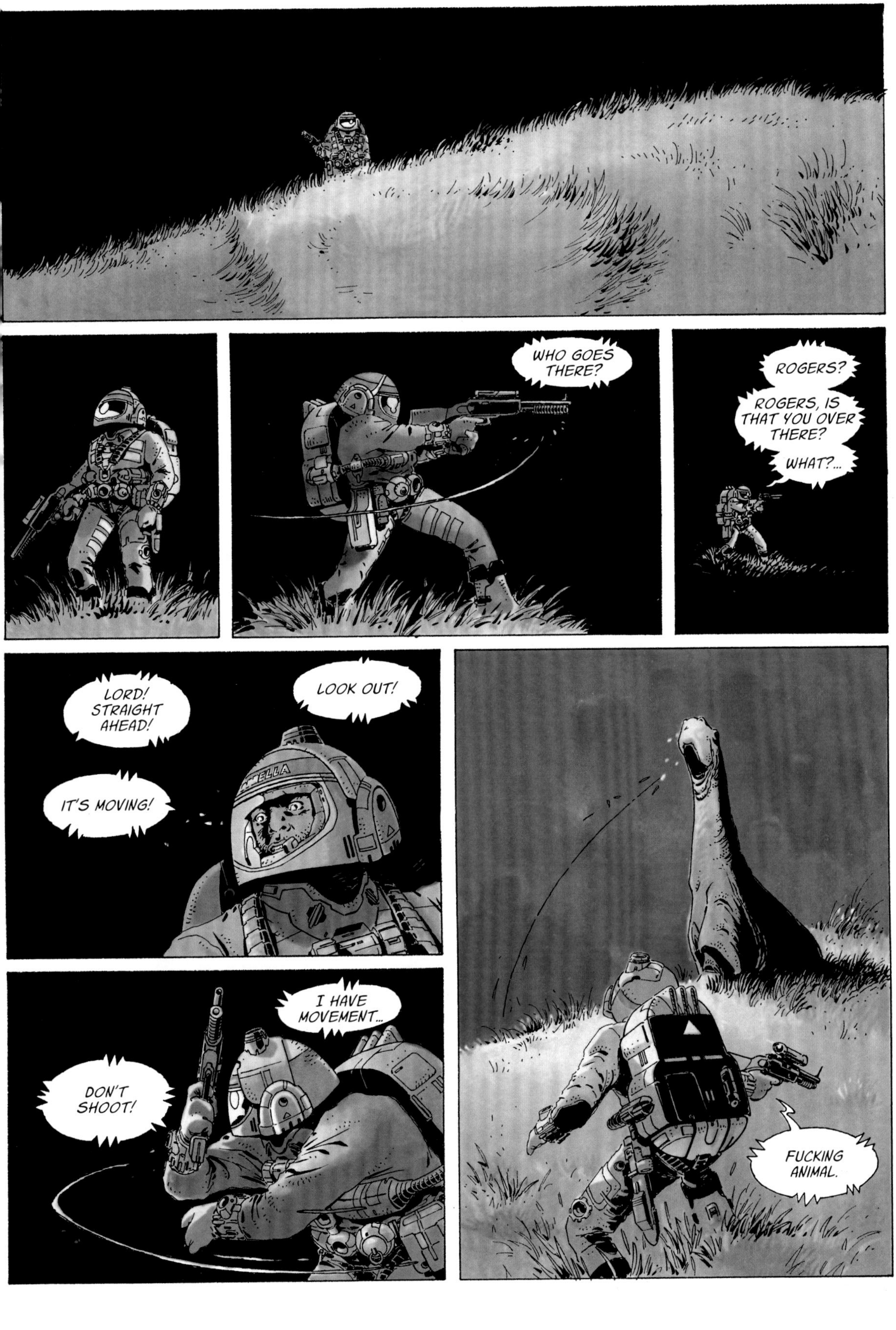
WHO GOES THERE?
ROGERS?
ROGERS, IS THAT YOU OVER THERE?
WHAT?...
LORD! STRAIGHT AHEAD!
LOOK OUT!
IT'S MOVING!
I HAVE MOVEMENT...
DON'T SHOOT!
FUCKING ANIMAL.

IT CHEWED CALMLY...   ALMOST WITHOUT MOVING...   STARING AT ME.   WAS IT TRYING TO COMMUNICATE...   OR TO DESTROY ME?

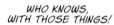

WHO KNOWS, WITH THOSE THINGS!

SERGEANT! HOLLISTER HERE. THEY'RE TRYING TO TELL US SOMETHING...

THEY'RE NOT AFRAID OF US... THEY THINK WE'RE... FUNNY!

THEY'RE CURIOUS, NOT DANGEROUS...

DON'T ASK ME HOW I KNOW. **I FEEL IT!**

HMM...

OKAY... CORTEZ HERE. I KNOW YOU'D LIKE TO SEE THEM DEAD FOR WHAT HAPPENED TO HO, BUT WE HAVE TO BE CAREFUL. LET THEM GRAZE IN PEACE.

I DIDN'T WANT TO SEE THEM DEAD. I DIDN'T WANT TO SEE THEM AT ALL.

AND THE FEELING SHOULD'VE BEEN MUTUAL... HOWEVER, THEY SEEMED TO WANT OUR COMPANY FOR SOME REASON.

WELL?

WHAT DO THESE CREATURES WANT? IT'S LIKE THEY FEEL SOMETHING!

YES, I...

JESUS! HOLLISTER HERE. GET DOWN! QUICK!

THE TAURANS!

MANDELLA

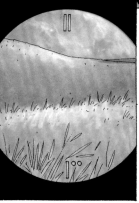

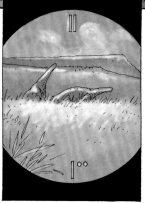

ENEMY VESSEL OVERHEAD.

MANDELLA

HIS VOICE WAS ALMOST LACONIC.

THE VESSEL WASN'T EXACTLY OVERHEAD. IT WAS SLIGHTLY TO THE NORTH, MOVING VERY SLOWLY.

FOR THE FIRST TIME, HUMAN EYES SAW AN ACTUAL TAURAN.

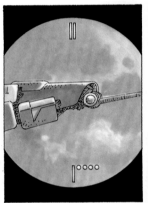

IT EITHER HADN'T SEEN US OR IT THOUGHT WE WERE PART OF THE HERD OF ANIMALS. IT DISAPPEARED IN THE DISTANCE.

CORTEZ HERE...

PLATOON LEADERS ASSEMBLE HERE...

EVERYONE ELSE, STAY ALERT -- MINDS OPEN.

ESPECIALLY YOU, HOLLISTER!

SEVERAL OF THE BEASTS SEEMED TO WANT TO TAKE PART IN THE BRIEFING...

WE TRIED TO IGNORE THEM...

PLUG IN YOUR SCREENS. I'LL SHOW YOU SOME IMAGES OF THE ENEMY BASE. THEY WERE TAKEN BY A DRONE SCOUT...

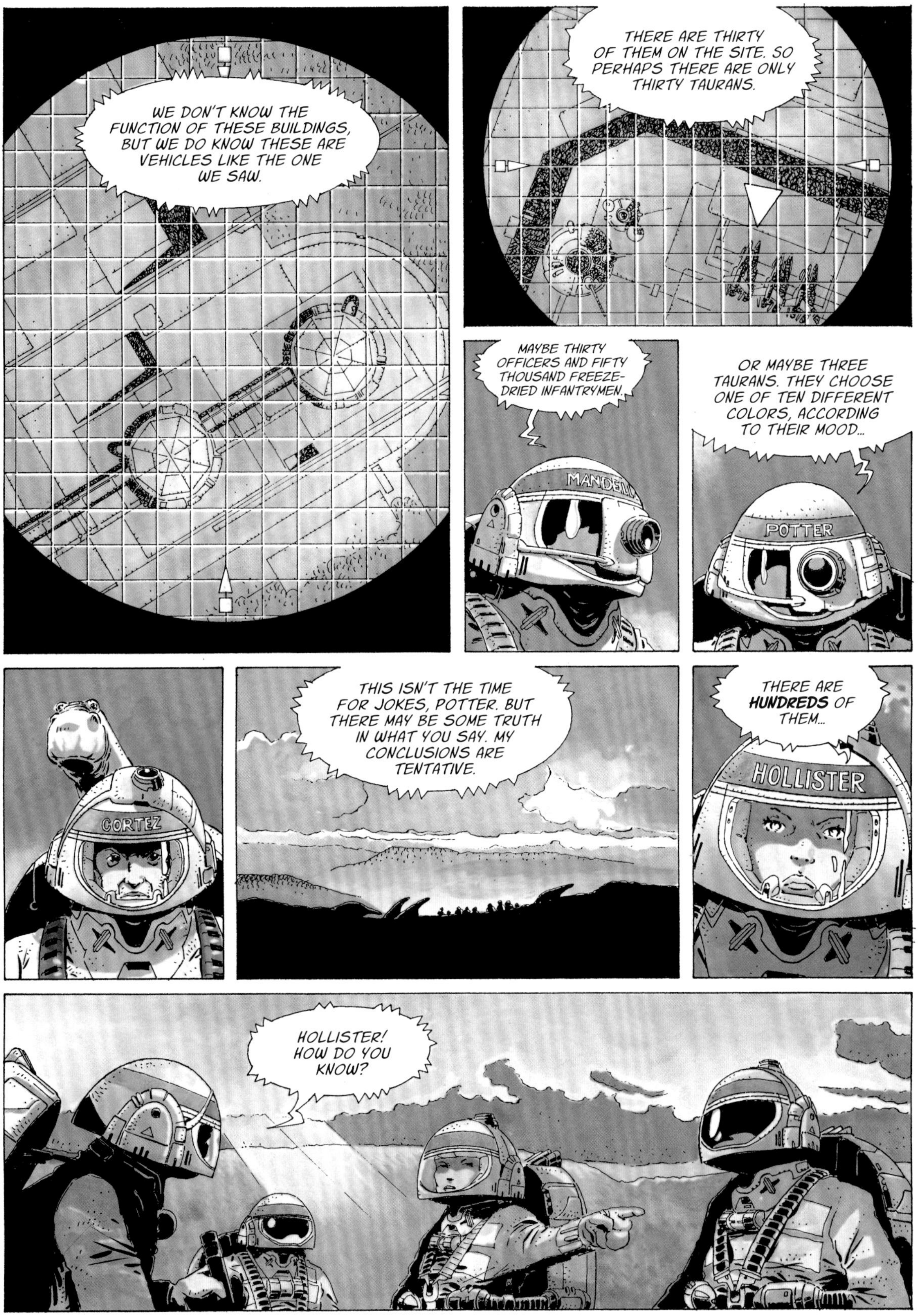
WE DON'T KNOW THE FUNCTION OF THESE BUILDINGS, BUT WE DO KNOW THESE ARE VEHICLES LIKE THE ONE WE SAW.
THERE ARE THIRTY OF THEM ON THE SITE. SO PERHAPS THERE ARE ONLY THIRTY TAURANS.
MAYBE THIRTY OFFICERS AND FIFTY THOUSAND FREEZE-DRIED INFANTRYMEN.
MANDELLA
OR MAYBE THREE TAURANS. THEY CHOOSE ONE OF TEN DIFFERENT COLORS, ACCORDING TO THEIR MOOD...
POTTER
CORTEZ
THIS ISN'T THE TIME FOR JOKES, POTTER. BUT THERE MAY BE SOME TRUTH IN WHAT YOU SAY. MY CONCLUSIONS ARE TENTATIVE.
THERE ARE **HUNDREDS** OF THEM...
HOLLISTER
HOLLISTER! HOW DO YOU KNOW?

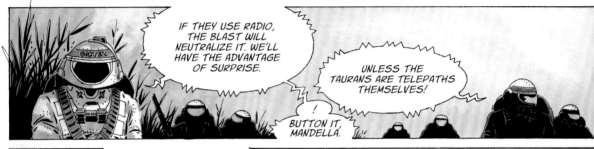

ALL RIGHT... LET'S SUPPOSE THEY HAVE AN ADVANTAGE IN NUMBERS. THE HOPE IS GOING TO SET OFF A NUCLEAR CHARGE IN THE UPPER LAYER OF THE ATMOSPHERE. WE'LL ATTACK AS SOON AS THEIR COMMUNICATION SYSTEM IS JAMMED.

IF THEY USE RADIO, THE BLAST WILL NEUTRALIZE IT. WE'LL HAVE THE ADVANTAGE OF SURPRISE.

UNLESS THE TAURANS ARE TELEPATHS THEMSELVES!

!

BUTTON IT, MANDELLA.

OKAY, WE'RE GOING TO OVERRUN THE BASE, LEAVING AS MUCH AS POSSIBLE INTACT. TAKE ONE PRISONER.

POTTER, HERE: YOU MEAN AT LEAST ONE PRISONER?

I 36B

I REPEAT: ONLY **ONE** PRISONER.

POTTER, I'M WITHDRAWING YOUR COMMAND. SEND ME CHAVEZ.

OKAY, SERGEANT.

THE RELIEF IN POTTER'S VOICE WAS UNMISTAKEABLE.

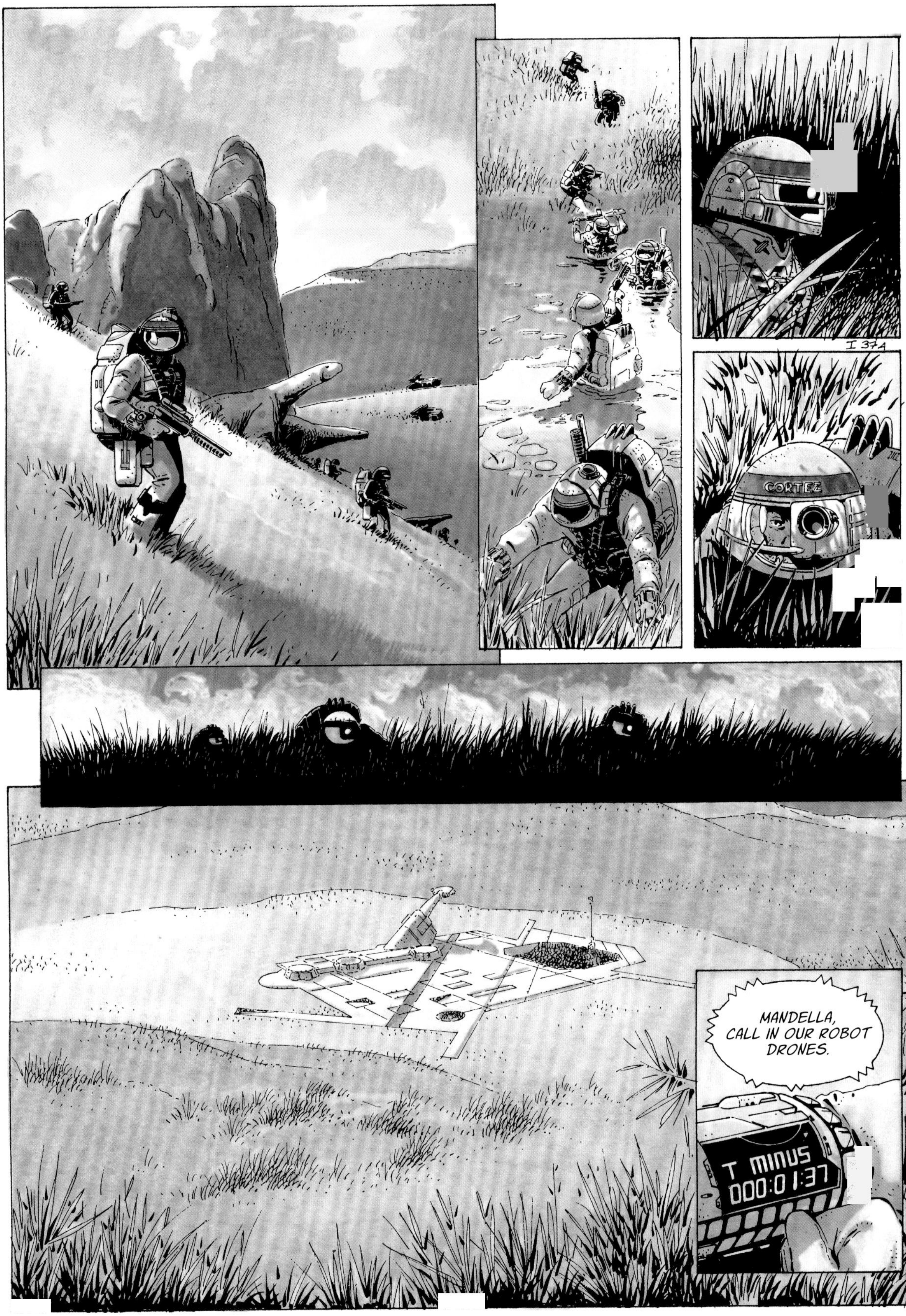
CORTEZ
MANDELLA, CALL IN OUR ROBOT DRONES.
T MINUS
000:01:37

LISTEN UP! MAYBE YOU'RE LIKE POTTER. YOU DON'T WANT TO BE INVOLVED IN A MASSACRE. THAT'S VERY CIVILIZED...

MINUS 0:01:02

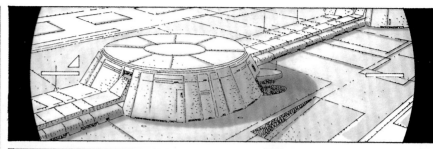

...BUT NONE OF US CAN AFFORD PITY. SO... I'M GOING TO ACTIVATE THE POST-HYPNOTIC SUGGESTION WE IMPLANTED IN ALL OF YOU DURING YOUR TRAINING...

MINUS 0:00:48

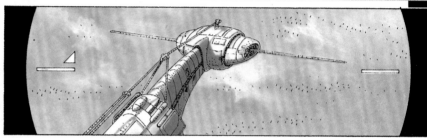

IT'S TEMPORARY. IT WILL HELP YOU DO YOUR JOB.

MINUS 0:00:17

SERGEANT!

QUIET! WE DON'T HAVE TIME TO DISCUSS IT!

MINUS 0:00:01

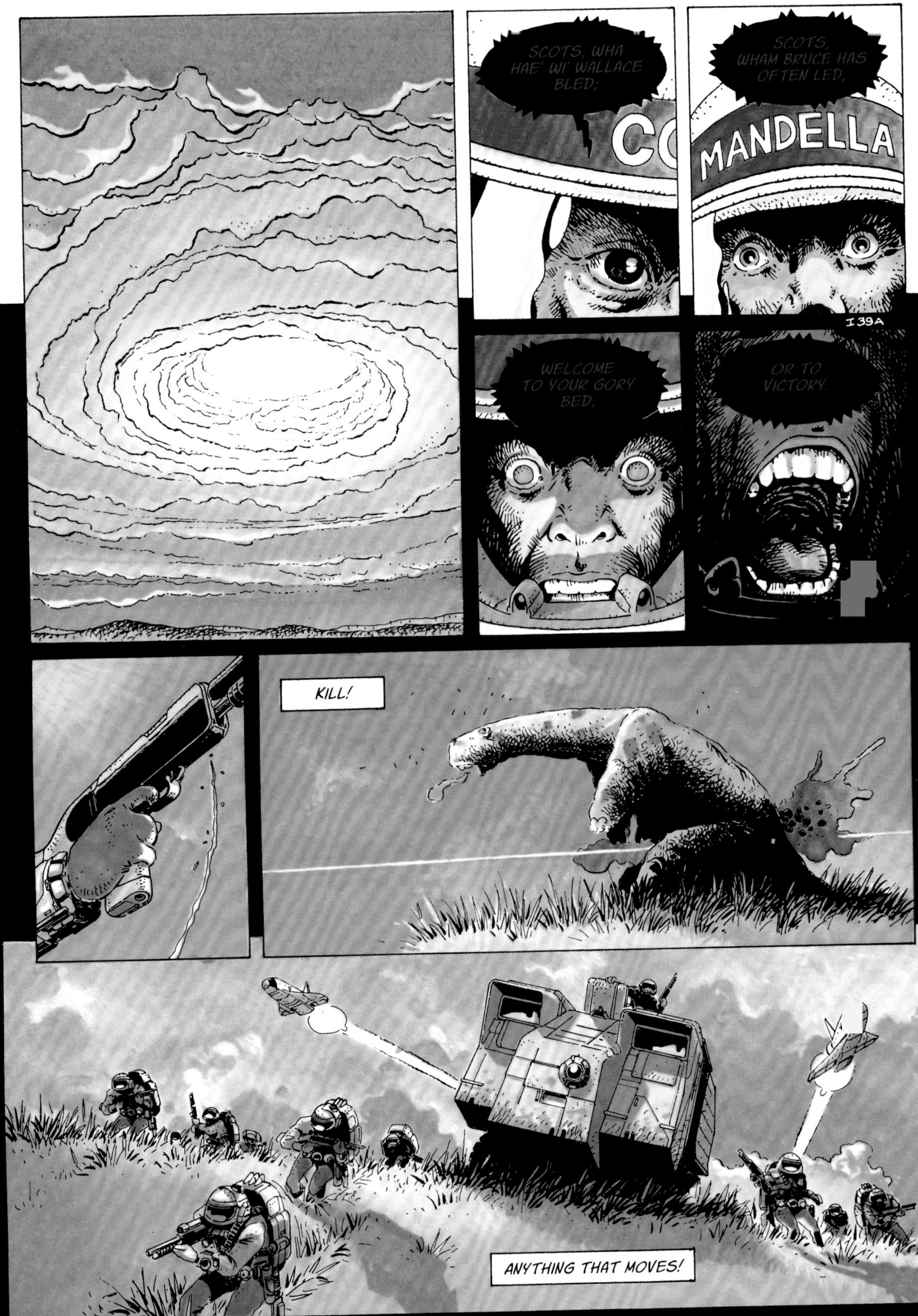
SCOTS, WHA HAE' WI' WALLACE BLED;
CO
SCOTS, WHAM BRUCE HAS OFTEN LED,
MANDELLA
I39A
WELCOME TO YOUR GORY BED,
OR TO VICTORY.
KILL!
ANYTHING THAT MOVES!

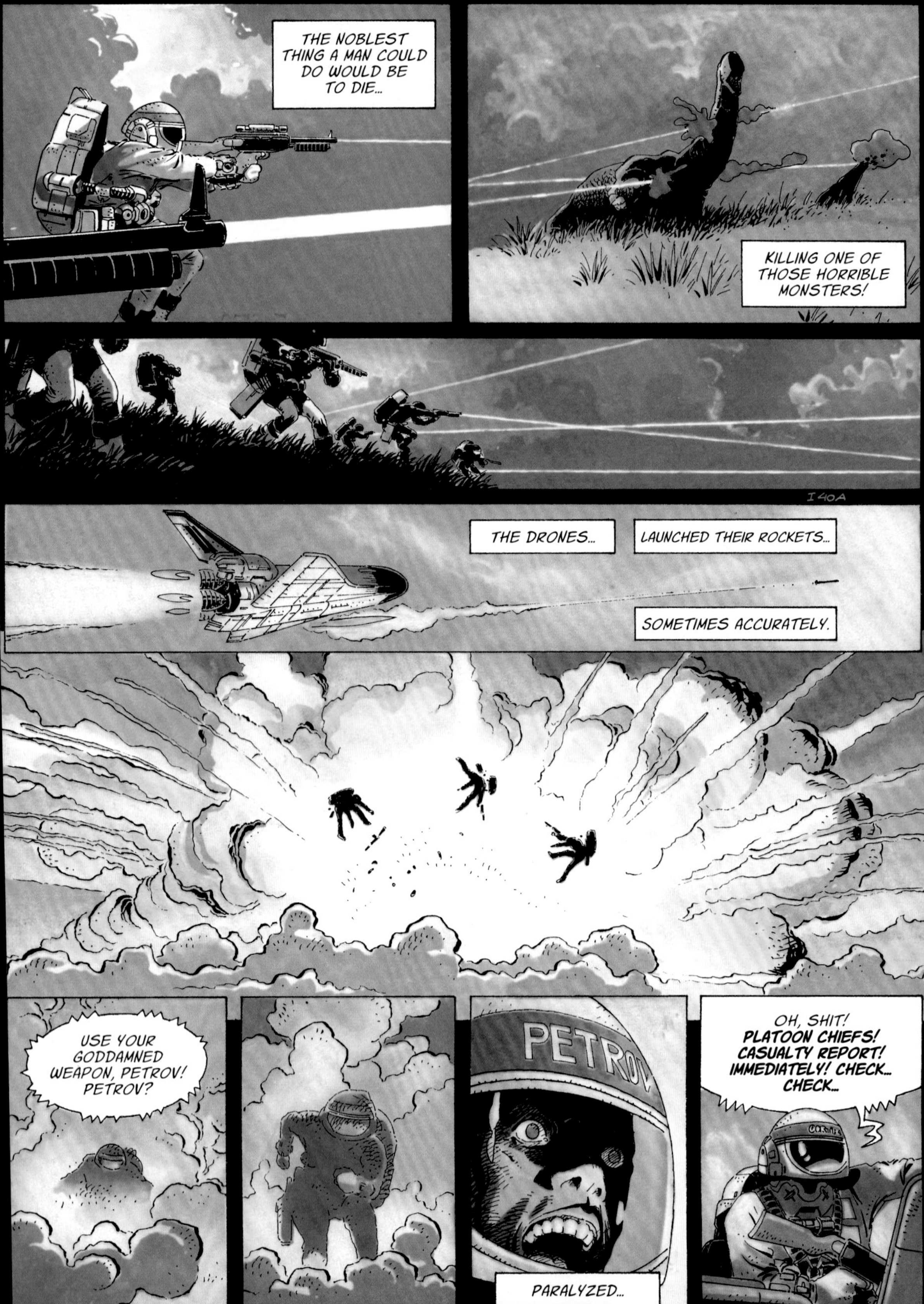
THE NOBLEST THING A MAN COULD DO WOULD BE TO DIE...
KILLING ONE OF THOSE HORRIBLE MONSTERS!
I 40A
THE DRONES...
LAUNCHED THEIR ROCKETS...
SOMETIMES ACCURATELY.
USE YOUR GODDAMNED WEAPON, PETROV! PETROV?
PETROV
PARALYZED...
OH, SHIT! PLATOON CHIEFS! CASUALTY REPORT! IMMEDIATELY! CHECK... CHECK...

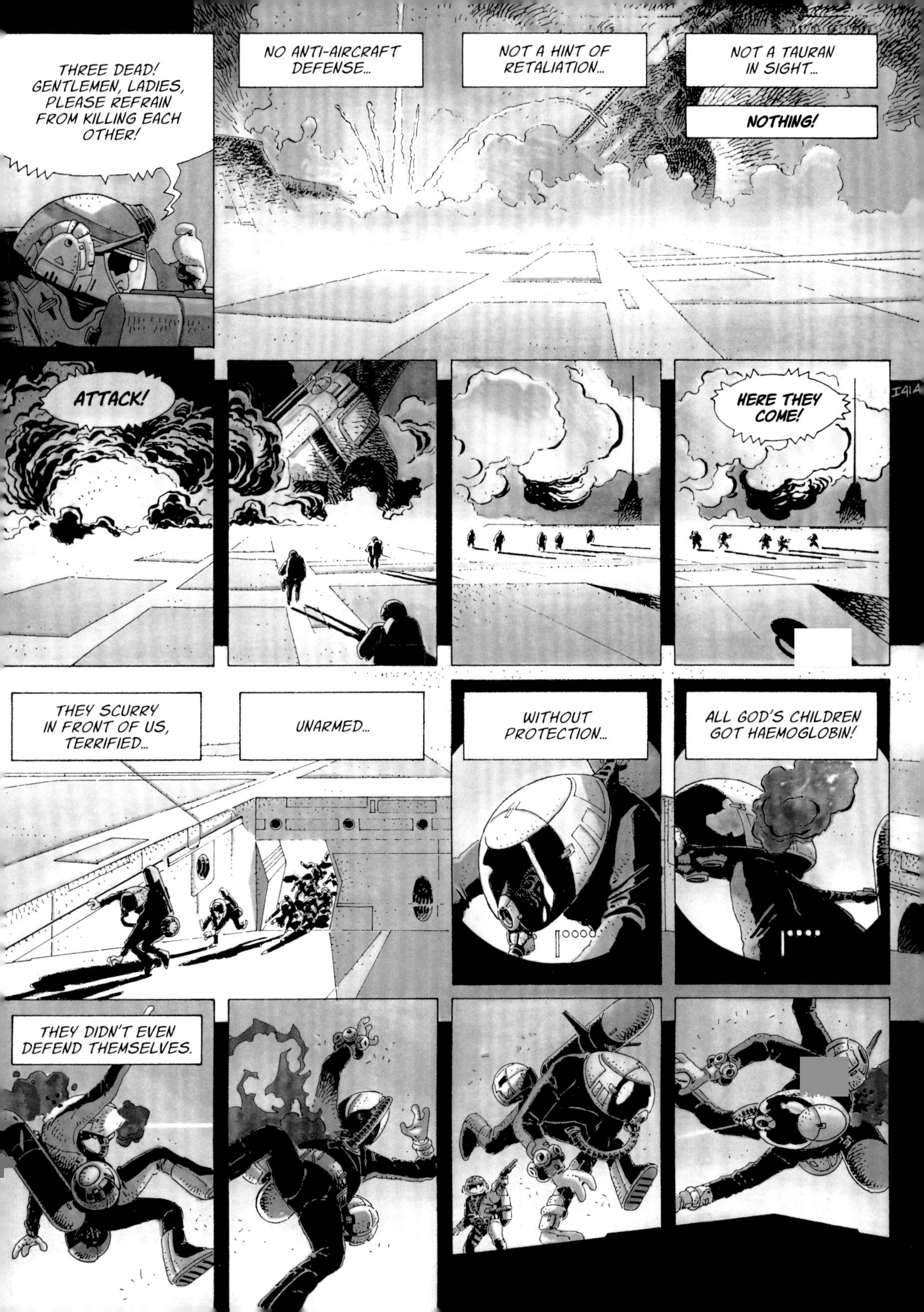
THREE DEAD! GENTLEMEN, LADIES, PLEASE REFRAIN FROM KILLING EACH OTHER!
NO ANTI-AIRCRAFT DEFENSE...
NOT A HINT OF RETALIATION...
NOT A TAURAN IN SIGHT...
NOTHING!
ATTACK!
HERE THEY COME!
THEY SCURRY IN FRONT OF US, TERRIFIED...
UNARMED...
WITHOUT PROTECTION...
ALL GOD'S CHILDREN GOT HAEMOGLOBIN!
THEY DIDN'T EVEN DEFEND THEMSELVES.

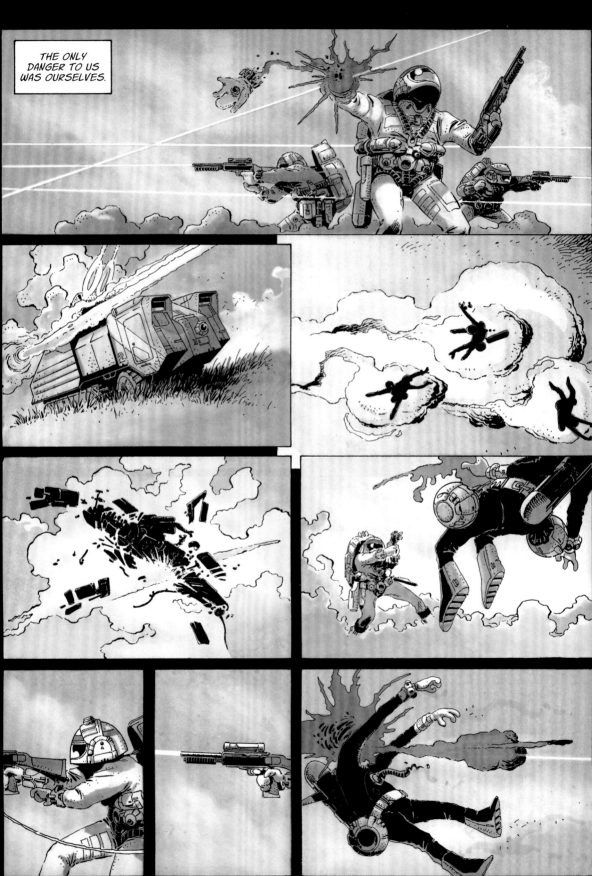

THE ONLY DANGER TO US WAS OURSELVES.

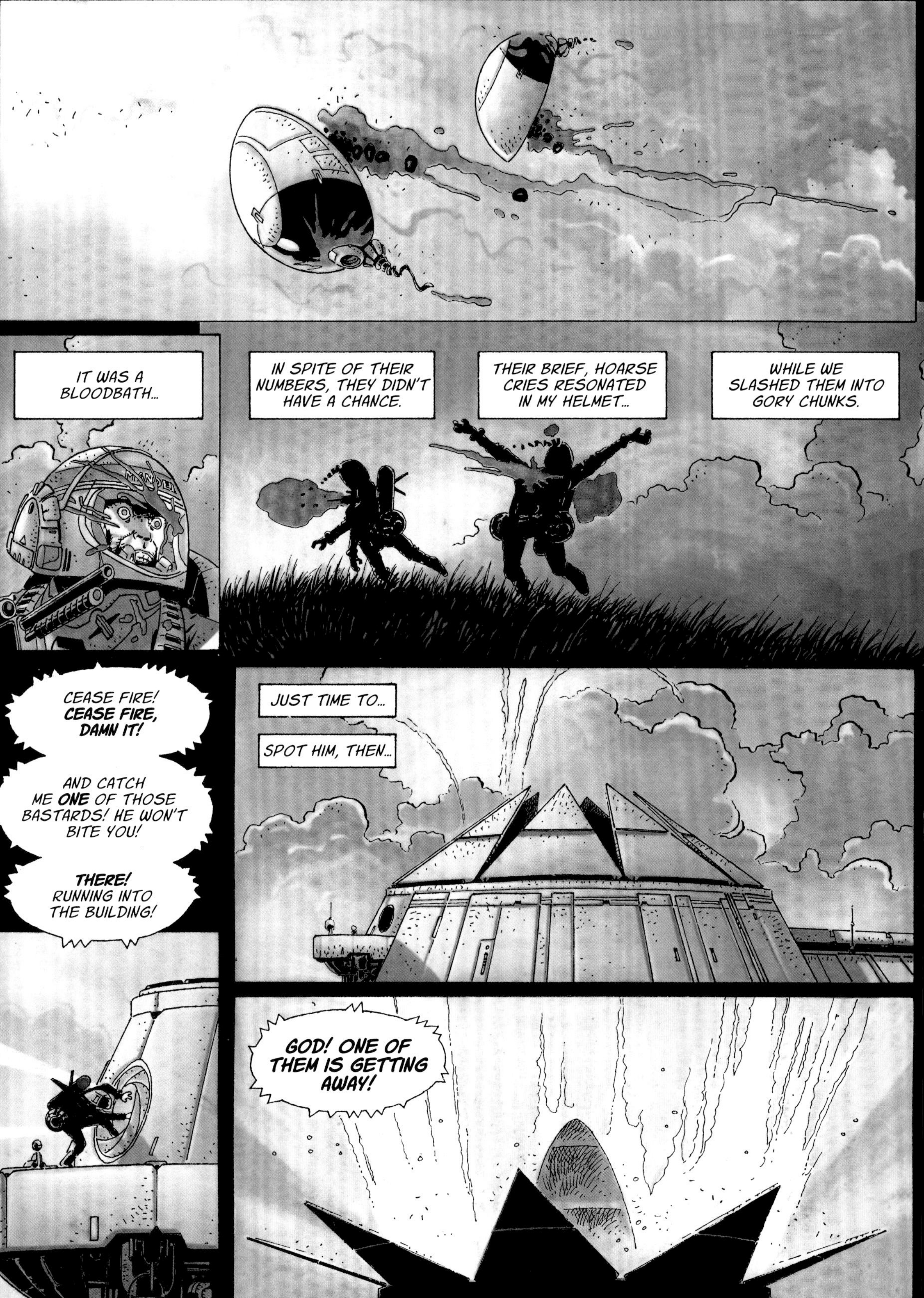
IT WAS A BLOODBATH...
IN SPITE OF THEIR NUMBERS, THEY DIDN'T HAVE A CHANCE.
THEIR BRIEF, HOARSE CRIES RESONATED IN MY HELMET...
WHILE WE SLASHED THEM INTO GORY CHUNKS.
CEASE FIRE! CEASE FIRE, DAMN IT!
AND CATCH ME ONE OF THOSE BASTARDS! HE WON'T BITE YOU!
THERE! RUNNING INTO THE BUILDING!
JUST TIME TO...
SPOT HIM, THEN...
GOD! ONE OF THEM IS GETTING AWAY!

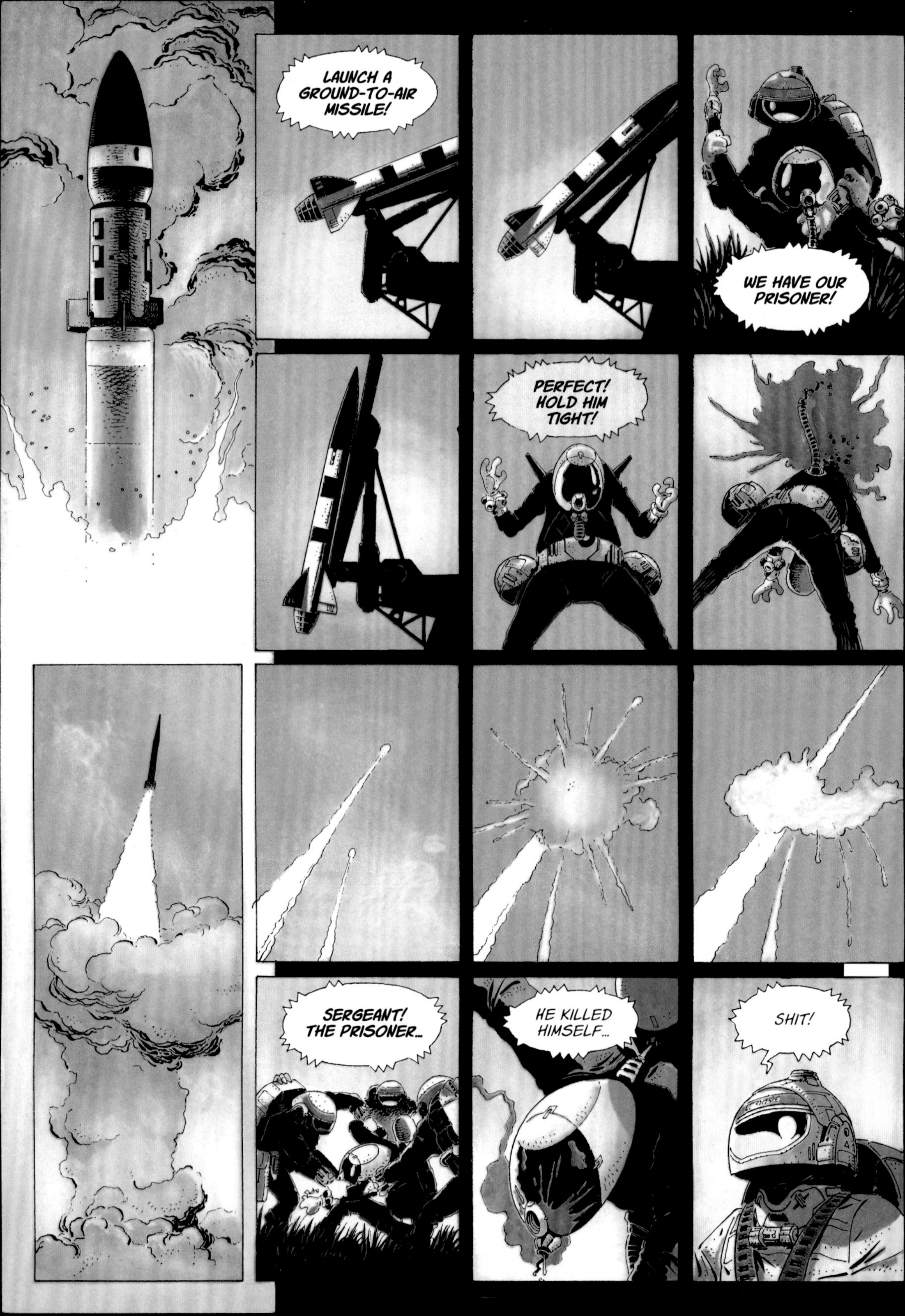
LAUNCH A GROUND-TO-AIR MISSILE!
WE HAVE OUR PRISONER!
PERFECT! HOLD HIM TIGHT!
SERGEANT! THE PRISONER...
HE KILLED HIMSELF...
SHIT!

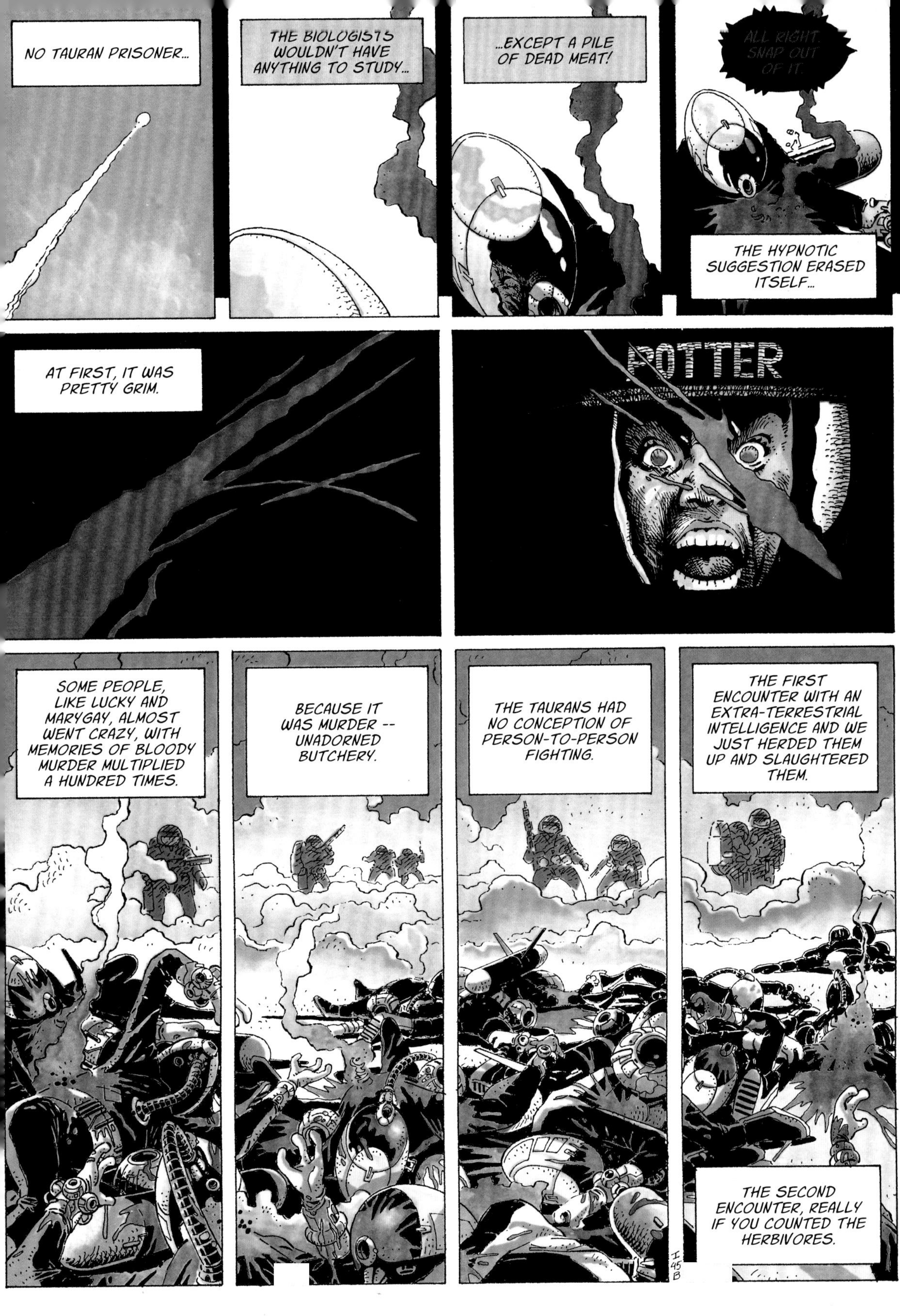
NO TAURAN PRISONER...
THE BIOLOGISTS WOULDN'T HAVE ANYTHING TO STUDY...
...EXCEPT A PILE OF DEAD MEAT!
ALL RIGHT. SNAP OUT OF IT.
THE HYPNOTIC SUGGESTION ERASED ITSELF...
AT FIRST, IT WAS PRETTY GRIM.
POTTER
SOME PEOPLE, LIKE LUCKY AND MARYGAY, ALMOST WENT CRAZY, WITH MEMORIES OF BLOODY MURDER MULTIPLIED A HUNDRED TIMES.
BECAUSE IT WAS MURDER -- UNADORNED BUTCHERY.
THE TAURANS HAD NO CONCEPTION OF PERSON-TO-PERSON FIGHTING.
THE FIRST ENCOUNTER WITH AN EXTRA-TERRESTRIAL INTELLIGENCE AND WE JUST HERDED THEM UP AND SLAUGHTERED THEM.
THE SECOND ENCOUNTER, REALLY IF YOU COUNTED THE HERBIVORES.

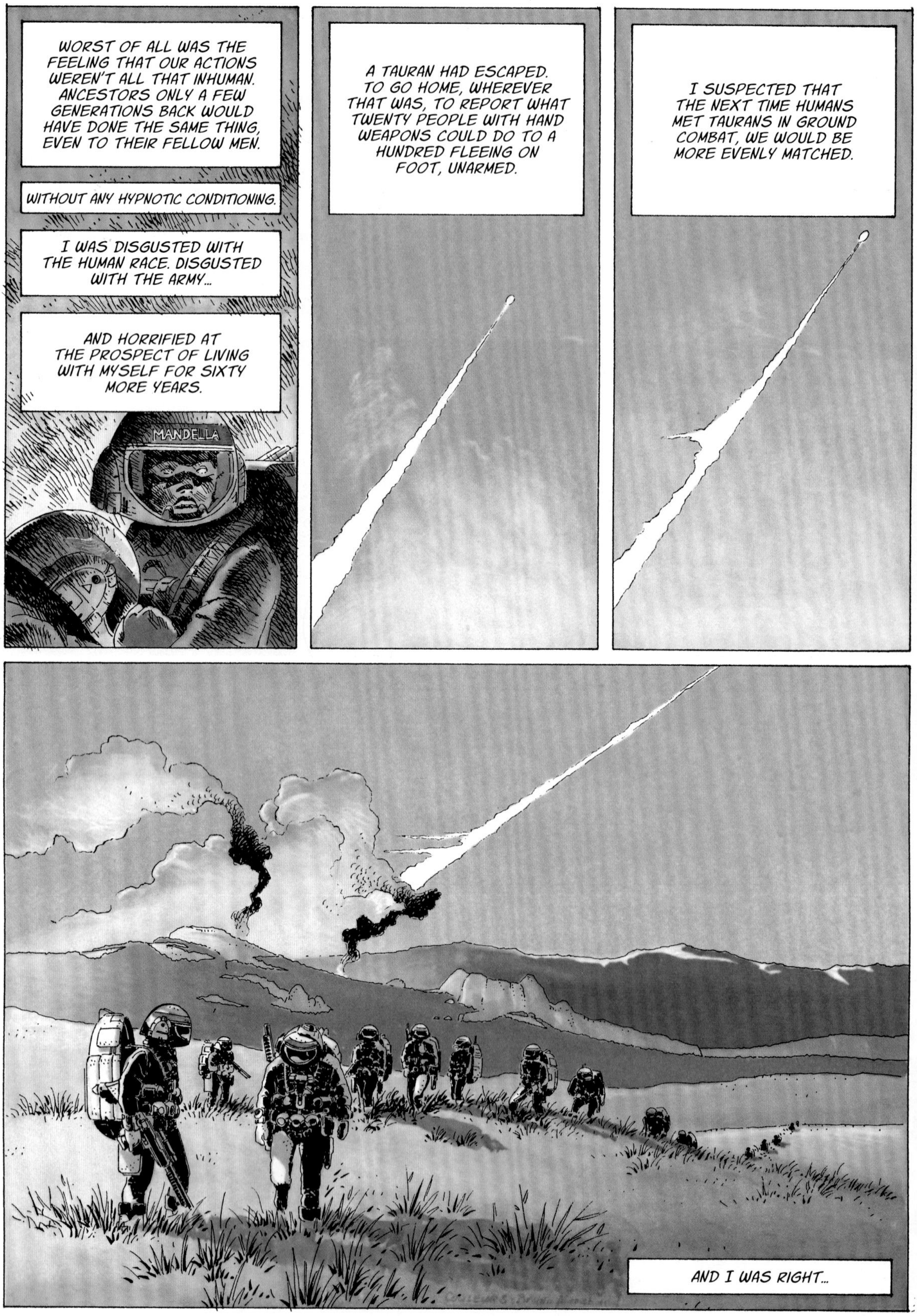
WORST OF ALL WAS THE FEELING THAT OUR ACTIONS WEREN'T ALL THAT INHUMAN. ANCESTORS ONLY A FEW GENERATIONS BACK WOULD HAVE DONE THE SAME THING, EVEN TO THEIR FELLOW MEN.
WITHOUT ANY HYPNOTIC CONDITIONING.
I WAS DISGUSTED WITH THE HUMAN RACE. DISGUSTED WITH THE ARMY...
AND HORRIFIED AT THE PROSPECT OF LIVING WITH MYSELF FOR SIXTY MORE YEARS.
MANDELLA
A TAURAN HAD ESCAPED. TO GO HOME, WHEREVER THAT WAS, TO REPORT WHAT TWENTY PEOPLE WITH HAND WEAPONS COULD DO TO A HUNDRED FLEEING ON FOOT, UNARMED.
I SUSPECTED THAT THE NEXT TIME HUMANS MET TAURANS IN GROUND COMBAT, WE WOULD BE MORE EVENLY MATCHED.
AND I WAS RIGHT...

WE WERE BEING FOLLOWED...

I WAS AFRAID.

WHO WOULDN'T BE AFRAID?

II 1A

ONLY A FOOL, A ROBOT, A SUICIDE...

II 1 B

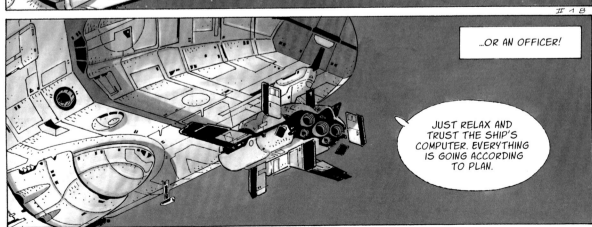

...OR AN OFFICER!

JUST RELAX AND TRUST THE SHIP'S COMPUTER. EVERYTHING IS GOING ACCORDING TO PLAN.

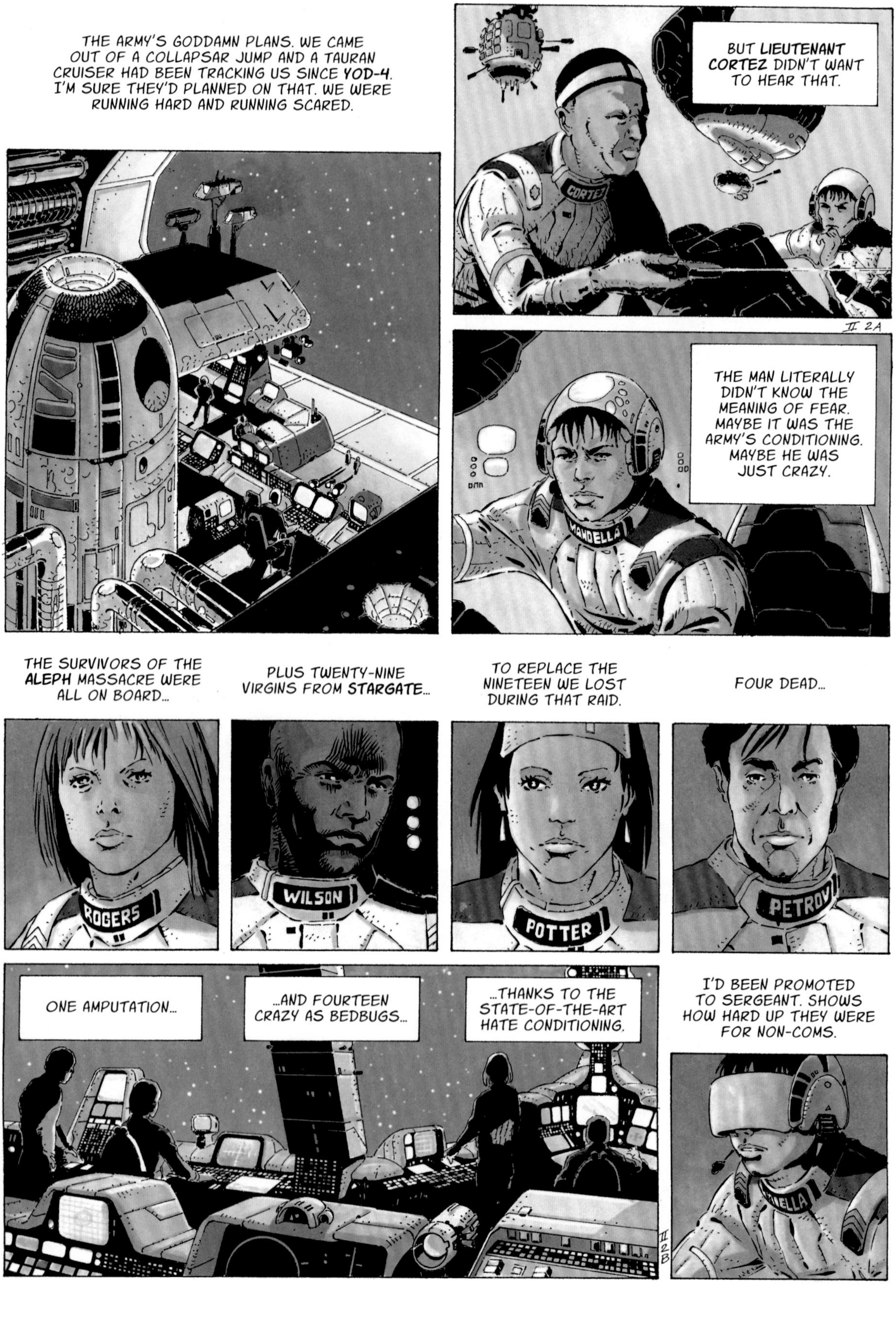
THE ARMY'S GODDAMN PLANS. WE CAME OUT OF A COLLAPSAR JUMP AND A TAURAN CRUISER HAD BEEN TRACKING US SINCE **YOD-4**. I'M SURE THEY'D PLANNED ON THAT. WE WERE RUNNING HARD AND RUNNING SCARED.
BUT **LIEUTENANT CORTEZ** DIDN'T WANT TO HEAR THAT.
CORTEZ
II 2A
THE MAN LITERALLY DIDN'T KNOW THE MEANING OF FEAR. MAYBE IT WAS THE ARMY'S CONDITIONING. MAYBE HE WAS JUST CRAZY.
MANDELLA
THE SURVIVORS OF THE **ALEPH** MASSACRE WERE ALL ON BOARD...
ROGERS
PLUS TWENTY-NINE VIRGINS FROM **STARGATE**...
WILSON
TO REPLACE THE NINETEEN WE LOST DURING THAT RAID.
POTTER
FOUR DEAD...
PETROV
ONE AMPUTATION...
...AND FOURTEEN CRAZY AS BEDBUGS...
...THANKS TO THE STATE-OF-THE-ART HATE CONDITIONING.
II 2B
I'D BEEN PROMOTED TO SERGEANT. SHOWS HOW HARD UP THEY WERE FOR NON-COMS.

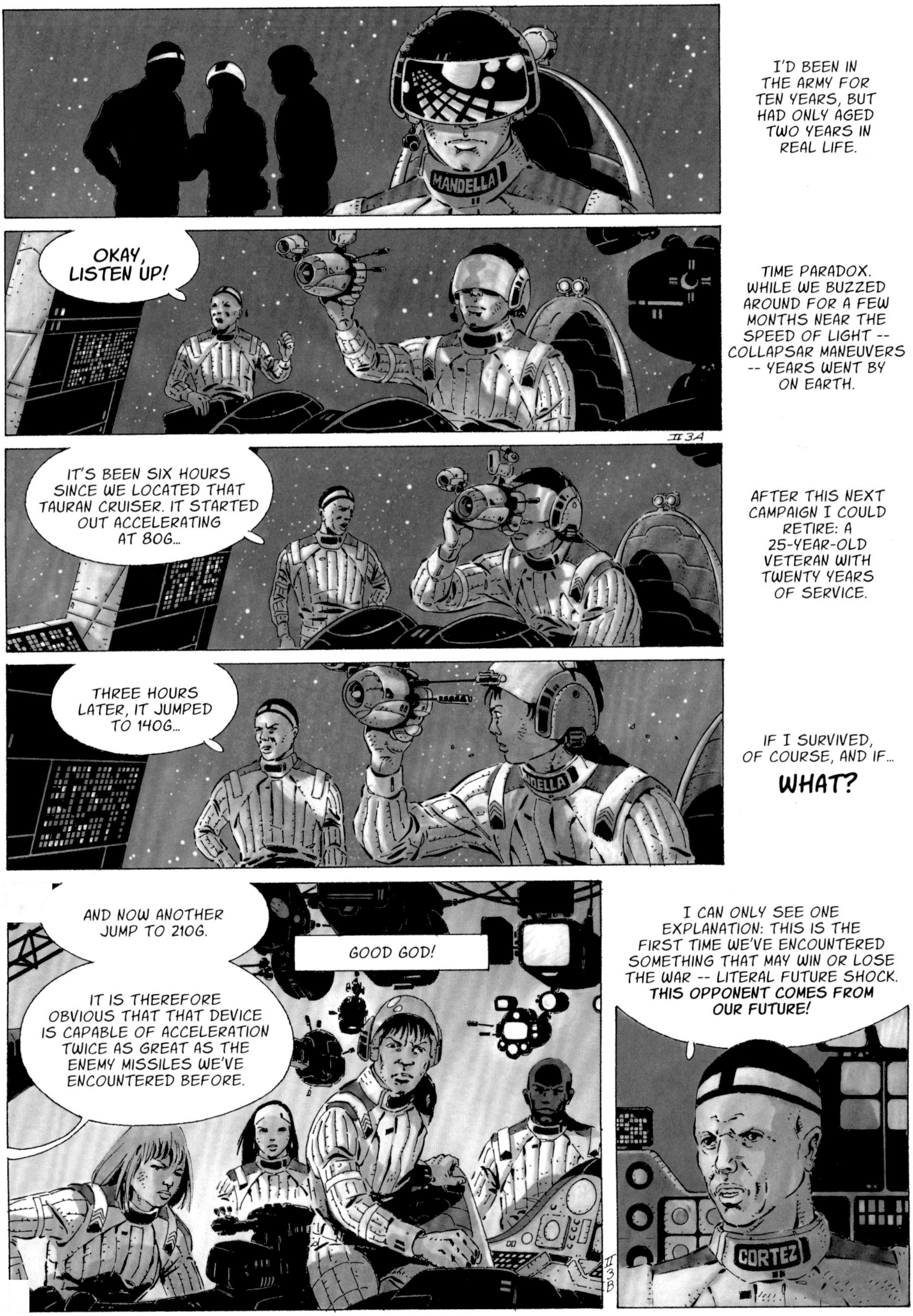
MANDELLA
I'D BEEN IN THE ARMY FOR TEN YEARS, BUT HAD ONLY AGED TWO YEARS IN REAL LIFE.
OKAY, LISTEN UP!
TIME PARADOX. WHILE WE BUZZED AROUND FOR A FEW MONTHS NEAR THE SPEED OF LIGHT -- COLLAPSAR MANEUVERS -- YEARS WENT BY ON EARTH.
IT'S BEEN SIX HOURS SINCE WE LOCATED THAT TAURAN CRUISER. IT STARTED OUT ACCELERATING AT 80G...
AFTER THIS NEXT CAMPAIGN I COULD RETIRE: A 25-YEAR-OLD VETERAN WITH TWENTY YEARS OF SERVICE.
THREE HOURS LATER, IT JUMPED TO 140G...
IF I SURVIVED, OF COURSE, AND IF...
WHAT?
AND NOW ANOTHER JUMP TO 210G.
GOOD GOD!
IT IS THEREFORE OBVIOUS THAT THAT DEVICE IS CAPABLE OF ACCELERATION TWICE AS GREAT AS THE ENEMY MISSILES WE'VE ENCOUNTERED BEFORE.
I CAN ONLY SEE ONE EXPLANATION: THIS IS THE FIRST TIME WE'VE ENCOUNTERED SOMETHING THAT MAY WIN OR LOSE THE WAR -- LITERAL FUTURE SHOCK. THIS OPPONENT COMES FROM OUR FUTURE!
CORTEZ

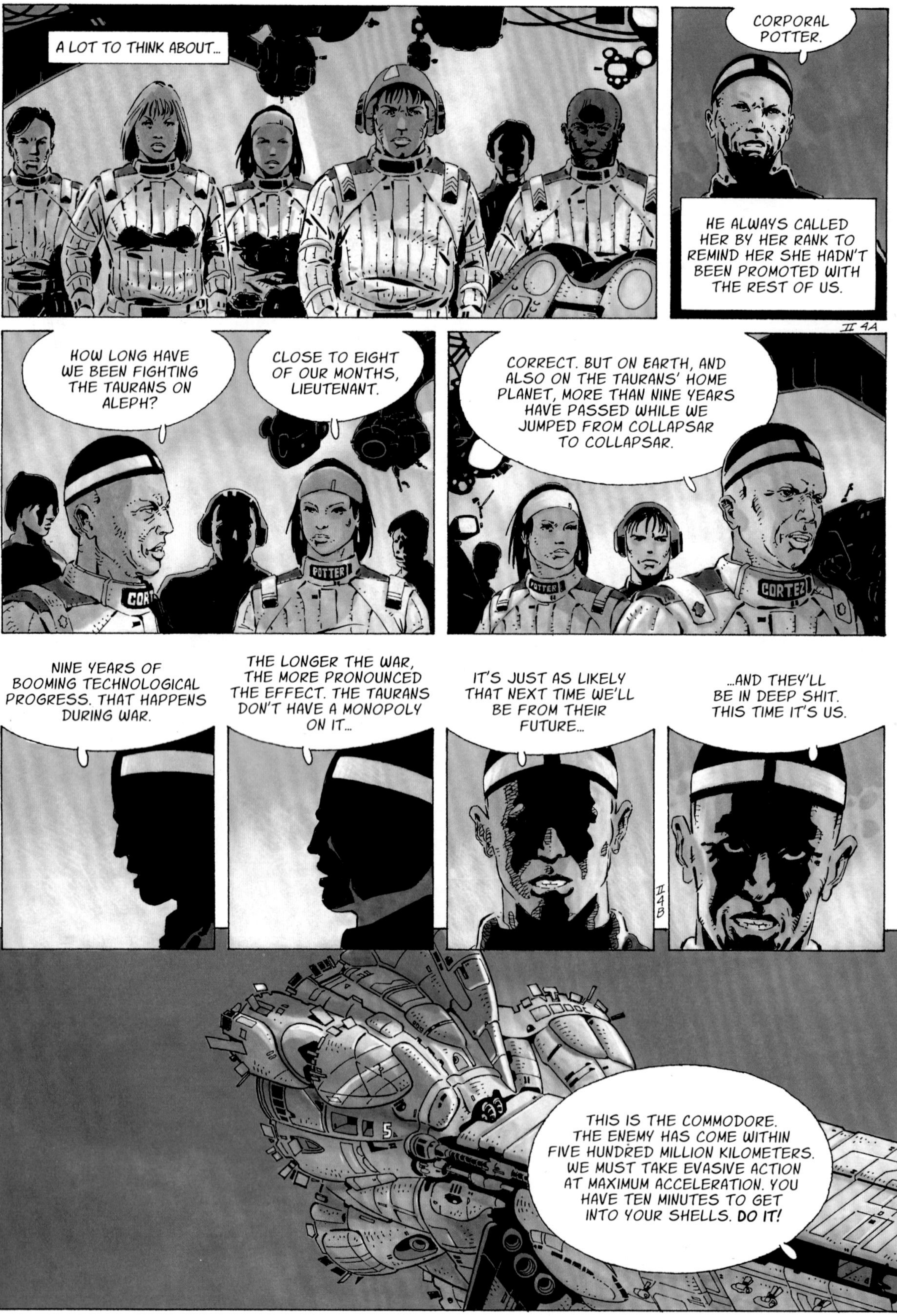
A LOT TO THINK ABOUT...
CORPORAL POTTER.
HE ALWAYS CALLED HER BY HER RANK TO REMIND HER SHE HADN'T BEEN PROMOTED WITH THE REST OF US.
HOW LONG HAVE WE BEEN FIGHTING THE TAURANS ON ALEPH?
CLOSE TO EIGHT OF OUR MONTHS, LIEUTENANT.
CORRECT. BUT ON EARTH, AND ALSO ON THE TAURANS' HOME PLANET, MORE THAN NINE YEARS HAVE PASSED WHILE WE JUMPED FROM COLLAPSAR TO COLLAPSAR.
POTTER
CORTEZ
NINE YEARS OF BOOMING TECHNOLOGICAL PROGRESS. THAT HAPPENS DURING WAR.
THE LONGER THE WAR, THE MORE PRONOUNCED THE EFFECT. THE TAURANS DON'T HAVE A MONOPOLY ON IT...
IT'S JUST AS LIKELY THAT NEXT TIME WE'LL BE FROM THEIR FUTURE...
...AND THEY'LL BE IN DEEP SHIT. THIS TIME IT'S US.
THIS IS THE COMMODORE. THE ENEMY HAS COME WITHIN FIVE HUNDRED MILLION KILOMETERS. WE MUST TAKE EVASIVE ACTION AT MAXIMUM ACCELERATION. YOU HAVE TEN MINUTES TO GET INTO YOUR SHELLS. DO IT!

THE ACCELERATION SHELLS WERE A NIGHTMARE EVEN WHEN IT WAS JUST PRACTICE...

A PENNY FOR YOUR THOUGHTS, MARYGAY.

WANT MY STRIPES?

I'M JUST A CORPORAL, SERGEANT. THEY DON'T PAY ME TO THINK.

I DON'T LIKE THIS AT ALL, WILLIAM.

ME NEITHER. I'D RATHER PLAY SOLDIER ON A PORTAL PLANET THAN LIE THERE HELPLESS, PUMPED UP, WAITING...

I KNOW...

WHILE THE COMPUTER MAKES A MILLION DECISIONS A SECOND. ALL OF THEM RIGHT, OF COURSE.

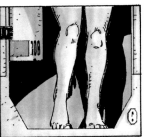

GOOD LUCK, WILL.

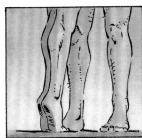

THE SAME TO YOU, MARYGAY.

THE ACCELERATION TANK: THE ARMY'S LATEST GADGET. IT MADE SURE THAT THE PRESSURE INSIDE OUR BODIES EQUALED THE PRESSURE OUTSIDE DURING EVASIVE ACTION -- EXTENDED PERIODS OF VIOLENTLY CHANGING ACCELERATION.

ON STARGATE, THEY'D IMPLANTED A REGULATOR ABOVE THE LEFT HIP, RIGHT OVER YOUR BLOOD TYPE TATTOO.

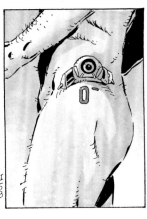

THIS DEVICE, AS WELL AS ALL THE NATURAL ORIFICES OF OUR BODIES, WAS HOOKED UP TO A HIGH-PRESSURE PUMP THAT FILLED US WITH SOME PALE BLUE STUFF THAT ALLOWED US TO SURVIVE THE DOZENS OF GEES WHILE THE SHIP ZIGZAGGED.

CORTEZ HERE.

IT'S 0520. WE'RE GOING TO SPEND ABOUT FOUR HOURS IN THE TANKS...

SECTION CHIEFS! CONNECT YOUR GROUP AT THE RED SIGNAL.

SO WE'D BE PASSIVE TARGETS FOR FOUR HOURS. ONLY A SMALL MAINTENANCE CREW HAD MOBILE TANKS.

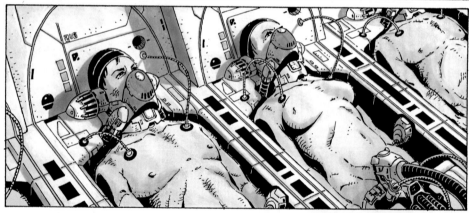

THE PRESSURE INSIDE HAD TO REMAIN EXACTLY THE SAME. IF THE SHIP WAS HIT AND THE OUTSIDE PRESSURE DROPPED, THE BODY WOULD EXPLODE LIKE A DROPPED MELON. IF IT WAS THE INSIDE PRESSURE, WE'D BE CRUSHED.

OTHERWISE, THE SYSTEM WAS PERFECT.

TROOP SHIP ANNIVERSARY PLACED UNDER ELECTRONIC CONTROL. OVER.

TAURAN CRUISER
APPROACHING
BEGIN EVASIVE
MANEUVERS

TAURAN CRUISER
APPROACHING

II 7A

TWO ENEMY MISSILES
FIRED
RANDOM ACCELERATION
BEGUN

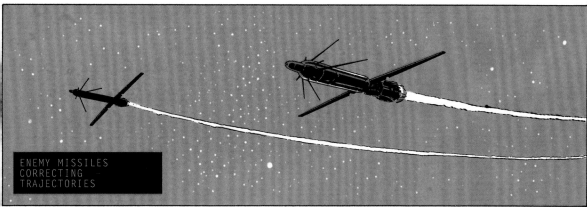

ENEMY MISSILES
CORRECTING
TRAJECTORIES

II 7B

FIRING EIGHT
PROJECTILES
INTERCEPTION
DISENGAGEMENT
IN PROCESS
FIRING COORDINATED
ON ENEMY SHIP

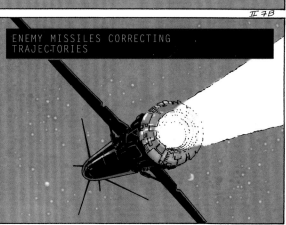

ENEMY MISSILES CORRECTING
TRAJECTORIES

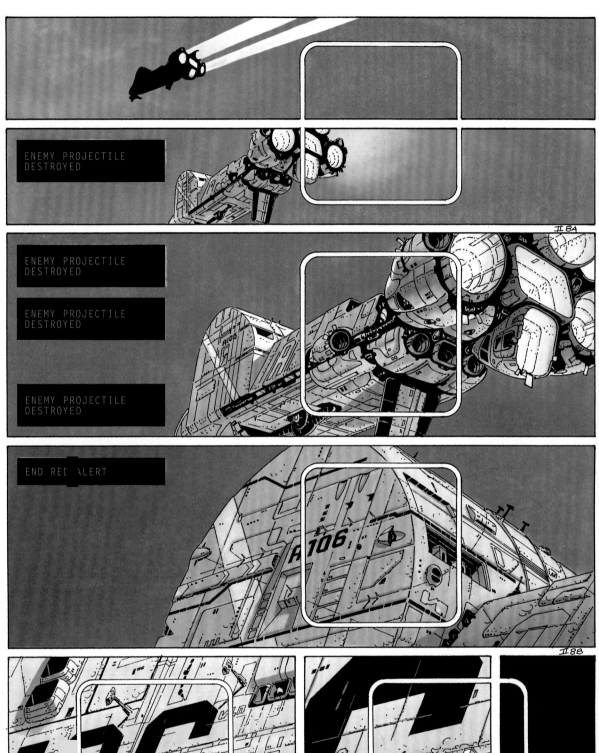

ENEMY PROJECTILE
DESTROYED

II 84

ENEMY PROJECTILE
DESTROYED

ENEMY PROJECTILE
DESTROYED

ENEMY PROJECTILE
DESTROYED

END RED ALERT

A106

II 88

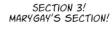

THE PRESSURE WAS ALMOST DOWN TO NORMAL BEFORE I REALIZED WE WERE ALIVE; WE HAD WON...

I WAS ONLY PARTLY RIGHT...

MANDELLA! ROGERS HERE! GO TO SECTION 3, THERE'S A PROBLEM. DALTON HAD TO DEPRESSURIZE IT FROM CONTROL.

SECTION 3! MARYGAY'S SECTION!

I CROSSED THE SHIP IN BARE FEET. THE SMELL WAS FRIGHTENING, BURNT METAL AND OZONE AND SOMETHING ELSE. PEOPLE WERE STAGGERING OUT OF THE SECTION...

PALE, CONFUSED, LURCHING...

INSIDE, SOMEONE WAS SHOUTING...

IT WAS **STRUVE**, MARYGAY'S ASSISTANT. HE WAS TALKING LOUD AND FAST INTO HIS TRANSMITTER.

MEDIC! MEDIC! QUICK!

AND GOD YES, WE NEED BLOOD!

MARYGAY STILL LAY IN HER TANK...

...AND I MEAN NOW!

EVERY CENTIMETER OF HER BODY WAS COVERED IN BLOOD.

A PINK FOAM RAN FROM HER MOUTH...

I POPPED HER TANK, MANUALLY, AND...

MANDELLA!

II 10 A

EACH TIME SHE BREATHED, WITH A HOARSE SOUND...

HEY, MANDELLA!

TURN HER OVER AND READ ME HER BLOOD TYPE.

GROUP O NEGATIVE, DAMN IT!

EXCUSE ME. TYPE O, RHESUS NEGATIVE.

406

I'D SEEN THAT TATTOO TEN THOUSAND TIMES!

DOC WILSON ARRIVED, WITH TWO NURSES.

SORRY YOU HAD TO WAIT... TOO MUCH WORK.

HIS VOICE WAS WEARY.

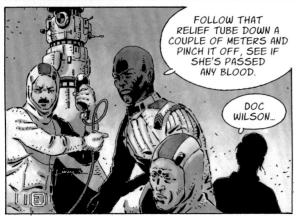

FOLLOW THAT RELIEF TUBE DOWN A COUPLE OF METERS AND PINCH IT OFF, SEE IF SHE'S PASSED ANY BLOOD.

DOC WILSON...

II 10 B

MORE PATIENTS, DOCTOR HARMONY?

NO. EXPLOSIVE DECOMPRESSION FOR THE OTHERS, CAN I HELP HERE?

THE OTHERS?!...

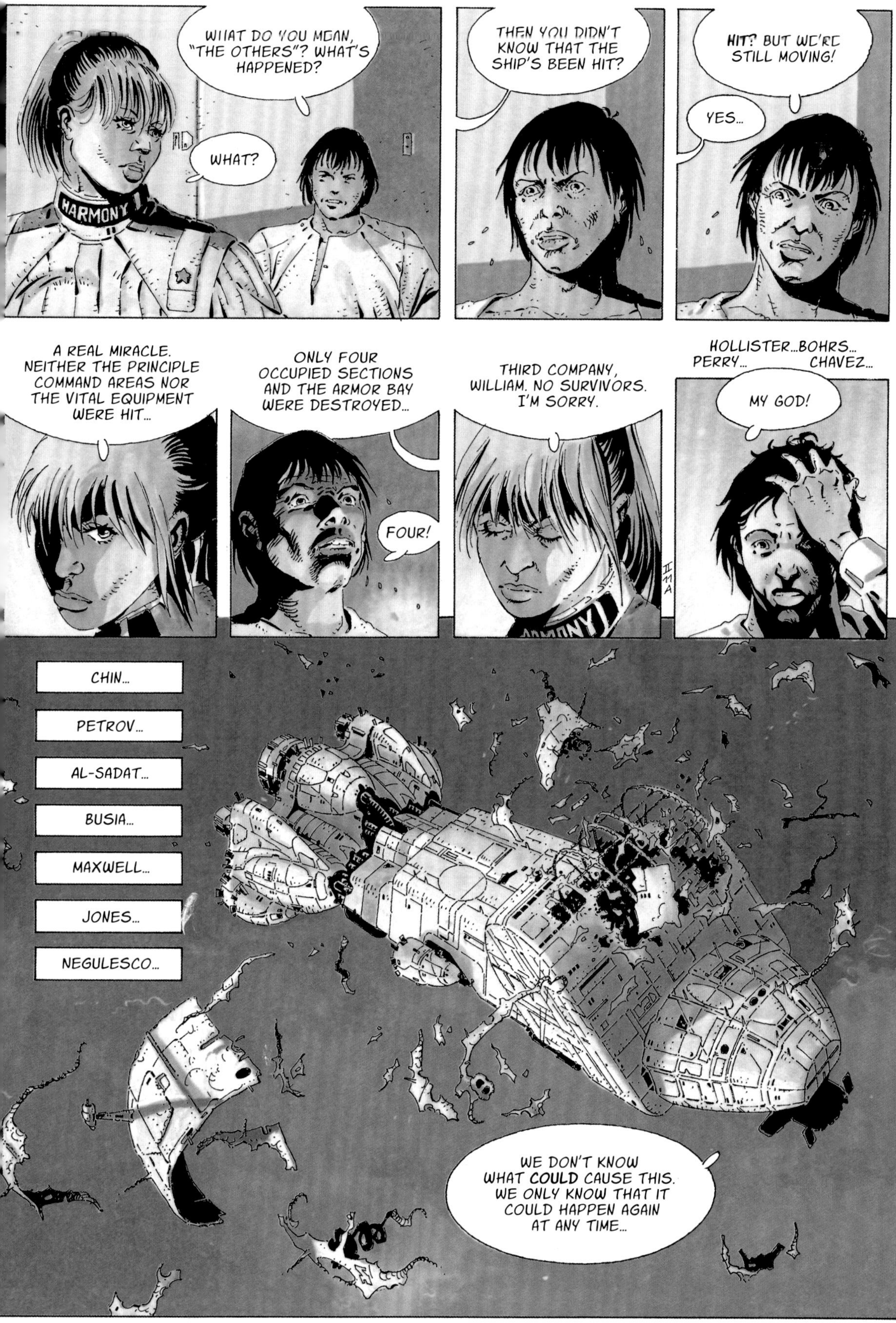
WHAT DO YOU MEAN, "THE OTHERS"? WHAT'S HAPPENED?
WHAT?
THEN YOU DIDN'T KNOW THAT THE SHIP'S BEEN HIT?
HIT? BUT WE'RE STILL MOVING!
YES...
A REAL MIRACLE. NEITHER THE PRINCIPLE COMMAND AREAS NOR THE VITAL EQUIPMENT WERE HIT...
ONLY FOUR OCCUPIED SECTIONS AND THE ARMOR BAY WERE DESTROYED...
FOUR!
THIRD COMPANY, WILLIAM. NO SURVIVORS. I'M SORRY.
HOLLISTER...BOHRS... PERRY... CHAVEZ...
MY GOD!
CHIN...
PETROV...
AL-SADAT...
BUSIA...
MAXWELL...
JONES...
NEGULESCO...
WE DON'T KNOW WHAT **COULD** CAUSE THIS. WE ONLY KNOW THAT IT COULD HAPPEN AGAIN AT ANY TIME...

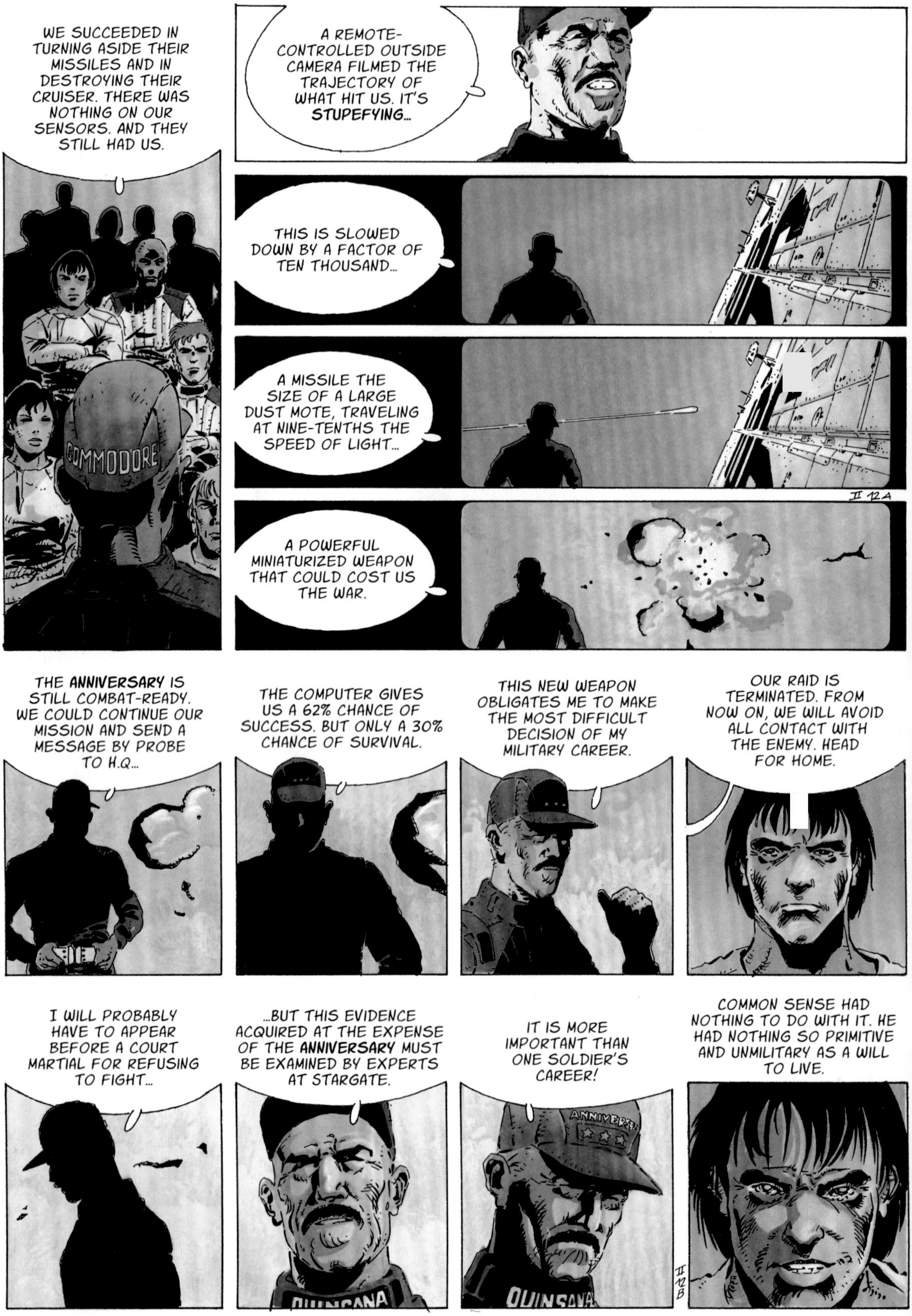
WE SUCCEEDED IN TURNING ASIDE THEIR MISSILES AND IN DESTROYING THEIR CRUISER. THERE WAS NOTHING ON OUR SENSORS. AND THEY STILL HAD US.
A REMOTE-CONTROLLED OUTSIDE CAMERA FILMED THE TRAJECTORY OF WHAT HIT US. IT'S STUPEFYING...
THIS IS SLOWED DOWN BY A FACTOR OF TEN THOUSAND...
A MISSILE THE SIZE OF A LARGE DUST MOTE, TRAVELING AT NINE-TENTHS THE SPEED OF LIGHT...
A POWERFUL MINIATURIZED WEAPON THAT COULD COST US THE WAR.
COMMODORE
II 12A
THE ANNIVERSARY IS STILL COMBAT-READY. WE COULD CONTINUE OUR MISSION AND SEND A MESSAGE BY PROBE TO H.Q...
THE COMPUTER GIVES US A 62% CHANCE OF SUCCESS. BUT ONLY A 30% CHANCE OF SURVIVAL.
THIS NEW WEAPON OBLIGATES ME TO MAKE THE MOST DIFFICULT DECISION OF MY MILITARY CAREER.
OUR RAID IS TERMINATED. FROM NOW ON, WE WILL AVOID ALL CONTACT WITH THE ENEMY. HEAD FOR HOME.
I WILL PROBABLY HAVE TO APPEAR BEFORE A COURT MARTIAL FOR REFUSING TO FIGHT...
...BUT THIS EVIDENCE ACQUIRED AT THE EXPENSE OF THE ANNIVERSARY MUST BE EXAMINED BY EXPERTS AT STARGATE.
QUINSANA
IT IS MORE IMPORTANT THAN ONE SOLDIER'S CAREER!
ANNIVERSA
QUINSANA
II 12 B
COMMON SENSE HAD NOTHING TO DO WITH IT. HE HAD NOTHING SO PRIMITIVE AND UNMILITARY AS A WILL TO LIVE.

WE SPENT THE REST OF THE VOYAGE PATCHING UP THE SHIP WITHOUT TOUCHING THE PRECIOUS EVIDENCE ON WHICH **COMMODORE QUINSANA** WAS GAMBLING HIS CAREER.

THE HARDEST PART WAS JETTISONING THE CADAVERS INTO SPACE.

ESPECIALLY THOSE THAT HAD EXPLODED IN THE TANKS.

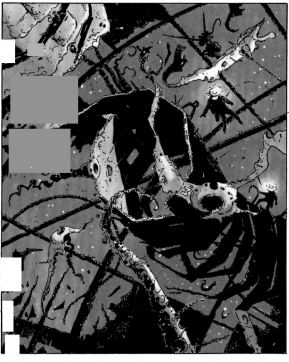

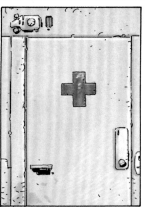

YES?

AH! WILLIAM...

HOW IS SHE?

IT WON'T DO YOU ANY GOOD TO SEE HER NOW.

A LITTLE ETHYL ALCOHOL?

IS SHE OUT OF DANGER?

ON EARTH, SHE WOULD BE. JUST SPRINKLE SOME MAGIC DUST IN THE ABDOMINAL CAVITY AND PASTE HER UP.

A PART OF HER LOWER INTESTINE WAS TORN. WE HAVE REPLACED AND RE-STITCHED THE ESSENTIAL PART.

STANDARD MEDICATION, TOO, WITH AN ARTIFICIAL CULTURE TO RE-ESTABLISH THE DEAD INTESTINAL FLORA KILLED BY STERILIZATION.

MM...

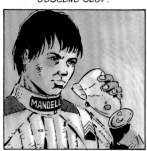

DOCTORS DON'T SEEM TO REALIZE MOST OF US COULD GET ALONG WITHOUT SEEING OURSELVES AS FRAGILE BAGS OF SKIN FILLED WITH OBSCENE GLOP.

MANDELLA

SHE'LL SOON BE ON HER FEET, BUT I DOUBT THAT HER DIGESTIVE TRACT WILL BE ABLE TO STAND ACCELERATIONS HIGHER THAN 2G...

BUT... WE'RE BOUND TO GO OVER TWO ON THE FINAL APPROACH!

I KNOW. I KNOW. WE CAN JUST HOPE SHE'LL BE MENDED BY THEN. IT'S SAD; SHE WAS SPECIAL TO YOU. BUT WE'VE HAD SO MUCH DEATH... YOU OUGHT TO BE GETTING USED TO IT. COME TO TERMS WITH IT.

YOU'RE GETTING PRETTY HARD-BOILED.

JUST REALISTIC. I HAVE A FEELING WE'RE HEADED FOR A LOT MORE DEATH AND SORROW.

MONY

NOT FOR ME. WE GET TO STARGATE AND I'M A CIVILIAN. MY TWO YEARS ARE UP.

I WOULDN'T BANK ON IT. THE JOKERS WHO SIGNED US UP COULD JUST AS WELL LENGTHEN THE SENTENCE. CHANGE IT TO FIVE YEARS...

OR SIX, OR TWENTY. OR THE DURATION. BUT THEY WON'T. IT WOULD BE MUTINY.

I DON'T KNOW. IF THEY COULD CONDITION US TO MURDER ON CUE --

HARMONY

THEY CAN CONDITION US TO DO ALMOST ANYTHING. ANYTHING!

ANYTHING? RE-ENLIST?

I FELT A COLD SHIVER DOWN MY BACK...

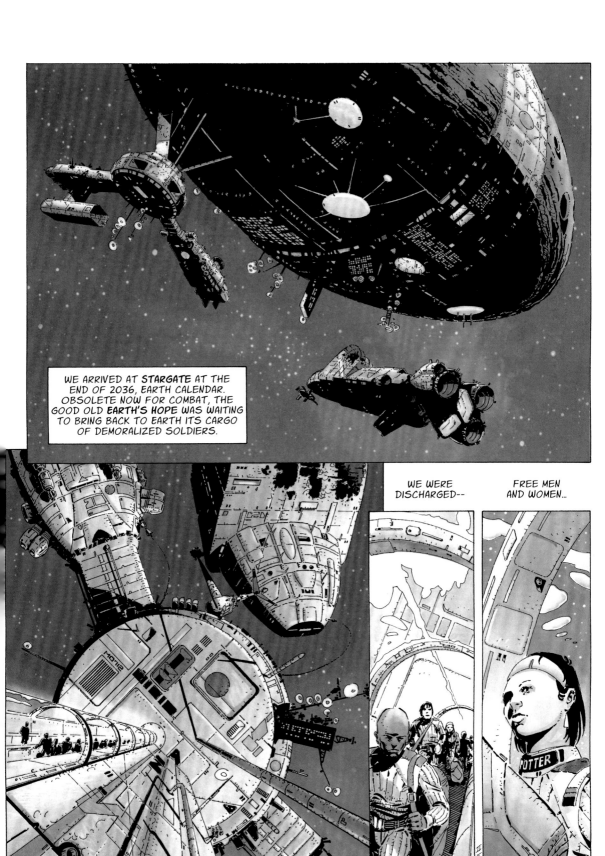

WE ARRIVED AT **STARGATE** AT THE END OF 2036, EARTH CALENDAR. OBSOLETE NOW FOR COMBAT, THE GOOD OLD **EARTH'S HOPE** WAS WAITING TO BRING BACK TO EARTH ITS CARGO OF DEMORALIZED SOLDIERS.

WE WERE DISCHARGED--

FREE MEN AND WOMEN...

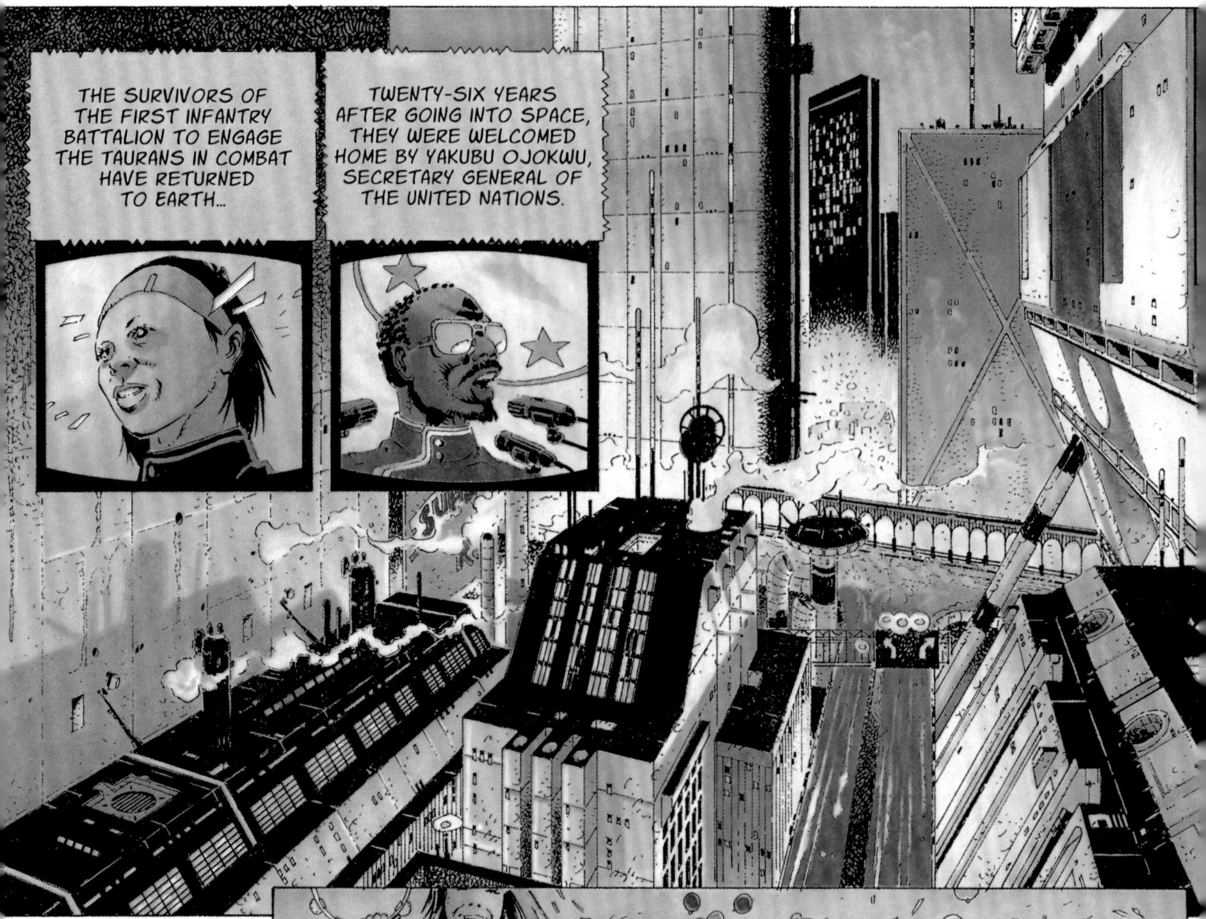
THE SURVIVORS OF THE FIRST INFANTRY BATTALION TO ENGAGE THE TAURANS IN COMBAT HAVE RETURNED TO EARTH...
TWENTY-SIX YEARS AFTER GOING INTO SPACE, THEY WERE WELCOMED HOME BY YAKUBU OJOKWU, SECRETARY GENERAL OF THE UNITED NATIONS.

WE HADN'T EVEN THOUGHT ABOUT IT, BUT HERE WE WERE CONSIDERED HEROES. NOT PAWNS, NOT VICTIMS. HEROES!

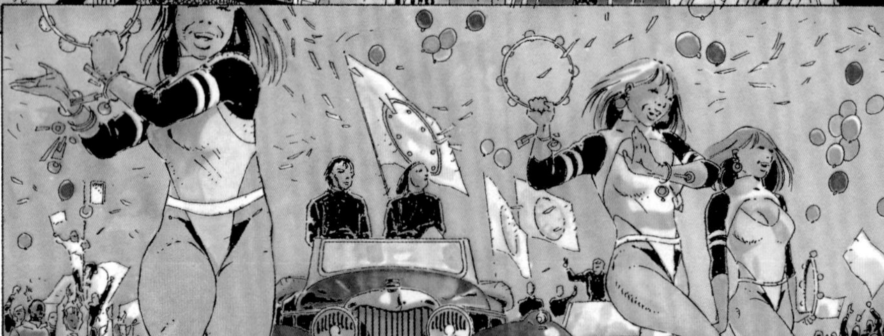

A DELIRIOUS CROWD CHEERED US. BUT IT WAS NO TRICK TO ROUND UP A FEW TENS OF THOUSANDS OF WARM BODIES WHEN MORE THAN HALF OF THE WORLD WAS UNEMPLOYED.

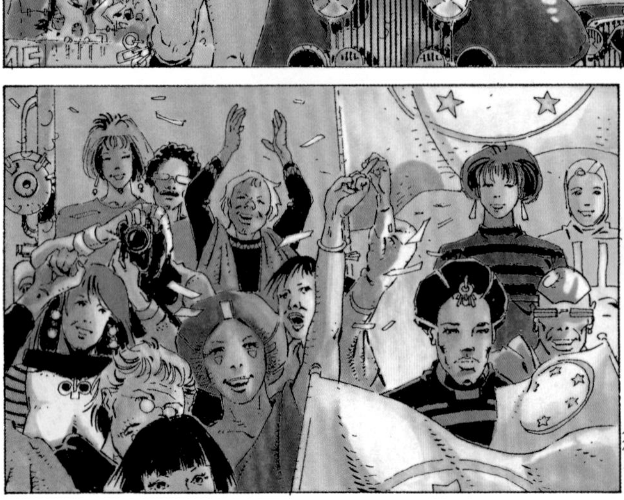

"EARTH IS NO LONGER AS YOU KNOW IT," CORTEZ HAD SAID TO US.

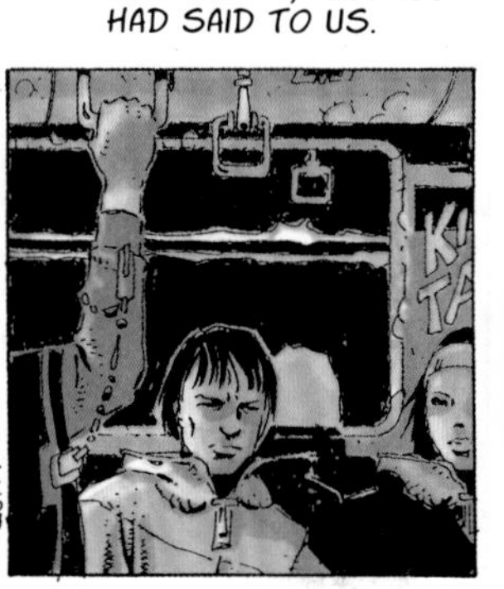

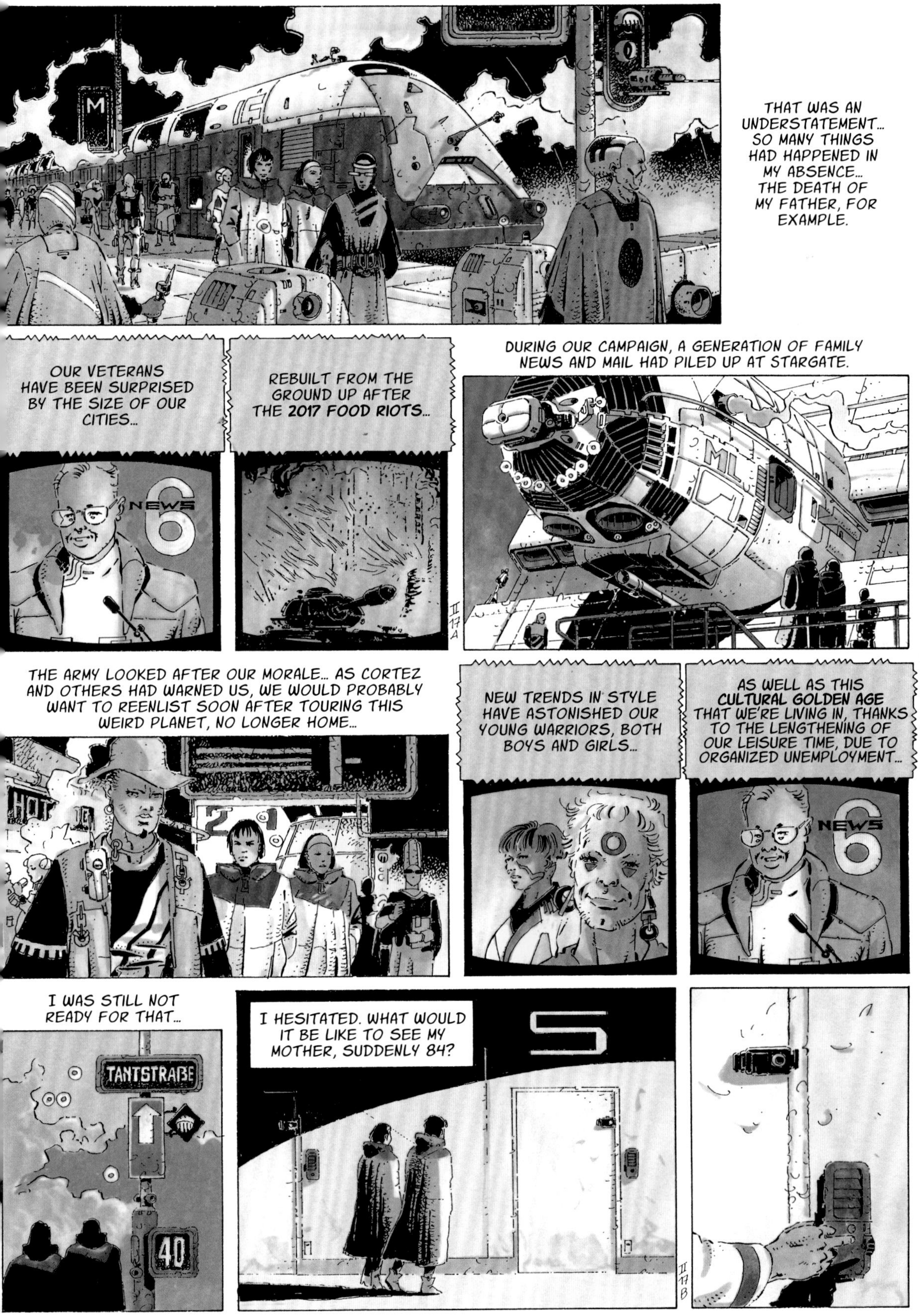
M
THAT WAS AN UNDERSTATEMENT... SO MANY THINGS HAD HAPPENED IN MY ABSENCE... THE DEATH OF MY FATHER, FOR EXAMPLE.
OUR VETERANS HAVE BEEN SURPRISED BY THE SIZE OF OUR CITIES...
NEWS 6
REBUILT FROM THE GROUND UP AFTER THE **2017 FOOD RIOTS**...
DURING OUR CAMPAIGN, A GENERATION OF FAMILY NEWS AND MAIL HAD PILED UP AT STARGATE.
ML
THE ARMY LOOKED AFTER OUR MORALE... AS CORTEZ AND OTHERS HAD WARNED US, WE WOULD PROBABLY WANT TO REENLIST SOON AFTER TOURING THIS WEIRD PLANET, NO LONGER HOME...
NEW TRENDS IN STYLE HAVE ASTONISHED OUR YOUNG WARRIORS, BOTH BOYS AND GIRLS...
AS WELL AS THIS **CULTURAL GOLDEN AGE** THAT WE'RE LIVING IN, THANKS TO THE LENGTHENING OF OUR LEISURE TIME, DUE TO ORGANIZED UNEMPLOYMENT...
NEWS 6
I WAS STILL NOT READY FOR THAT...
TANTSTRAßE
40
I HESITATED. WHAT WOULD IT BE LIKE TO SEE MY MOTHER, SUDDENLY 84?
5

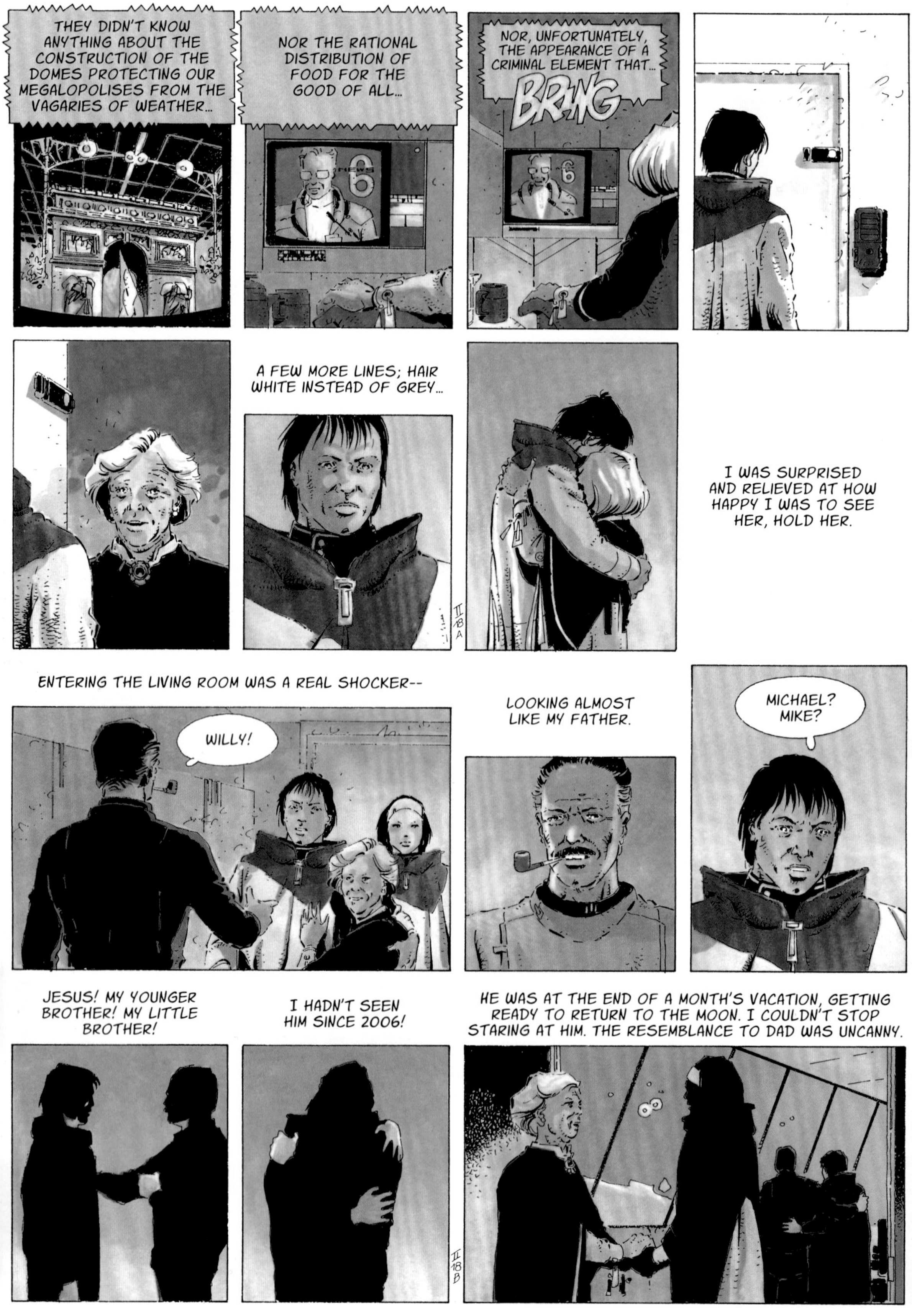
THEY DIDN'T KNOW ANYTHING ABOUT THE CONSTRUCTION OF THE DOMES PROTECTING OUR MEGALOPOLISES FROM THE VAGARIES OF WEATHER...
NOR THE RATIONAL DISTRIBUTION OF FOOD FOR THE GOOD OF ALL...
NOR, UNFORTUNATELY, THE APPEARANCE OF A CRIMINAL ELEMENT THAT...
BRING
A FEW MORE LINES; HAIR WHITE INSTEAD OF GREY...
I WAS SURPRISED AND RELIEVED AT HOW HAPPY I WAS TO SEE HER, HOLD HER.
ENTERING THE LIVING ROOM WAS A REAL SHOCKER--
WILLY!
LOOKING ALMOST LIKE MY FATHER.
MICHAEL? MIKE?
JESUS! MY YOUNGER BROTHER! MY LITTLE BROTHER!
I HADN'T SEEN HIM SINCE 2006!
HE WAS AT THE END OF A MONTH'S VACATION, GETTING READY TO RETURN TO THE MOON. I COULDN'T STOP STARING AT HIM. THE RESEMBLANCE TO DAD WAS UNCANNY.

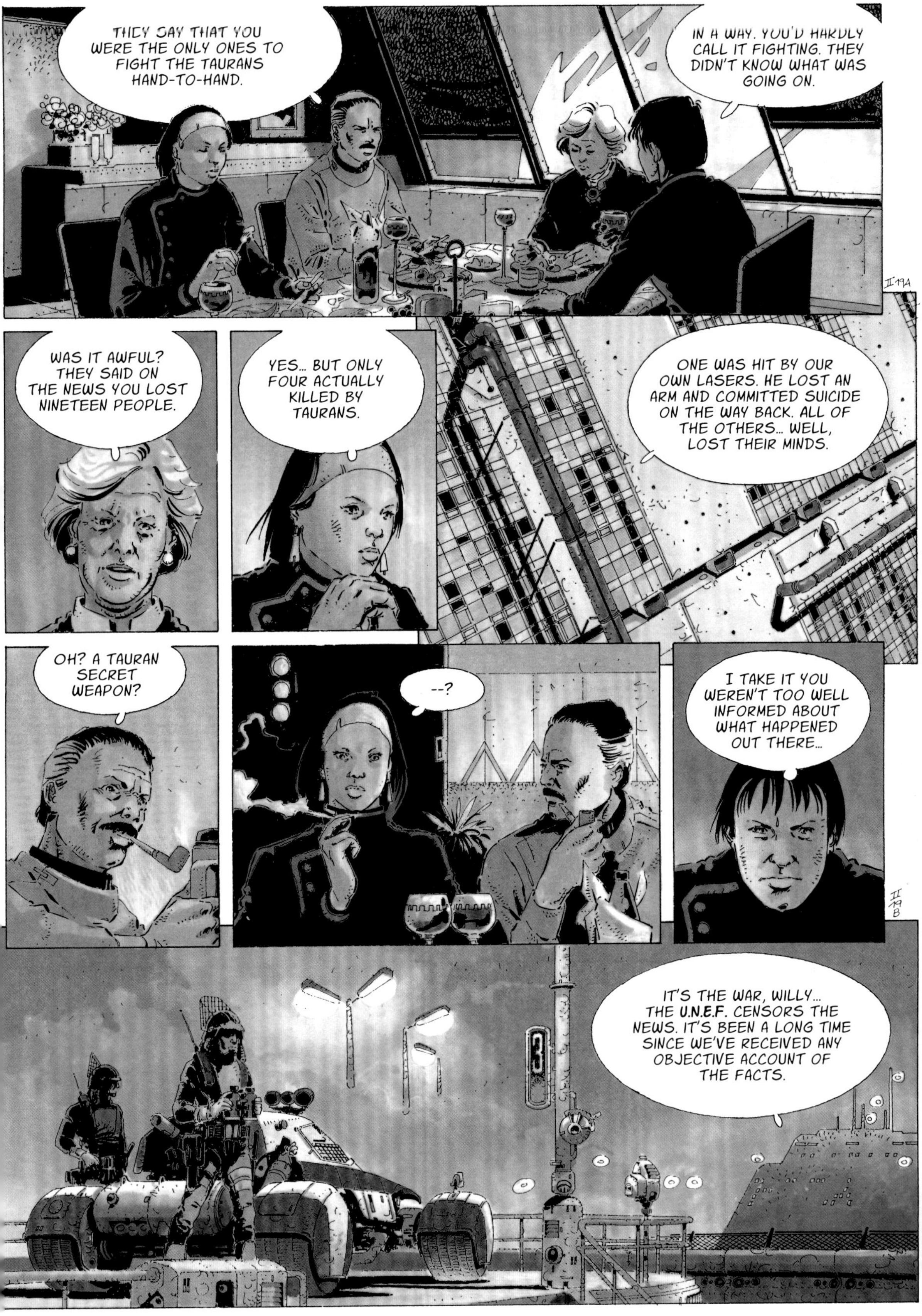
THEY SAY THAT YOU WERE THE ONLY ONES TO FIGHT THE TAURANS HAND-TO-HAND.
IN A WAY. YOU'D HARDLY CALL IT FIGHTING. THEY DIDN'T KNOW WHAT WAS GOING ON.
WAS IT AWFUL? THEY SAID ON THE NEWS YOU LOST NINETEEN PEOPLE.
YES... BUT ONLY FOUR ACTUALLY KILLED BY TAURANS.
ONE WAS HIT BY OUR OWN LASERS. HE LOST AN ARM AND COMMITTED SUICIDE ON THE WAY BACK. ALL OF THE OTHERS... WELL, LOST THEIR MINDS.
OH? A TAURAN SECRET WEAPON?
--?
I TAKE IT YOU WEREN'T TOO WELL INFORMED ABOUT WHAT HAPPENED OUT THERE...
IT'S THE WAR, WILLY... THE U.N.E.F. CENSORS THE NEWS. IT'S BEEN A LONG TIME SINCE WE'VE RECEIVED ANY OBJECTIVE ACCOUNT OF THE FACTS.

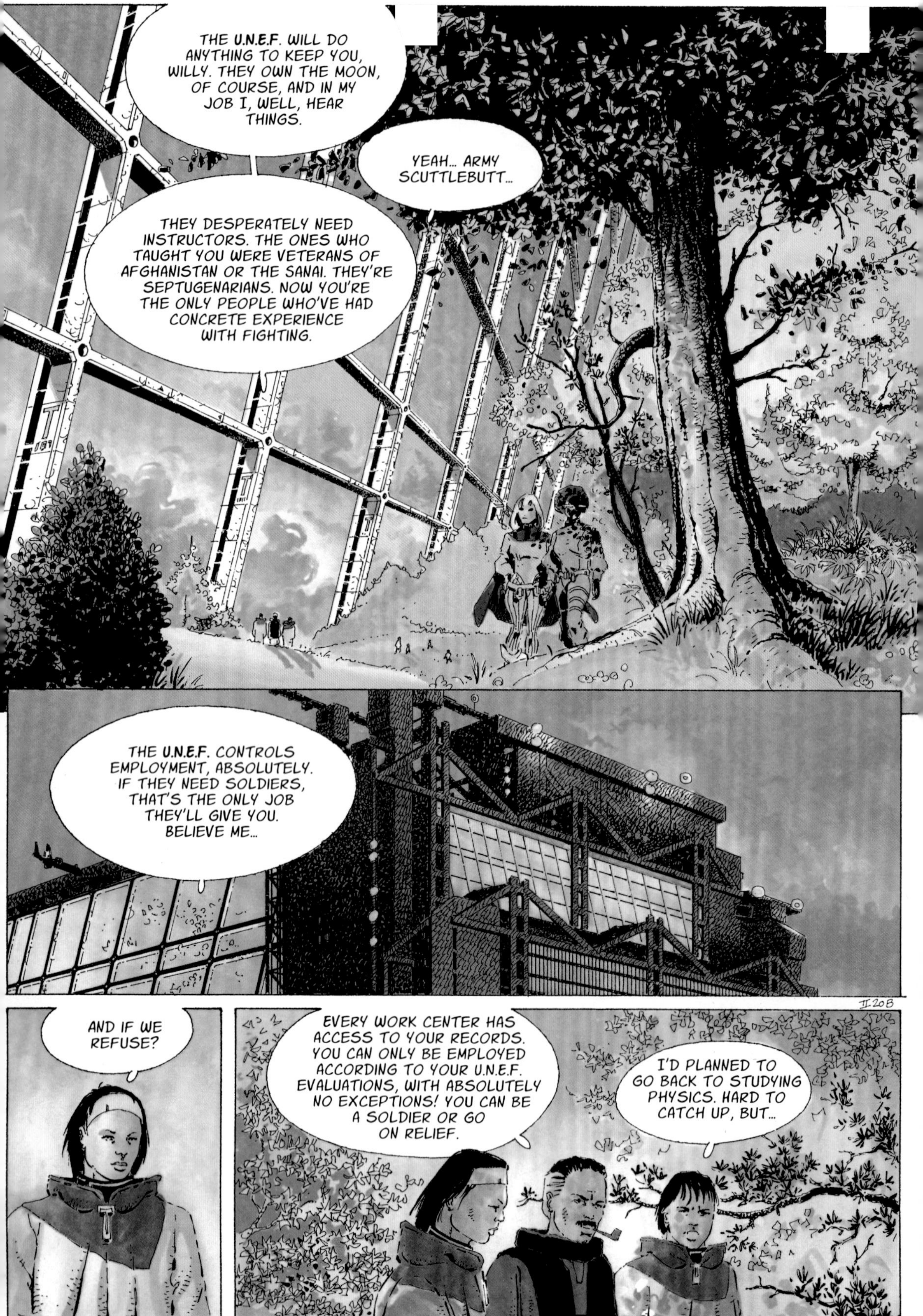
THE U.N.E.F. WILL DO ANYTHING TO KEEP YOU, WILLY. THEY OWN THE MOON, OF COURSE, AND IN MY JOB I, WELL, HEAR THINGS.
YEAH... ARMY SCUTTLEBUTT...
THEY DESPERATELY NEED INSTRUCTORS. THE ONES WHO TAUGHT YOU WERE VETERANS OF AFGHANISTAN OR THE SANAI. THEY'RE SEPTUGENARIANS. NOW YOU'RE THE ONLY PEOPLE WHO'VE HAD CONCRETE EXPERIENCE WITH FIGHTING.
THE U.N.E.F. CONTROLS EMPLOYMENT, ABSOLUTELY. IF THEY NEED SOLDIERS, THAT'S THE ONLY JOB THEY'LL GIVE YOU. BELIEVE ME...
II 20 B
AND IF WE REFUSE?
EVERY WORK CENTER HAS ACCESS TO YOUR RECORDS. YOU CAN ONLY BE EMPLOYED ACCORDING TO YOUR U.N.E.F. EVALUATIONS, WITH ABSOLUTELY NO EXCEPTIONS! YOU CAN BE A SOLDIER OR GO ON RELIEF.
I'D PLANNED TO GO BACK TO STUDYING PHYSICS. HARD TO CATCH UP, BUT...

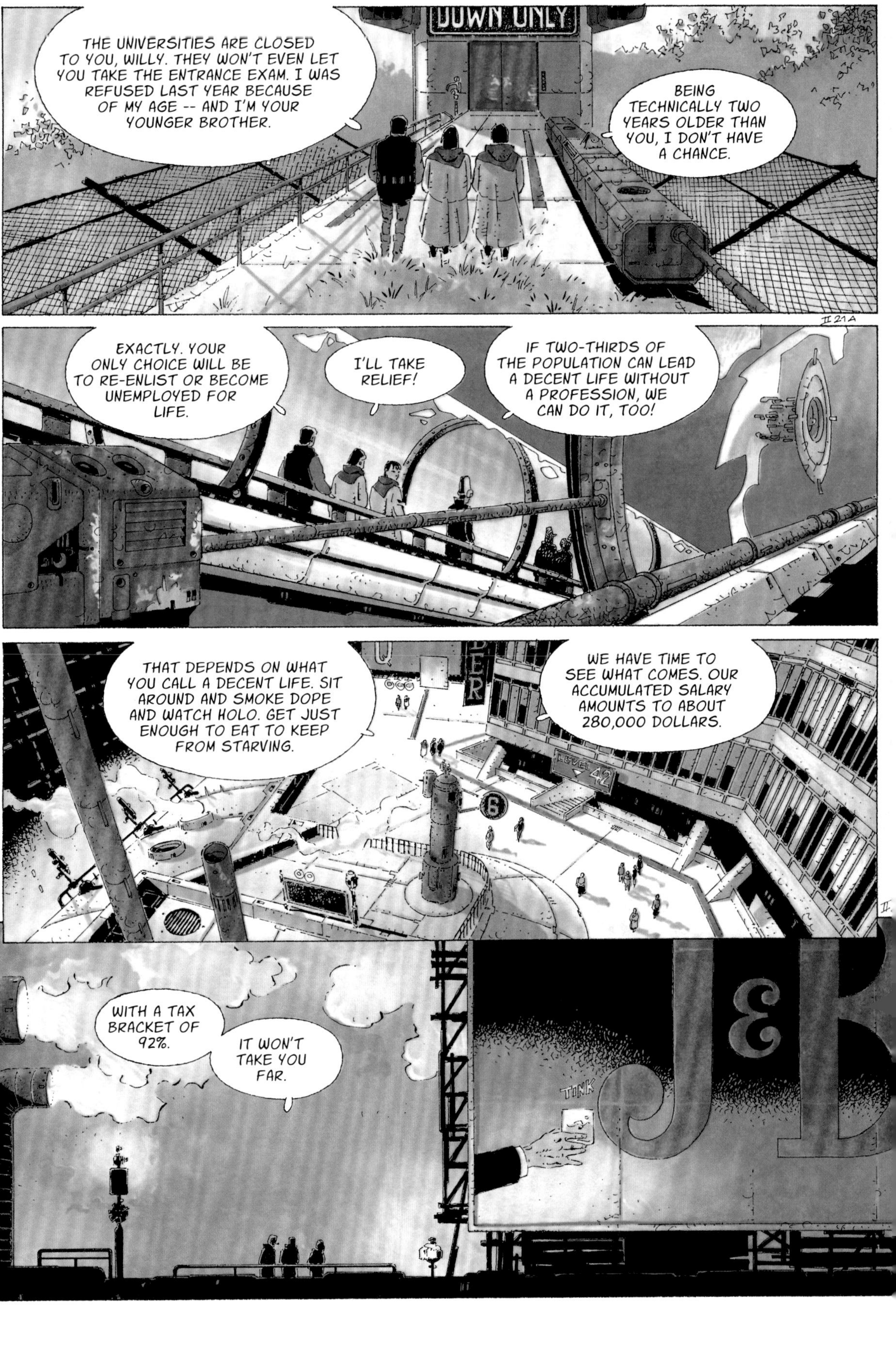
DOWN ONLY
THE UNIVERSITIES ARE CLOSED TO YOU, WILLY. THEY WON'T EVEN LET YOU TAKE THE ENTRANCE EXAM. I WAS REFUSED LAST YEAR BECAUSE OF MY AGE -- AND I'M YOUR YOUNGER BROTHER.
BEING TECHNICALLY TWO YEARS OLDER THAN YOU, I DON'T HAVE A CHANCE.
EXACTLY. YOUR ONLY CHOICE WILL BE TO RE-ENLIST OR BECOME UNEMPLOYED FOR LIFE.
I'LL TAKE RELIEF!
IF TWO-THIRDS OF THE POPULATION CAN LEAD A DECENT LIFE WITHOUT A PROFESSION, WE CAN DO IT, TOO!
THAT DEPENDS ON WHAT YOU CALL A DECENT LIFE. SIT AROUND AND SMOKE DOPE AND WATCH HOLO. GET JUST ENOUGH TO EAT TO KEEP FROM STARVING.
WE HAVE TIME TO SEE WHAT COMES. OUR ACCUMULATED SALARY AMOUNTS TO ABOUT 280,000 DOLLARS.
LEVEL 42
6
WITH A TAX BRACKET OF 92%.
IT WON'T TAKE YOU FAR.
TINK

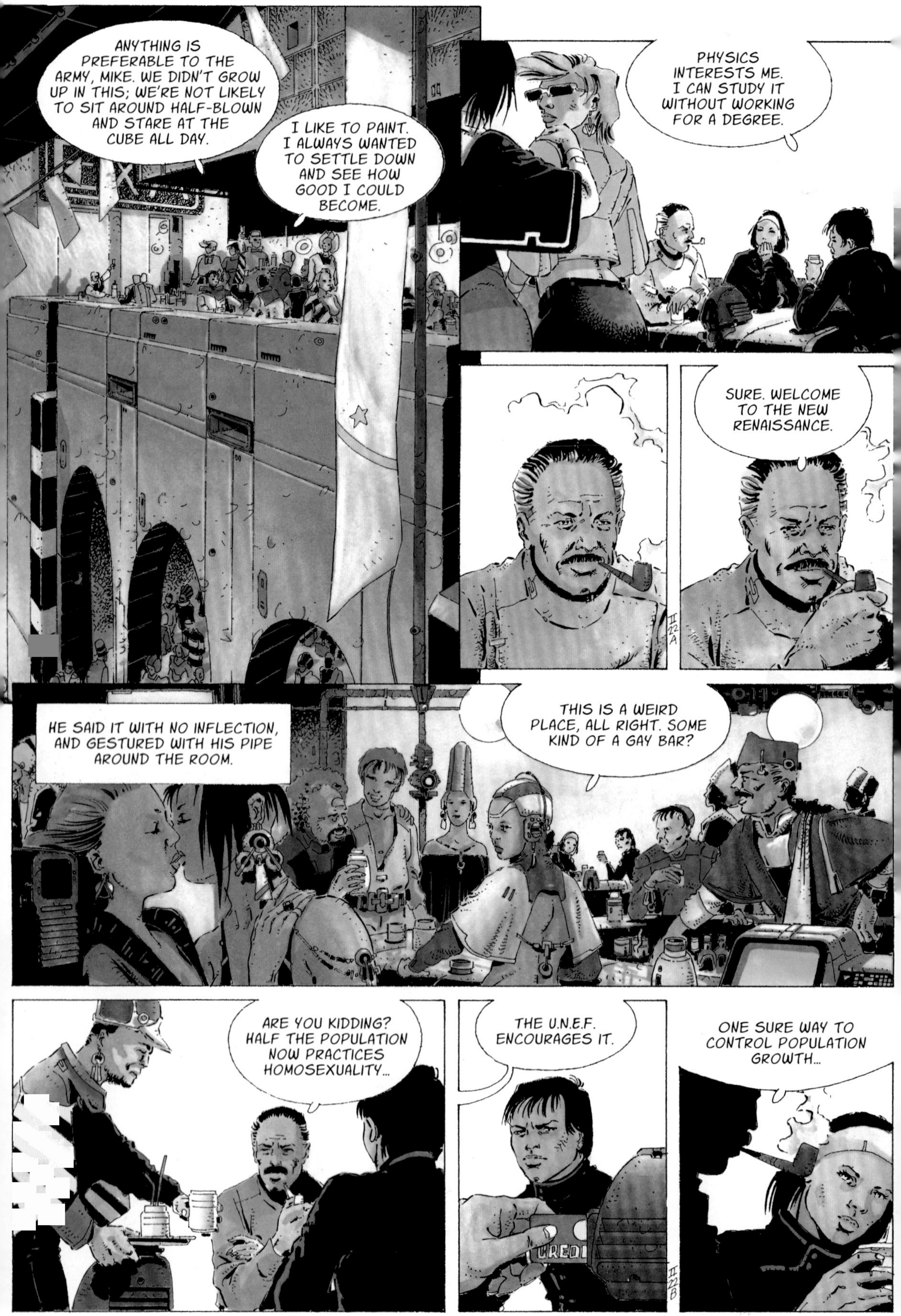
ANYTHING IS PREFERABLE TO THE ARMY, MIKE. WE DIDN'T GROW UP IN THIS; WE'RE NOT LIKELY TO SIT AROUND HALF-BLOWN AND STARE AT THE CUBE ALL DAY.
I LIKE TO PAINT. I ALWAYS WANTED TO SETTLE DOWN AND SEE HOW GOOD I COULD BECOME.
PHYSICS INTERESTS ME. I CAN STUDY IT WITHOUT WORKING FOR A DEGREE.
SURE. WELCOME TO THE NEW RENAISSANCE.
II 22 A
HE SAID IT WITH NO INFLECTION, AND GESTURED WITH HIS PIPE AROUND THE ROOM.
THIS IS A WEIRD PLACE, ALL RIGHT. SOME KIND OF A GAY BAR?
ARE YOU KIDDING? HALF THE POPULATION NOW PRACTICES HOMOSEXUALITY...
THE U.N.E.F. ENCOURAGES IT.
II 22 B
ONE SURE WAY TO CONTROL POPULATION GROWTH...

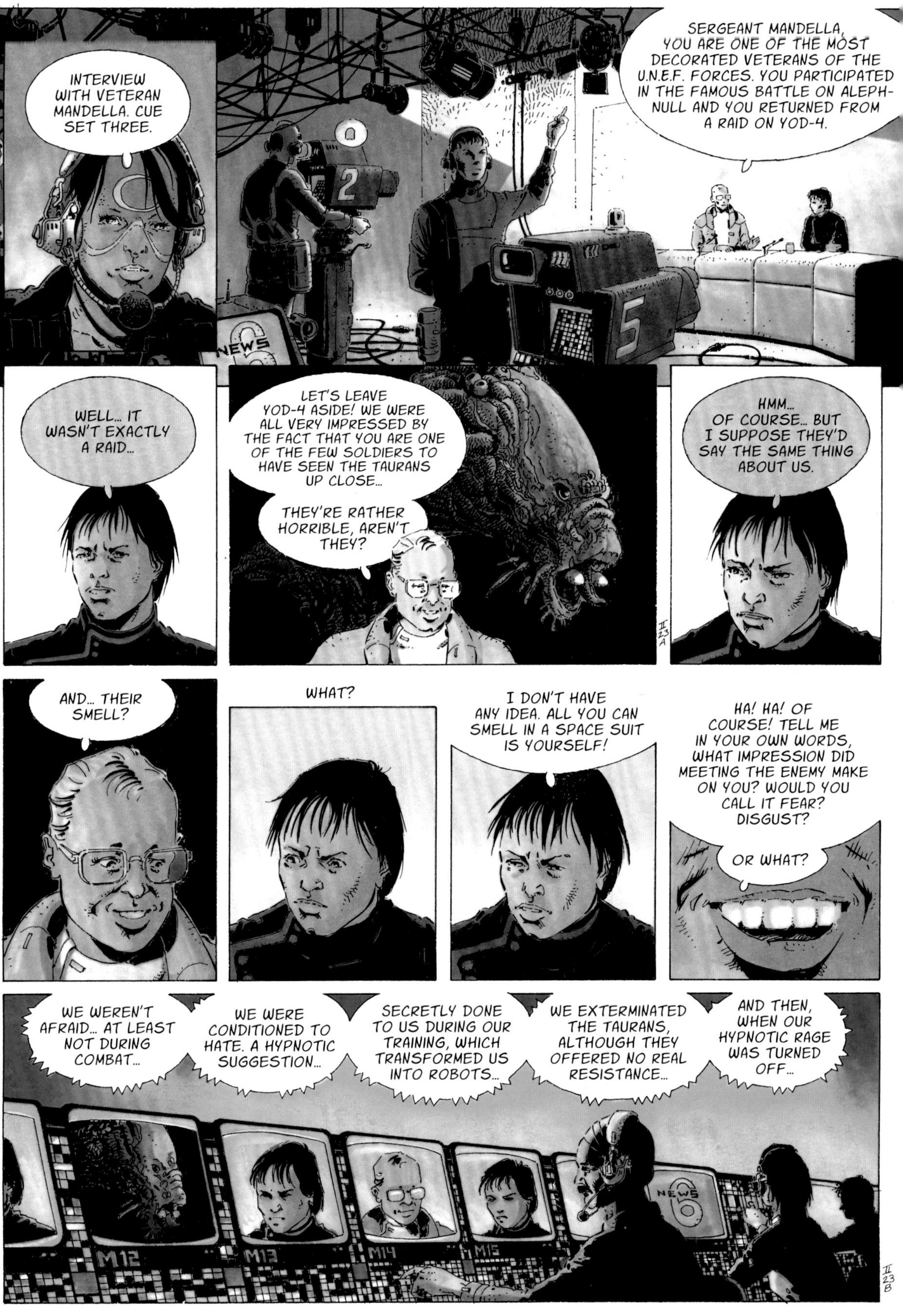
INTERVIEW WITH VETERAN MANDELLA. CUE SET THREE.
NEWS 6
2
5
SERGEANT MANDELLA, YOU ARE ONE OF THE MOST DECORATED VETERANS OF THE U.N.E.F. FORCES. YOU PARTICIPATED IN THE FAMOUS BATTLE ON ALEPH-NULL AND YOU RETURNED FROM A RAID ON YOD-4.
WELL... IT WASN'T EXACTLY A RAID...
LET'S LEAVE YOD-4 ASIDE! WE WERE ALL VERY IMPRESSED BY THE FACT THAT YOU ARE ONE OF THE FEW SOLDIERS TO HAVE SEEN THE TAURANS UP CLOSE...
THEY'RE RATHER HORRIBLE, AREN'T THEY?
II 23 A
HMM... OF COURSE... BUT I SUPPOSE THEY'D SAY THE SAME THING ABOUT US.
AND... THEIR SMELL?
WHAT?
I DON'T HAVE ANY IDEA. ALL YOU CAN SMELL IN A SPACE SUIT IS YOURSELF!
HA! HA! OF COURSE! TELL ME IN YOUR OWN WORDS, WHAT IMPRESSION DID MEETING THE ENEMY MAKE ON YOU? WOULD YOU CALL IT FEAR? DISGUST?
OR WHAT?
WE WEREN'T AFRAID... AT LEAST NOT DURING COMBAT...
WE WERE CONDITIONED TO HATE. A HYPNOTIC SUGGESTION...
SECRETLY DONE TO US DURING OUR TRAINING, WHICH TRANSFORMED US INTO ROBOTS...
WE EXTERMINATED THE TAURANS, ALTHOUGH THEY OFFERED NO REAL RESISTANCE...
AND THEN, WHEN OUR HYPNOTIC RAGE WAS TURNED OFF...
M12
M13
M14
M15
NEWS 6
II 23 B

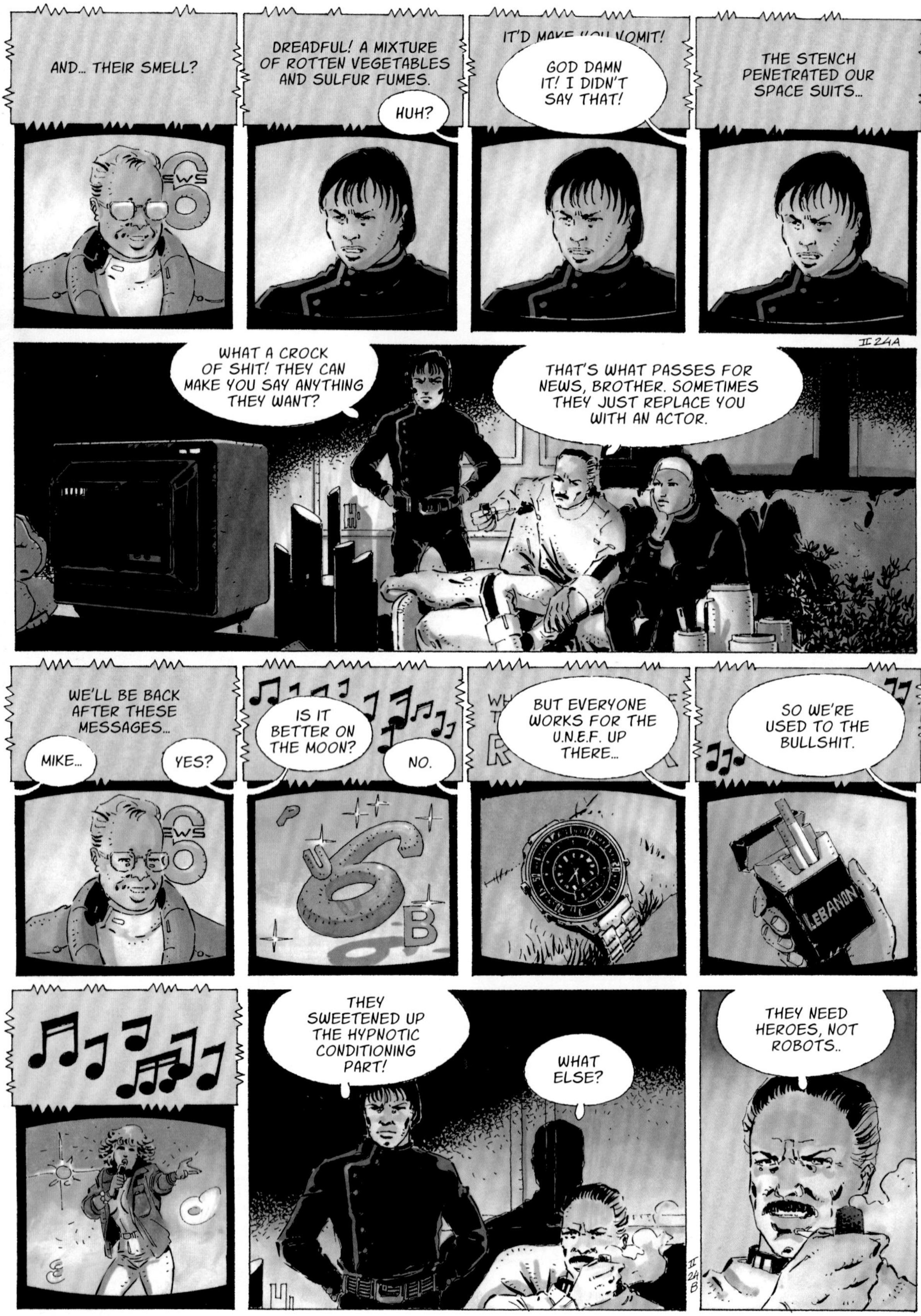
AND... THEIR SMELL?
DREADFUL! A MIXTURE OF ROTTEN VEGETABLES AND SULFUR FUMES.
HUH?
GOD DAMN IT! I DIDN'T SAY THAT!
THE STENCH PENETRATED OUR SPACE SUITS...
II 24A
WHAT A CROCK OF SHIT! THEY CAN MAKE YOU SAY ANYTHING THEY WANT?
THAT'S WHAT PASSES FOR NEWS, BROTHER. SOMETIMES THEY JUST REPLACE YOU WITH AN ACTOR.
WE'LL BE BACK AFTER THESE MESSAGES...
MIKE...
YES?
IS IT BETTER ON THE MOON?
NO.
BUT EVERYONE WORKS FOR THE U.N.E.F. UP THERE...
SO WE'RE USED TO THE BULLSHIT.
LEBANON
THEY SWEETENED UP THE HYPNOTIC CONDITIONING PART!
WHAT ELSE?
THEY NEED HEROES, NOT ROBOTS..
II 24B

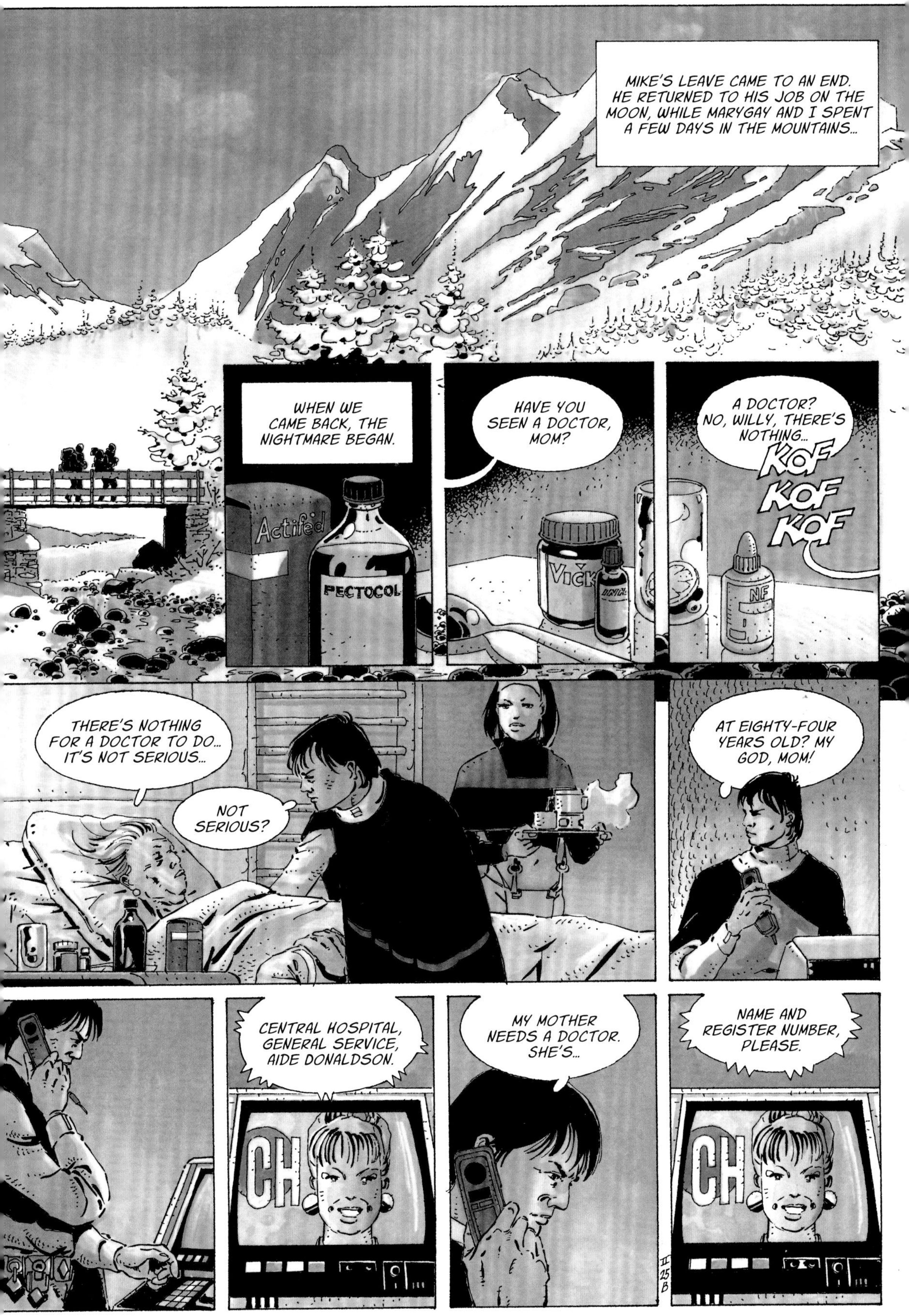
MIKE'S LEAVE CAME TO AN END. HE RETURNED TO HIS JOB ON THE MOON, WHILE MARYGAY AND I SPENT A FEW DAYS IN THE MOUNTAINS...
WHEN WE CAME BACK, THE NIGHTMARE BEGAN.
Actifed
PECTOCOL
HAVE YOU SEEN A DOCTOR, MOM?
VICK
A DOCTOR? NO, WILLY, THERE'S NOTHING...
KOF KOF KOF
NF
THERE'S NOTHING FOR A DOCTOR TO DO... IT'S NOT SERIOUS...
NOT SERIOUS?
AT EIGHTY-FOUR YEARS OLD? MY GOD, MOM!
CENTRAL HOSPITAL, GENERAL SERVICE, AIDE DONALDSON.
CH
MY MOTHER NEEDS A DOCTOR. SHE'S...
NAME AND REGISTER NUMBER, PLEASE.
CH
II 25 B

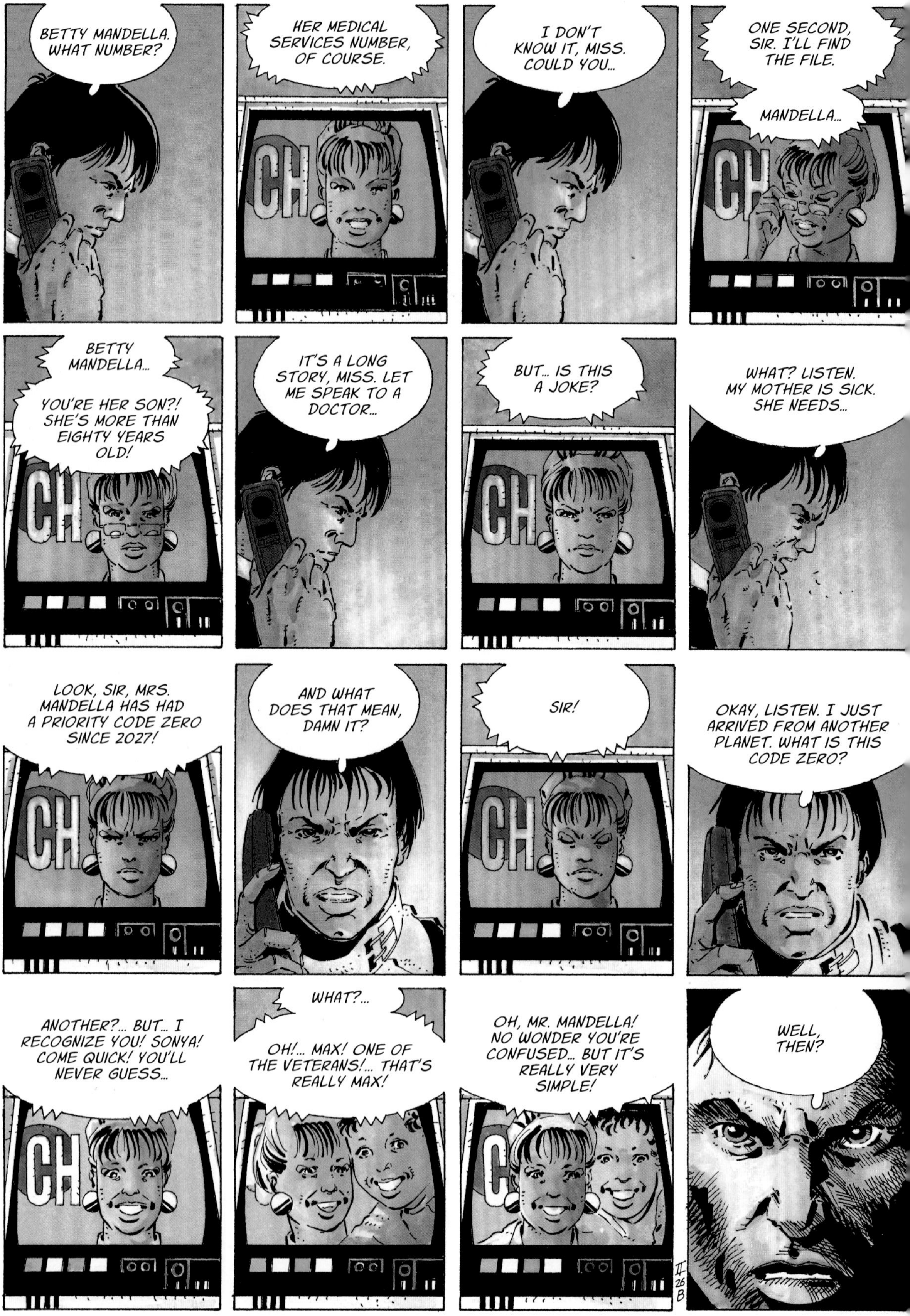
BETTY MANDELLA. WHAT NUMBER?
HER MEDICAL SERVICES NUMBER, OF COURSE.
I DON'T KNOW IT, MISS. COULD YOU...
ONE SECOND, SIR. I'LL FIND THE FILE.
MANDELLA...
BETTY MANDELLA...
YOU'RE HER SON?! SHE'S MORE THAN EIGHTY YEARS OLD!
IT'S A LONG STORY, MISS. LET ME SPEAK TO A DOCTOR...
BUT... IS THIS A JOKE?
WHAT? LISTEN. MY MOTHER IS SICK. SHE NEEDS...
LOOK, SIR, MRS. MANDELLA HAS HAD A PRIORITY CODE ZERO SINCE 2027!
AND WHAT DOES THAT MEAN, DAMN IT?
SIR!
OKAY, LISTEN. I JUST ARRIVED FROM ANOTHER PLANET. WHAT IS THIS CODE ZERO?
ANOTHER?... BUT... I RECOGNIZE YOU! SONYA! COME QUICK! YOU'LL NEVER GUESS...
WHAT?...
OH!... MAX! ONE OF THE VETERANS!... THAT'S REALLY MAX!
OH, MR. MANDELLA! NO WONDER YOU'RE CONFUSED... BUT IT'S REALLY VERY SIMPLE!
WELL, THEN?
II 26 B

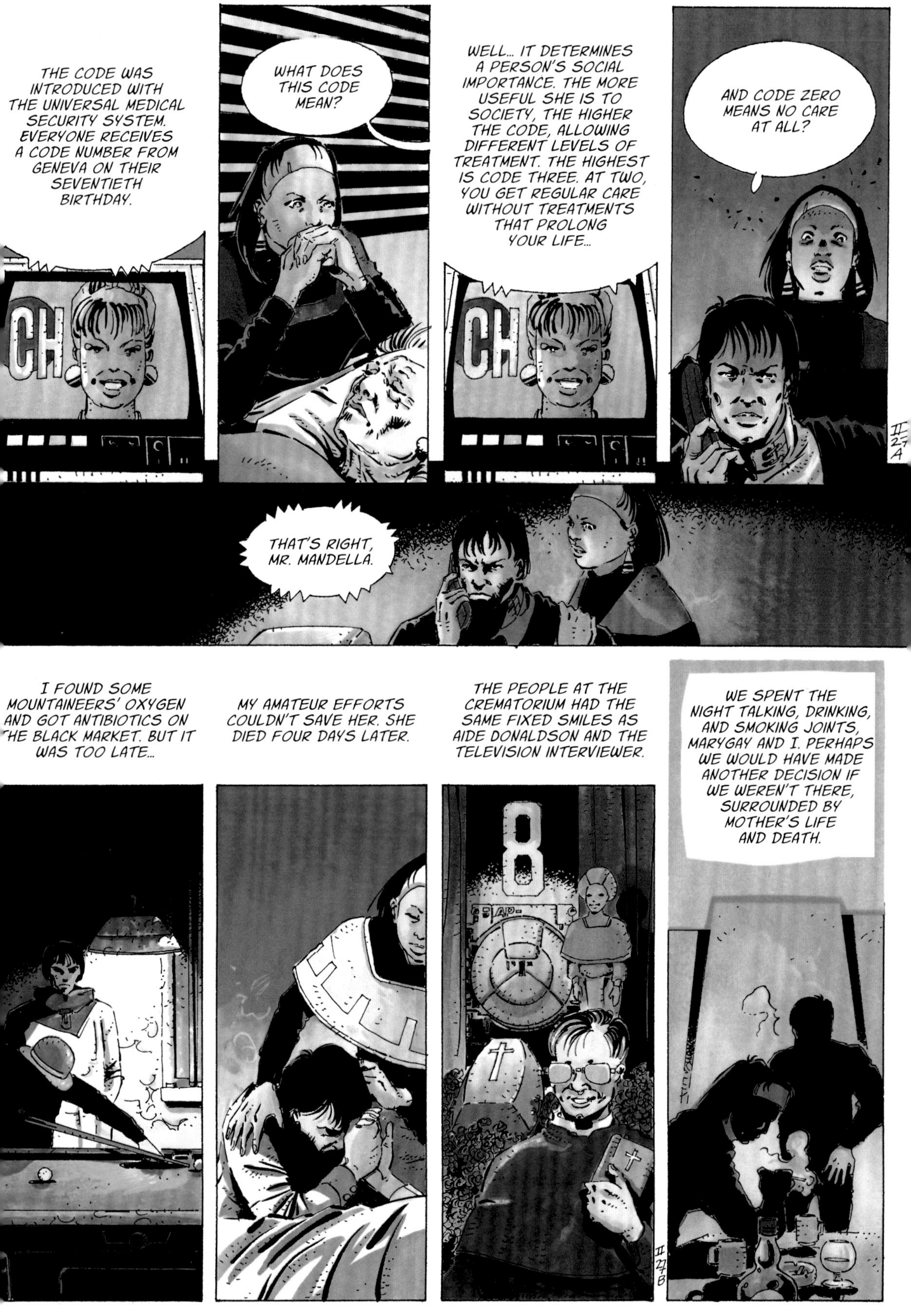
THE CODE WAS INTRODUCED WITH THE UNIVERSAL MEDICAL SECURITY SYSTEM. EVERYONE RECEIVES A CODE NUMBER FROM GENEVA ON THEIR SEVENTIETH BIRTHDAY.
WHAT DOES THIS CODE MEAN?
WELL... IT DETERMINES A PERSON'S SOCIAL IMPORTANCE. THE MORE USEFUL SHE IS TO SOCIETY, THE HIGHER THE CODE, ALLOWING DIFFERENT LEVELS OF TREATMENT. THE HIGHEST IS CODE THREE. AT TWO, YOU GET REGULAR CARE WITHOUT TREATMENTS THAT PROLONG YOUR LIFE...
AND CODE ZERO MEANS NO CARE AT ALL?
THAT'S RIGHT, MR. MANDELLA.
I FOUND SOME MOUNTAINEERS' OXYGEN AND GOT ANTIBIOTICS ON THE BLACK MARKET. BUT IT WAS TOO LATE...
MY AMATEUR EFFORTS COULDN'T SAVE HER. SHE DIED FOUR DAYS LATER.
THE PEOPLE AT THE CREMATORIUM HAD THE SAME FIXED SMILES AS AIDE DONALDSON AND THE TELEVISION INTERVIEWER.
WE SPENT THE NIGHT TALKING, DRINKING, AND SMOKING JOINTS, MARYGAY AND I. PERHAPS WE WOULD HAVE MADE ANOTHER DECISION IF WE WEREN'T THERE, SURROUNDED BY MOTHER'S LIFE AND DEATH.

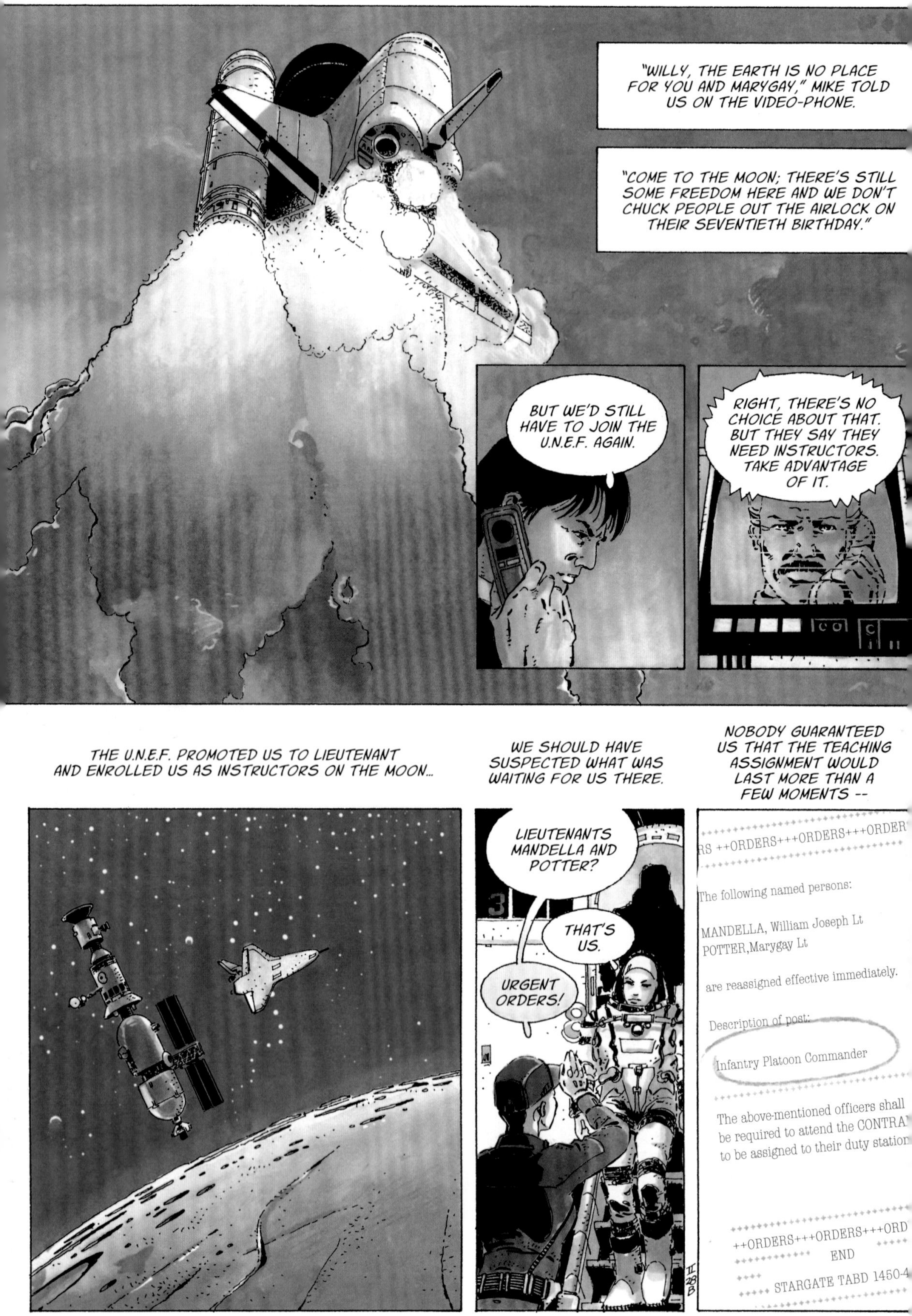
"WILLY, THE EARTH IS NO PLACE FOR YOU AND MARYGAY," MIKE TOLD US ON THE VIDEO-PHONE.
"COME TO THE MOON; THERE'S STILL SOME FREEDOM HERE AND WE DON'T CHUCK PEOPLE OUT THE AIRLOCK ON THEIR SEVENTIETH BIRTHDAY."
BUT WE'D STILL HAVE TO JOIN THE U.N.E.F. AGAIN.
RIGHT, THERE'S NO CHOICE ABOUT THAT. BUT THEY SAY THEY NEED INSTRUCTORS. TAKE ADVANTAGE OF IT.
THE U.N.E.F. PROMOTED US TO LIEUTENANT AND ENROLLED US AS INSTRUCTORS ON THE MOON...
WE SHOULD HAVE SUSPECTED WHAT WAS WAITING FOR US THERE.
LIEUTENANTS MANDELLA AND POTTER?
THAT'S US.
URGENT ORDERS!
NOBODY GUARANTEED US THAT THE TEACHING ASSIGNMENT WOULD LAST MORE THAN A FEW MOMENTS --
RS ++ORDERS+++ORDERS+++ORDER
The following named persons:
MANDELLA, William Joseph Lt
POTTER,Marygay Lt
are reassigned effective immediately.
Description of post:
Infantry Platoon Commander
The above-mentioned officers shall be required to attend the CONTRA
to be assigned to their duty station
++ORDERS+++ORDERS+++ORD
END
STARGATE TABD 1450-4

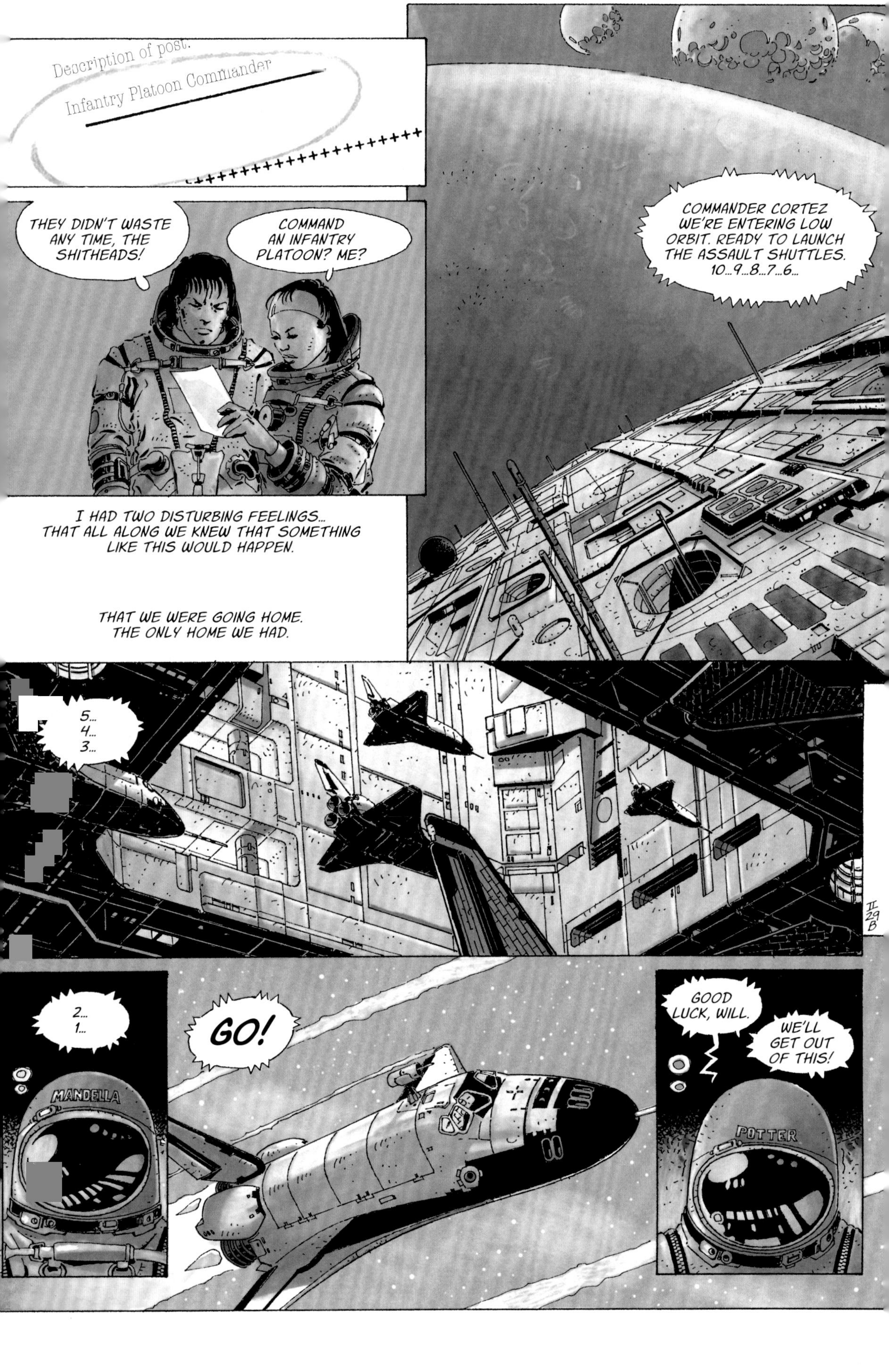

Description of post.
Infantry Platoon Commander
THEY DIDN'T WASTE ANY TIME, THE SHITHEADS!
COMMAND AN INFANTRY PLATOON? ME?
I HAD TWO DISTURBING FEELINGS... THAT ALL ALONG WE KNEW THAT SOMETHING LIKE THIS WOULD HAPPEN.
THAT WE WERE GOING HOME. THE ONLY HOME WE HAD.
COMMANDER CORTEZ WE'RE ENTERING LOW ORBIT. READY TO LAUNCH THE ASSAULT SHUTTLES. 10...9...8...7...6...
5... 4... 3...
II 29 B
2... 1...
MANDELLA
GO!
GOOD LUCK, WILL.
WE'LL GET OUT OF THIS!
POTTER

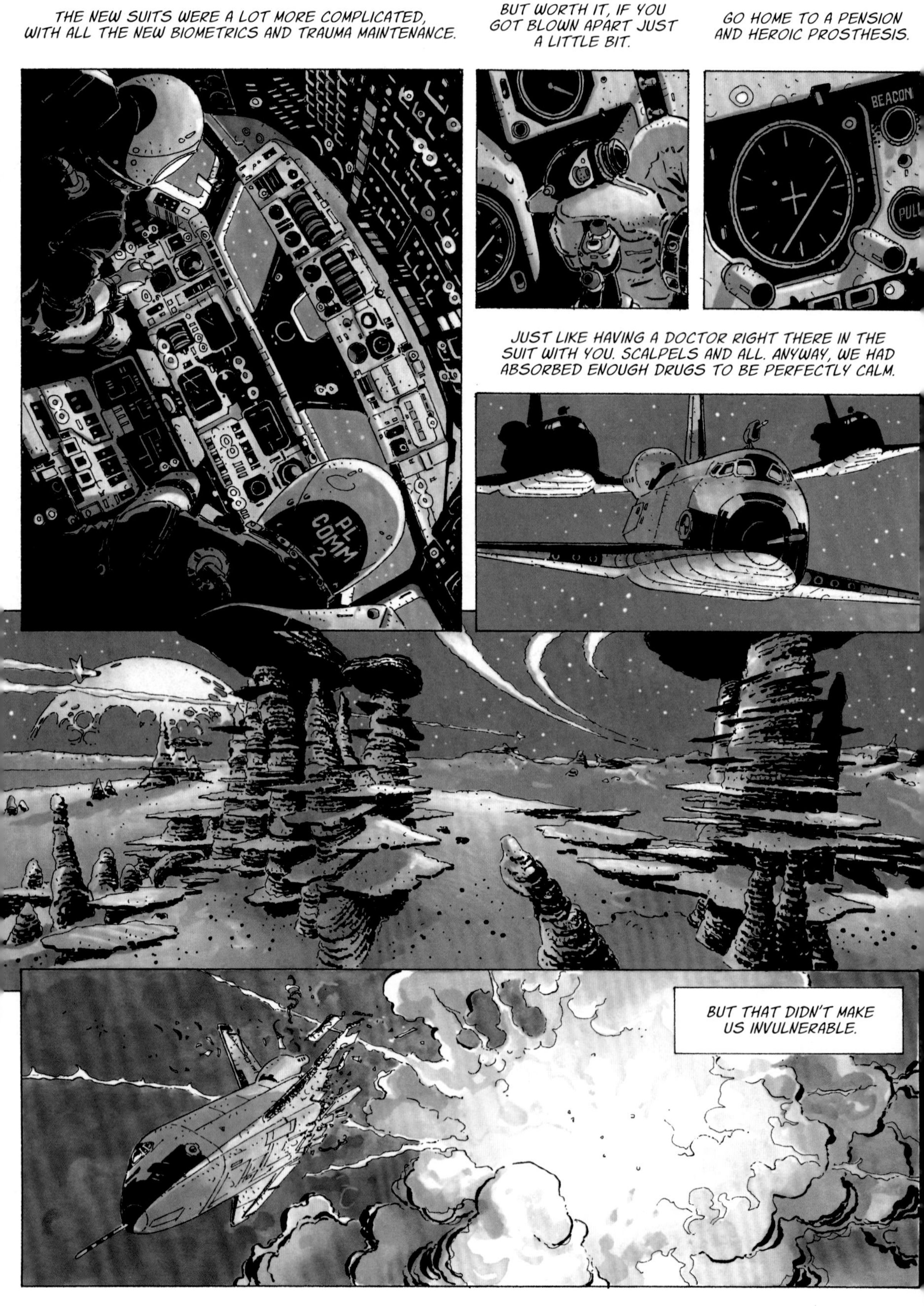
THE NEW SUITS WERE A LOT MORE COMPLICATED, WITH ALL THE NEW BIOMETRICS AND TRAUMA MAINTENANCE.
PL COMM 2
BUT WORTH IT, IF YOU GOT BLOWN APART JUST A LITTLE BIT.
GO HOME TO A PENSION AND HEROIC PROSTHESIS.
BEACON
JUST LIKE HAVING A DOCTOR RIGHT THERE IN THE SUIT WITH YOU. SCALPELS AND ALL. ANYWAY, WE HAD ABSORBED ENOUGH DRUGS TO BE PERFECTLY CALM.
BUT THAT DIDN'T MAKE US INVULNERABLE.

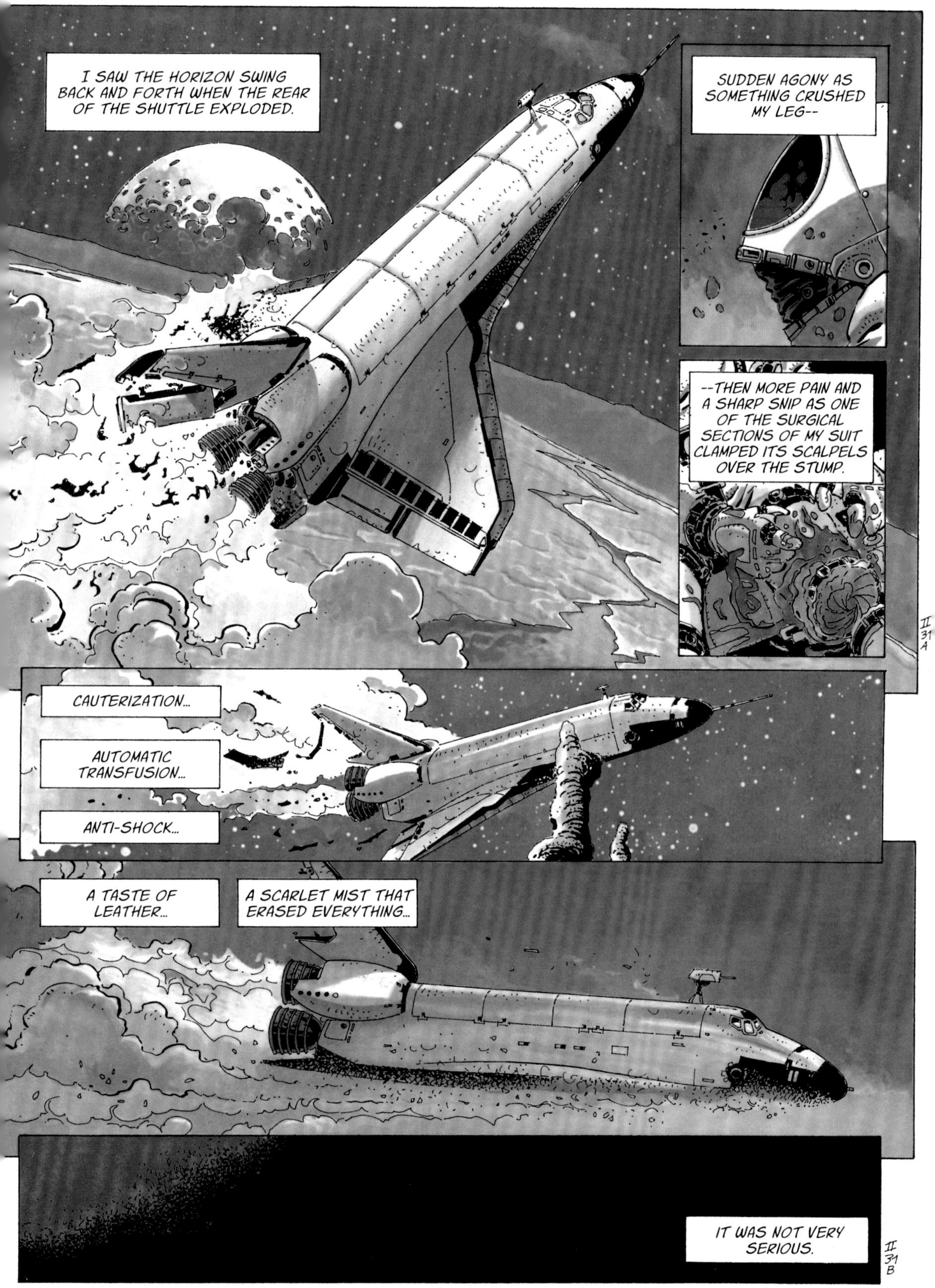
I SAW THE HORIZON SWING BACK AND FORTH WHEN THE REAR OF THE SHUTTLE EXPLODED.
SUDDEN AGONY AS SOMETHING CRUSHED MY LEG--
--THEN MORE PAIN AND A SHARP SNIP AS ONE OF THE SURGICAL SECTIONS OF MY SUIT CLAMPED ITS SCALPELS OVER THE STUMP.
II 31 A
CAUTERIZATION...
AUTOMATIC TRANSFUSION...
ANTI-SHOCK...
A TASTE OF LEATHER...
A SCARLET MIST THAT ERASED EVERYTHING...
IT WAS NOT VERY SERIOUS.
II 31 B

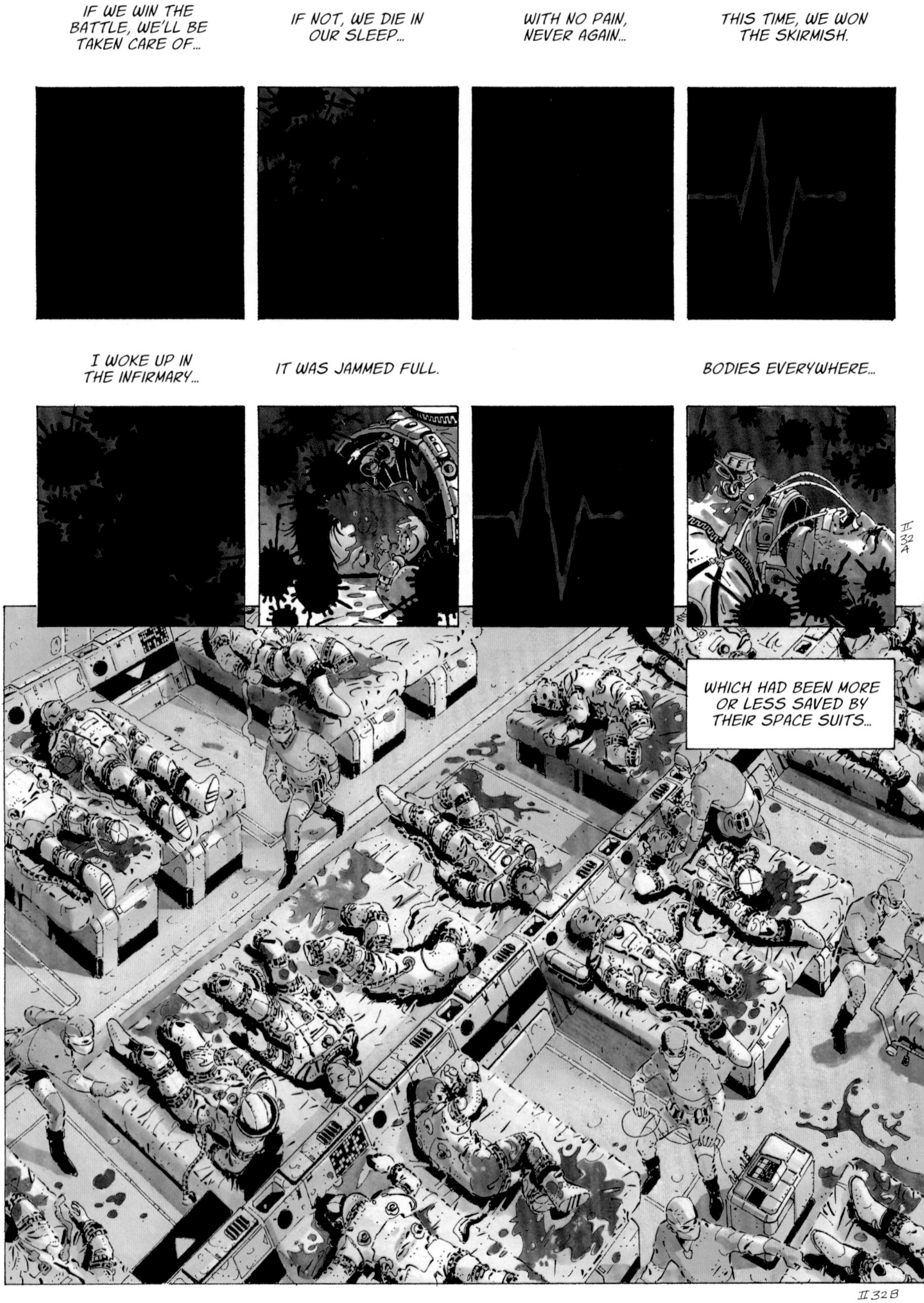
IF WE WIN THE BATTLE, WE'LL BE TAKEN CARE OF...
IF NOT, WE DIE IN OUR SLEEP...
WITH NO PAIN, NEVER AGAIN...
THIS TIME, WE WON THE SKIRMISH.
I WOKE UP IN THE INFIRMARY...
IT WAS JAMMED FULL.
BODIES EVERYWHERE...
II 32 A
WHICH HAD BEEN MORE OR LESS SAVED BY THEIR SPACE SUITS...
II 32 B

WE WEREN'T
THE FIRST BATCH.
UNDER THE HARSH
LIGHT, THE DOCTORS
WERE ABSORBED IN
BLOOD RITUALS --

THE BLOOD ON THEIR
GREEN TUNICS COULD HAVE
BEEN GREASE...

THE SWATHED
BODIES, ODD
SOFT MACHINES
THAT THEY WERE
FIXING.

BUT THE MACHINES
WOULD CRY OUT IN
THEIR SLEEP...

...AND THE MECHANICS
MUTTERED REASSURANCES...

...WHILE THEY PLIED
THEIR GREASY TOOLS.

I SLEPT, AND WOKE
IN PAIN, AND TRIED TO
SLEEP AGAIN --

THOUGH EVEN MY
DREAMS WERE FULL OF
BLOOD AND PAIN.

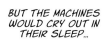

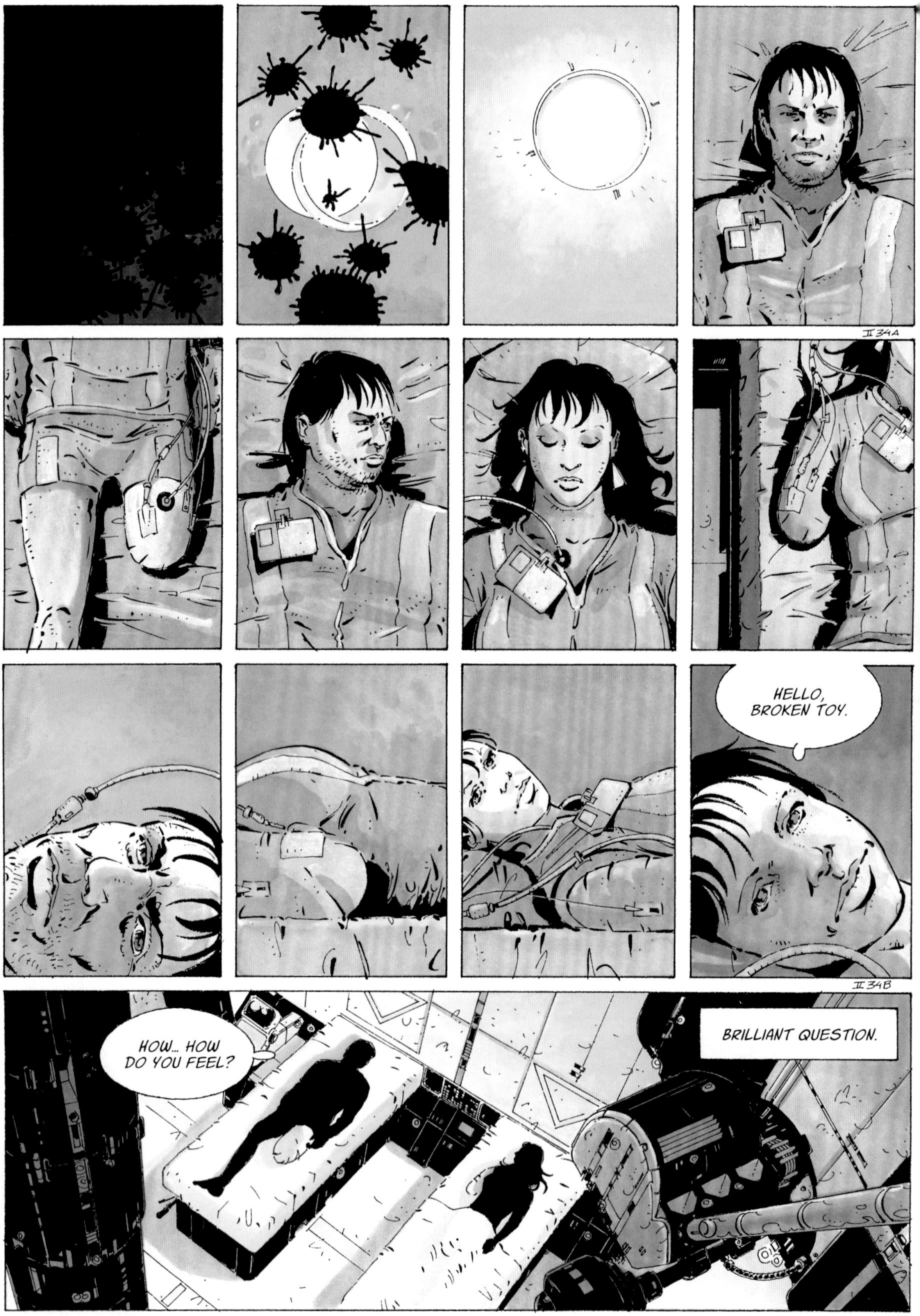
II 34A
HELLO, BROKEN TOY.
II 34B
HOW... HOW DO YOU FEEL?
BRILLIANT QUESTION.

DOC WILSON CAME IN.

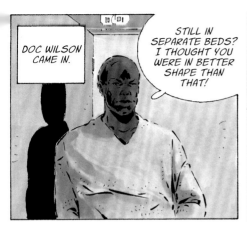

STILL IN SEPARATE BEDS? I THOUGHT YOU WERE IN BETTER SHAPE THAN THAT!

I'LL GIVE IT TO YOU STRAIGHT. YOU'RE ON HAPPY JUICE UP TO YOUR EARS, AND THE LOSS YOU'VE SUSTAINED WON'T BOTHER YOU UNTIL YOU'RE OFF IT.

FOR MY OWN CONVENIENCE, I HAVE TO KEEP YOU IN THIS STATE. WE HAVE TWENTY-ONE AMPUTEES --

-- AND WE CAN'T HANDLE TWENTY-ONE PSYCHIATRIC CASES.

WE WILL FIT YOUR PROSTHESES WHEN WE ARRIVE AT **HEAVEN**.

AT HEAVEN?!

HEAVEN, THE U.N.E.F.'S NEW HOSPITAL PLANET. AN IDEAL SPOT TO PUT YOU BOTH BACK TOGETHER.

WE'LL BE THERE FOR THREE MONTHS, REAL TIME. ENJOY YOUR PEACE OF MIND WHILE YOU HAVE IT...

...BECAUSE EVENTUALLY, EVERY TIME YOU LOOK AT HER ARTIFICIAL ARM...

...AND YOU HIS MECHANICAL LEG...

YOU WILL EACH THINK THAT THE OTHER HAD BETTER LUCK.

YOU MAY BE AT EACH OTHER'S THROATS IN A COUPLE OF WEEKS...

...OR YOU MIGHT STAY TOGETHER OUT OF MUTUAL PITY.

OR TRANSCEND IT. GIVE EACH OTHER STRENGTH.

JUST DON'T KID YOURSELVES IF IT DOESN'T WORK OUT.

NO SPACE SHIP WENT DIRECTLY TO HEAVEN...

...EVEN IF IT COST A NUMBER OF EXTRA LIVES EN ROUTE.

EARTH AND HEAVEN WERE THE TWO PLANETS...

...THAT THE TAURANS MUST NEVER DISCOVER.

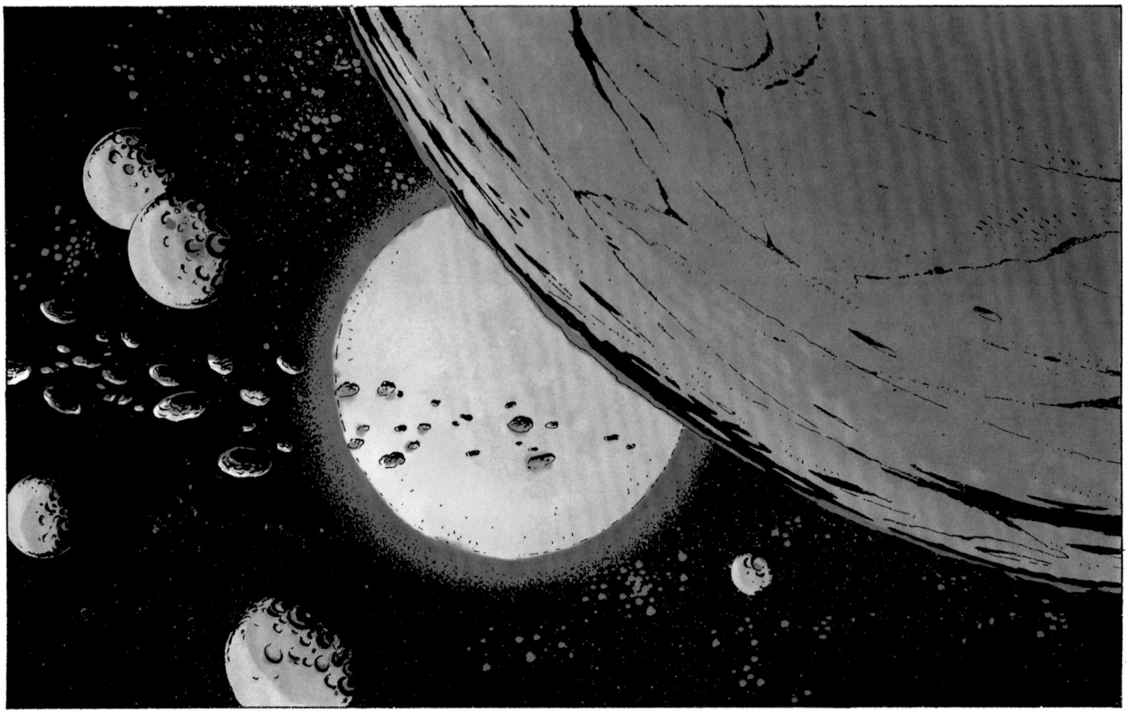

HEAVEN RESEMBLED EARTH...

AT LEAST, WHAT SHE WOULD HAVE BEEN...

...IF HUMANS HAD TREATED HER WITH RESPECT RATHER THAN WITH GREED.

IT WAS 2202... I WAS 213 YEARS OLD WHEN I ARRIVED ON HEAVEN.

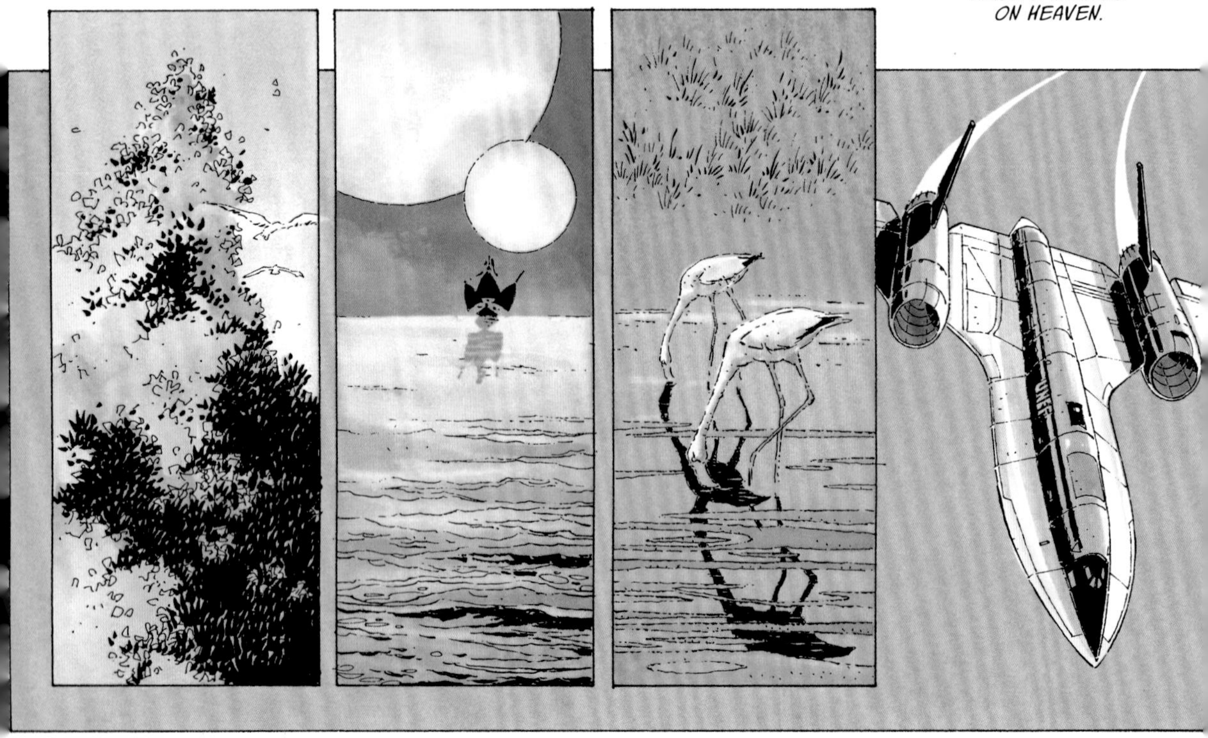

THE SCIENCE
OF PROSTHESIS
HAD ADVANCED
CONSIDERABLY
IN TWO CENTURIES...

I WAS GROWING
A REAL LEG.

GOOD MORNING,
SIR. AND THE LEG
IS COMING?

ALMOST UNBREAKABLE
METAL BONES!

BUT THE TREATMENT
CAUSED NUMEROUS LOCAL
CANCERS...

THAT HAD TO BE
TREATED SEPARATELY,
PAINFULLY.

I DON'T
RECOGNIZE YOUR
ACCENT, HOBSON.
WHERE ARE YOU
FROM?

A MAN HAS TO TALK
ABOUT SOMETHING.

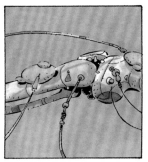
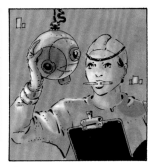

ARE YOU BEING
IN THE SERVICE
A LONG TIME,
SIR?

I HAVEN'T SEEN EARTH
IN MORE THAN A CENTURY.
DO ALL ENGLISH SPEAKERS
ON EARTH HAVE THIS NEW
THICK ACCENT? I'D HAVE TO
GO BACK TO SCHOOL
TO RELEARN MY OWN
LANGUAGE!

THE EARTH
I KNEW WAS
COMICALLY
UGLY.

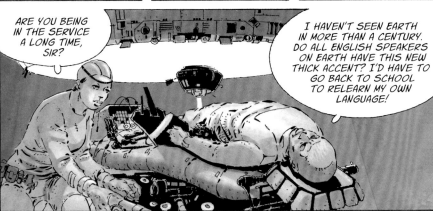

SORRY TO
SEEM SO
BITTER...

NO IMPORT,
SIR. MOST OF THE
OTHERS, SAME.

ME, I AM NEVER
BEEN THERE.

NOT SURPRISING
THAT I COULDN'T PLACE
HER ACCENT!

YOU MEAN...

A THIRD GENERATION ANGEL, SIR.

POKED, BORN, AND DRAFTED ON HEAVEN.

DON'T MOVE, SIR.

HER GRANDPARENTS CAME FROM EARTH WHEN I WAS A YOUNG PUNK OF A HUNDRED. HOW MANY OTHER WORLDS HAD THEY COLONIZED WHILE MY BACK WAS TURNED?

MARYGAY WAS ALREADY UP. WHEN HER SCHEDULE PERMITTED, SHE CAME TO KEEP ME COMPANY. WE TALKED, READ, PLAYED CHESS...HER ARM WAS ABOUT AS PRETTY AS MY LEG, BUT GROWING.

THEY TRANSFERRED US TO ORTHOPEDICS, FOR "RANGE AND MOTION REPATTERNING"...

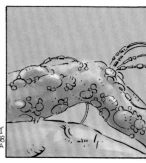

A FANCY NAME FOR SLOW TORTURE...

THEY STRAP YOU INTO A MACHINE THAT TWISTS THE OLD LEG AND THE NEW ONE AT THE SAME TIME.

THE NEW ONE RESISTS.

WE BOTH BEGAN SWIMMING. I STILL LIMPED ON LAND, BUT GOT AROUND OKAY IN THE WATER.

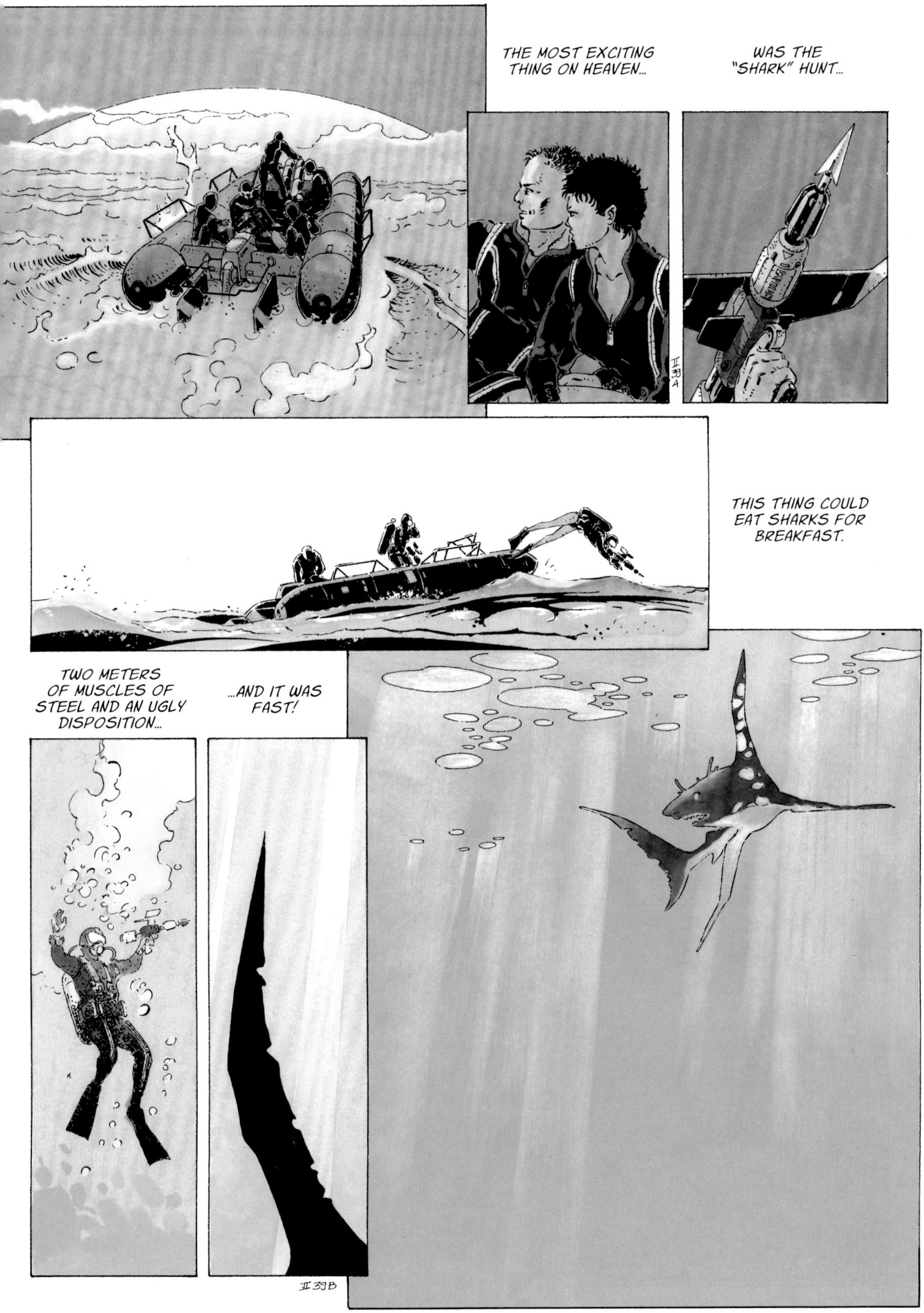
THE MOST EXCITING THING ON HEAVEN...
WAS THE "SHARK" HUNT...
THIS THING COULD EAT SHARKS FOR BREAKFAST.
TWO METERS OF MUSCLES OF STEEL AND AN UGLY DISPOSITION...
...AND IT WAS FAST!

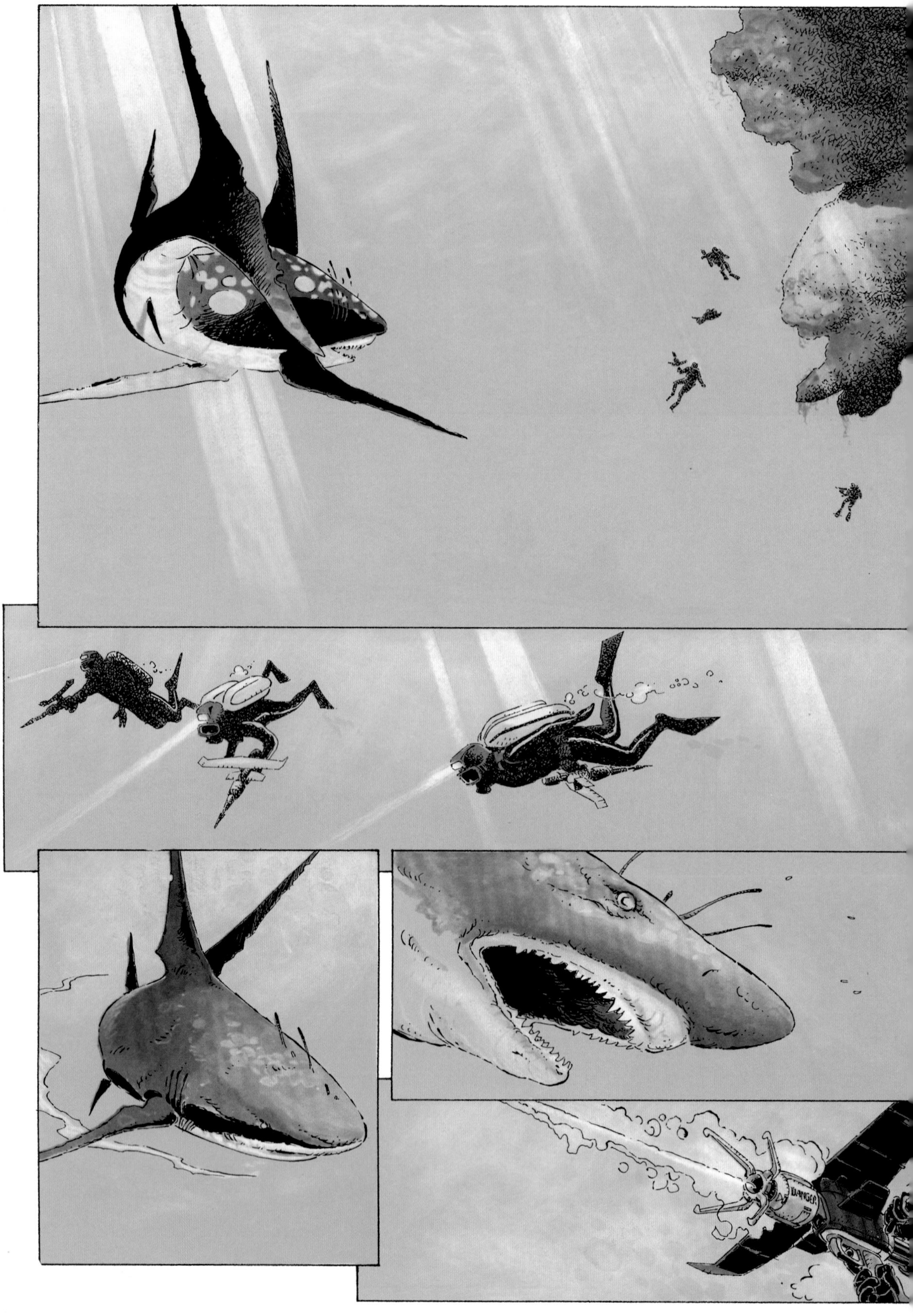
DANGER

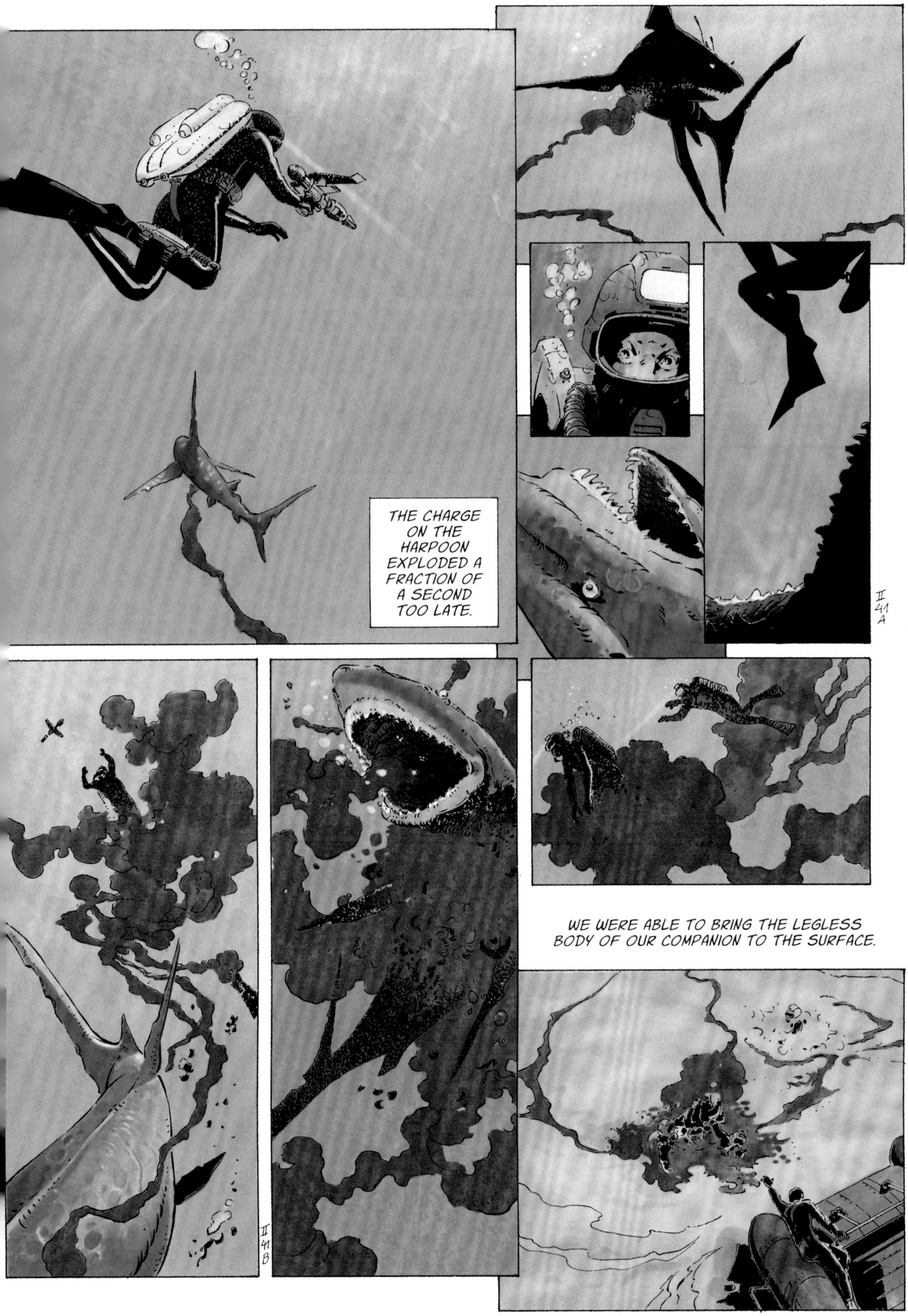
THE CHARGE ON THE HARPOON EXPLODED A FRACTION OF A SECOND TOO LATE.
II 41 A
II 41 B
WE WERE ABLE TO BRING THE LEGLESS BODY OF OUR COMPANION TO THE SURFACE.

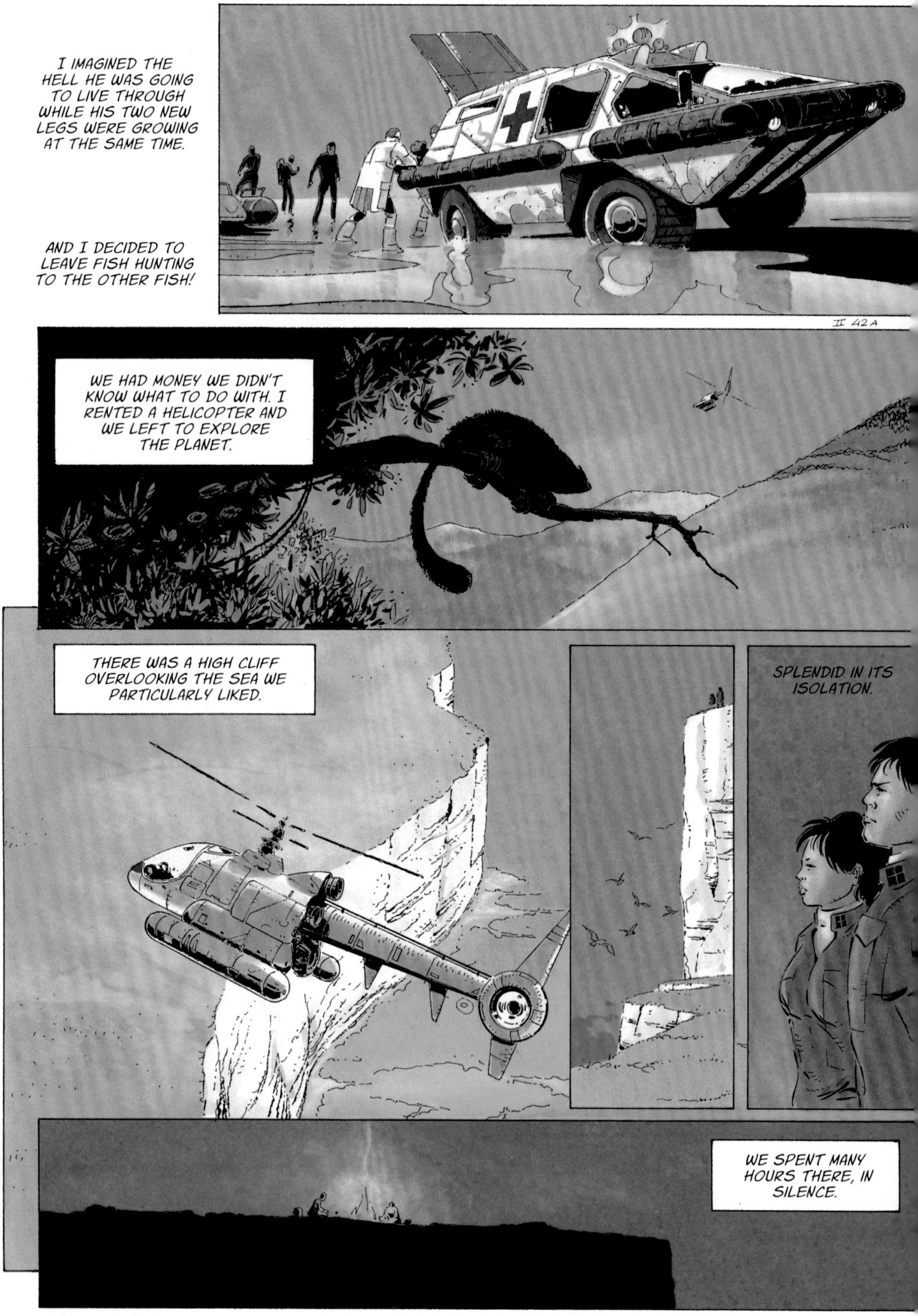
I IMAGINED THE HELL HE WAS GOING TO LIVE THROUGH WHILE HIS TWO NEW LEGS WERE GROWING AT THE SAME TIME.
AND I DECIDED TO LEAVE FISH HUNTING TO THE OTHER FISH!
II 42A
WE HAD MONEY WE DIDN'T KNOW WHAT TO DO WITH. I RENTED A HELICOPTER AND WE LEFT TO EXPLORE THE PLANET.
THERE WAS A HIGH CLIFF OVERLOOKING THE SEA WE PARTICULARLY LIKED.
SPLENDID IN ITS ISOLATION.
WE SPENT MANY HOURS THERE, IN SILENCE.

BUT WE WERE STILL
IN THE ARMY...

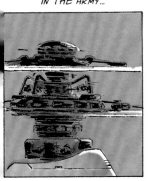

IN THE VAST
MILITARY MACHINE,
WE WERE JUST USED
PARTS THAT, ONCE
RECONDITIONED, MUST
RETURN TO THEIR
POSITION ON THE
FRONT LINE.

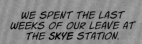

WE SPENT THE LAST
WEEKS OF OUR LEAVE AT
THE *SKYE* STATION.

II 43.A

WE EXPECTED
ANYTHING...

...EXCEPT WHAT WE
FOUND...

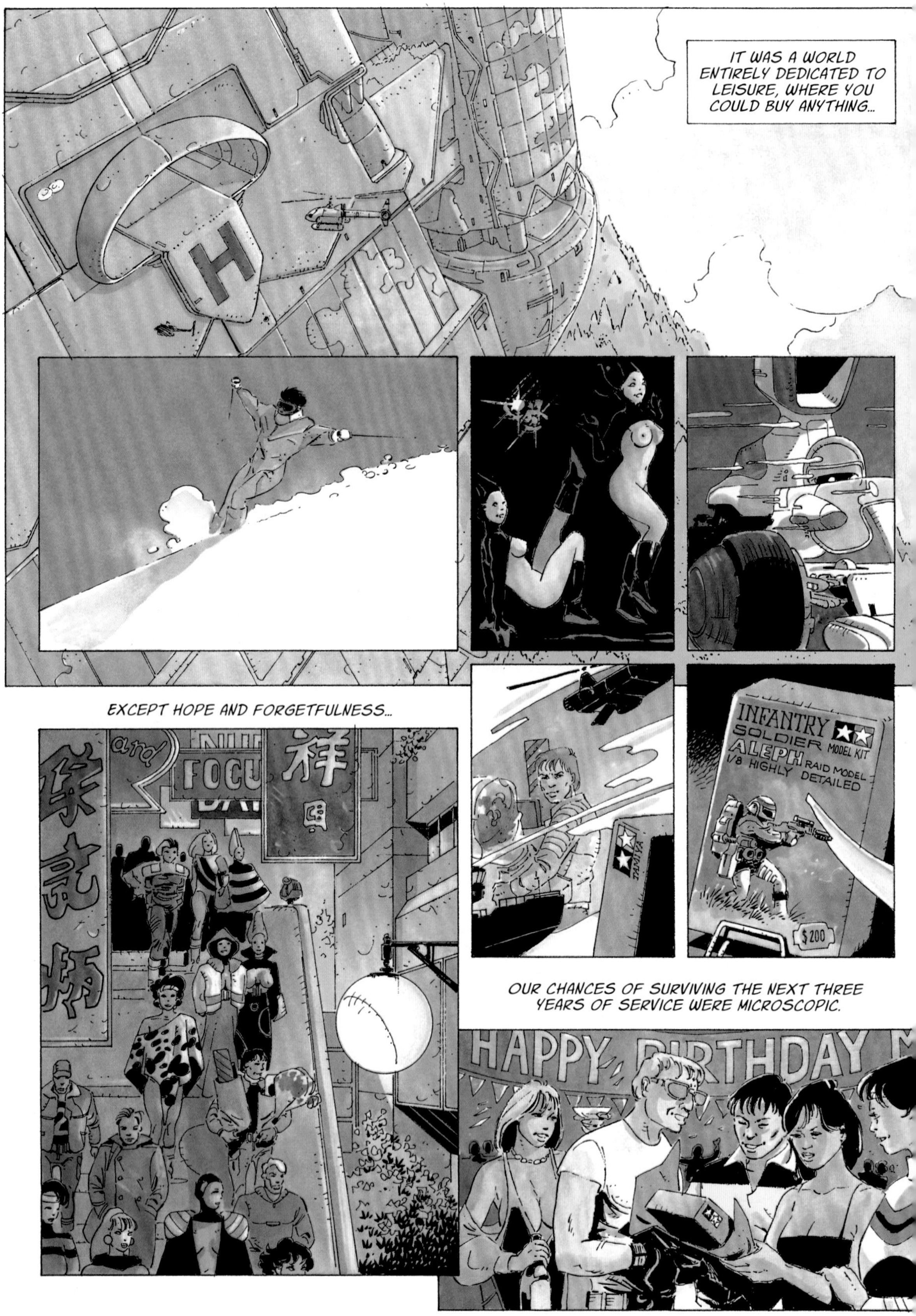
IT WAS A WORLD ENTIRELY DEDICATED TO LEISURE, WHERE YOU COULD BUY ANYTHING...
EXCEPT HOPE AND FORGETFULNESS...
INFANTRY SOLDIER MODEL KIT
ALEPH RAID MODEL
1/8 HIGHLY DETAILED
$200
OUR CHANCES OF SURVIVING THE NEXT THREE YEARS OF SERVICE WERE MICROSCOPIC.
HAPPY BIRTHDAY

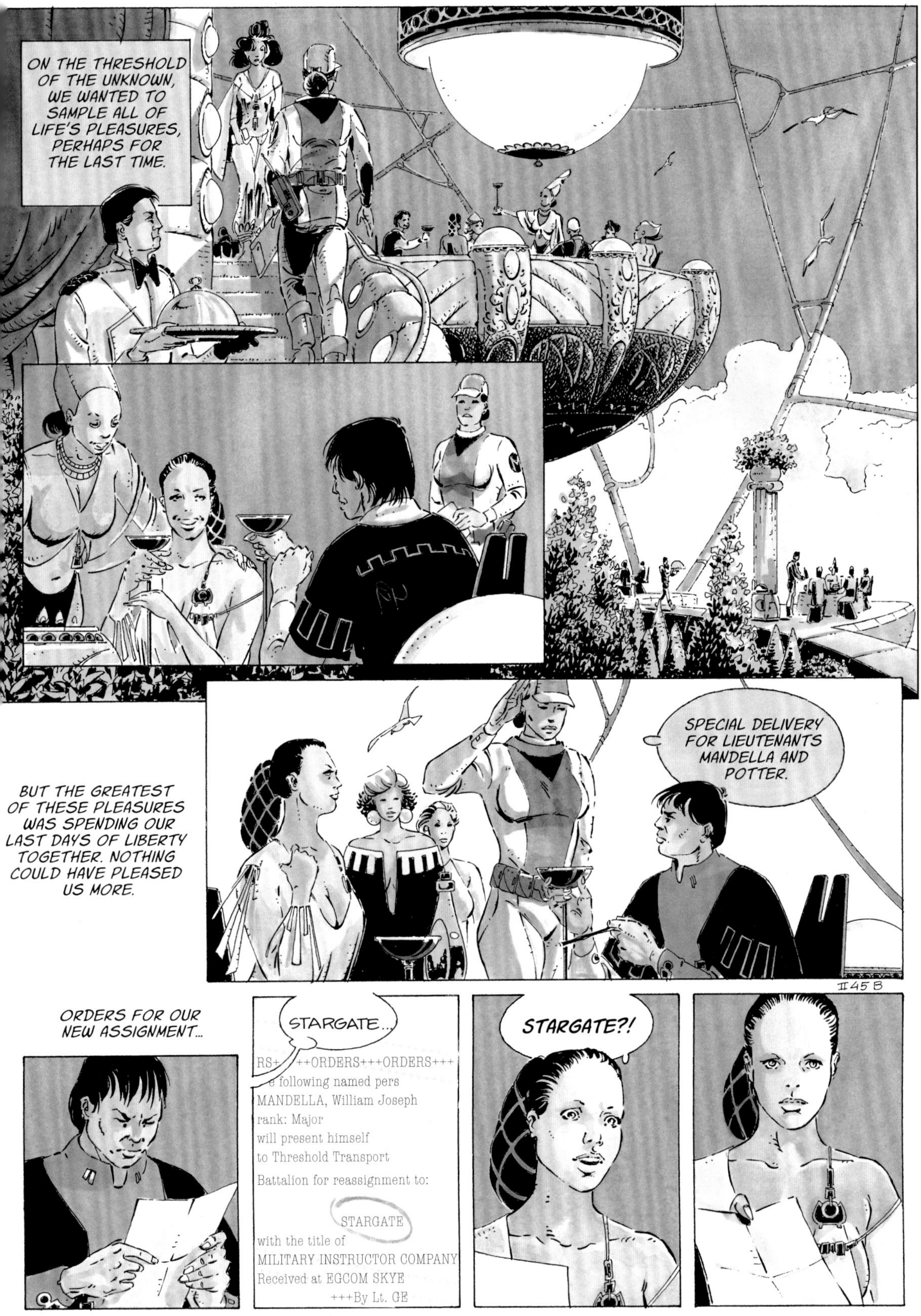

ON THE THRESHOLD OF THE UNKNOWN, WE WANTED TO SAMPLE ALL OF LIFE'S PLEASURES, PERHAPS FOR THE LAST TIME.
BUT THE GREATEST OF THESE PLEASURES WAS SPENDING OUR LAST DAYS OF LIBERTY TOGETHER. NOTHING COULD HAVE PLEASED US MORE.
SPECIAL DELIVERY FOR LIEUTENANTS MANDELLA AND POTTER.
II 45 B
ORDERS FOR OUR NEW ASSIGNMENT...
STARGATE...
RS+ ++ORDERS+++ORDERS+++
e following named pers
MANDELLA, William Joseph
rank: Major
will present himself
to Threshold Transport
Battalion for reassignment to:
STARGATE
with the title of
MILITARY INSTRUCTOR COMPANY
Received at EGCOM SKYE
+++By Lt. GE
STARGATE?!

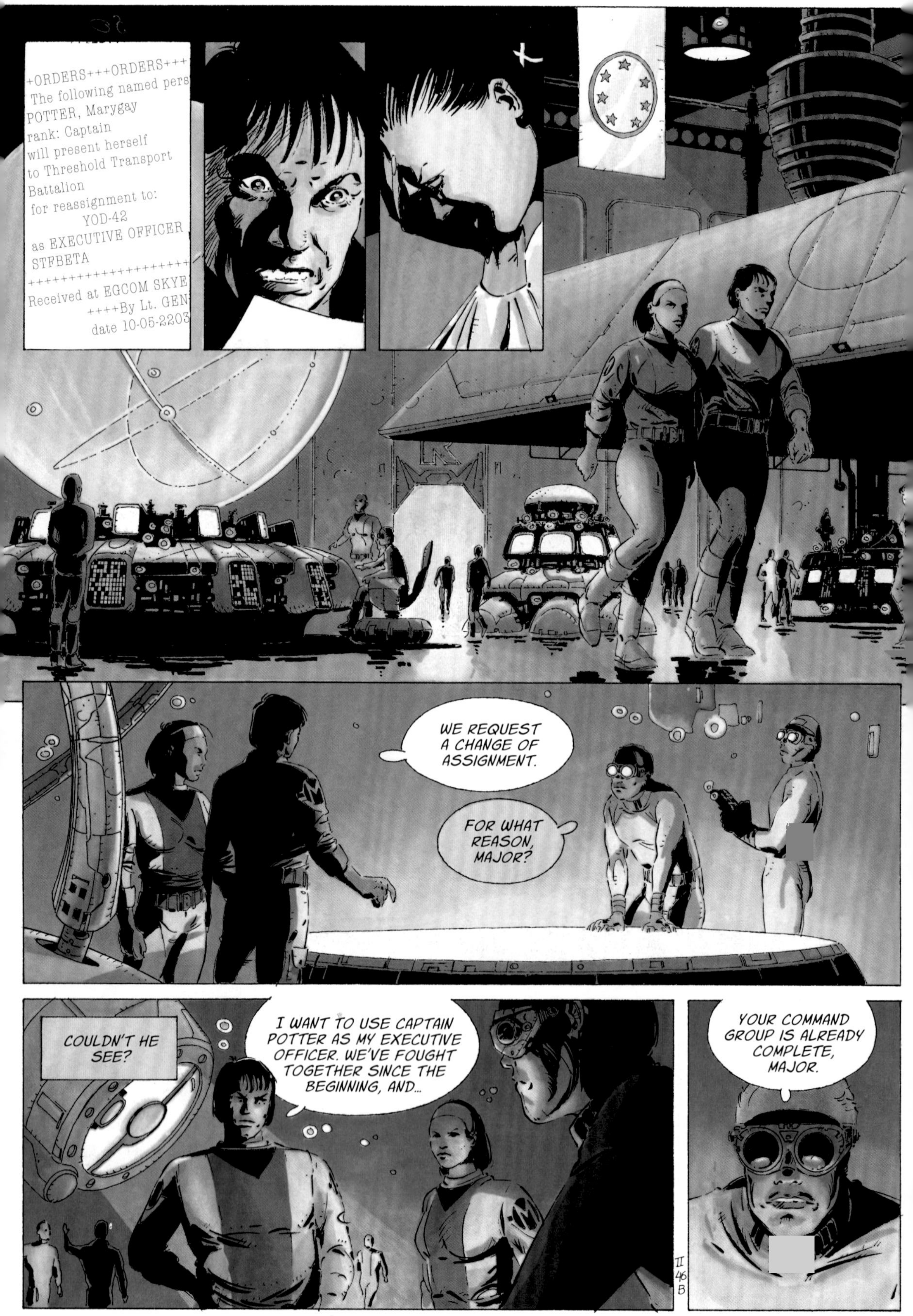
+ORDERS+++ORDERS+++
The following named pers
POTTER, Marygay
rank: Captain
will present herself
to Threshold Transport
Battalion
for reassignment to:
YOD-42
as EXECUTIVE OFFICER
STFBETA
++++++++++++++++++++
Received at EGCOM SKYE
++++By Lt. GEN
date 10-05-2203
WE REQUEST A CHANGE OF ASSIGNMENT.
FOR WHAT REASON, MAJOR?
COULDN'T HE SEE?
I WANT TO USE CAPTAIN POTTER AS MY EXECUTIVE OFFICER. WE'VE FOUGHT TOGETHER SINCE THE BEGINNING, AND...
YOUR COMMAND GROUP IS ALREADY COMPLETE, MAJOR.
II 46 B

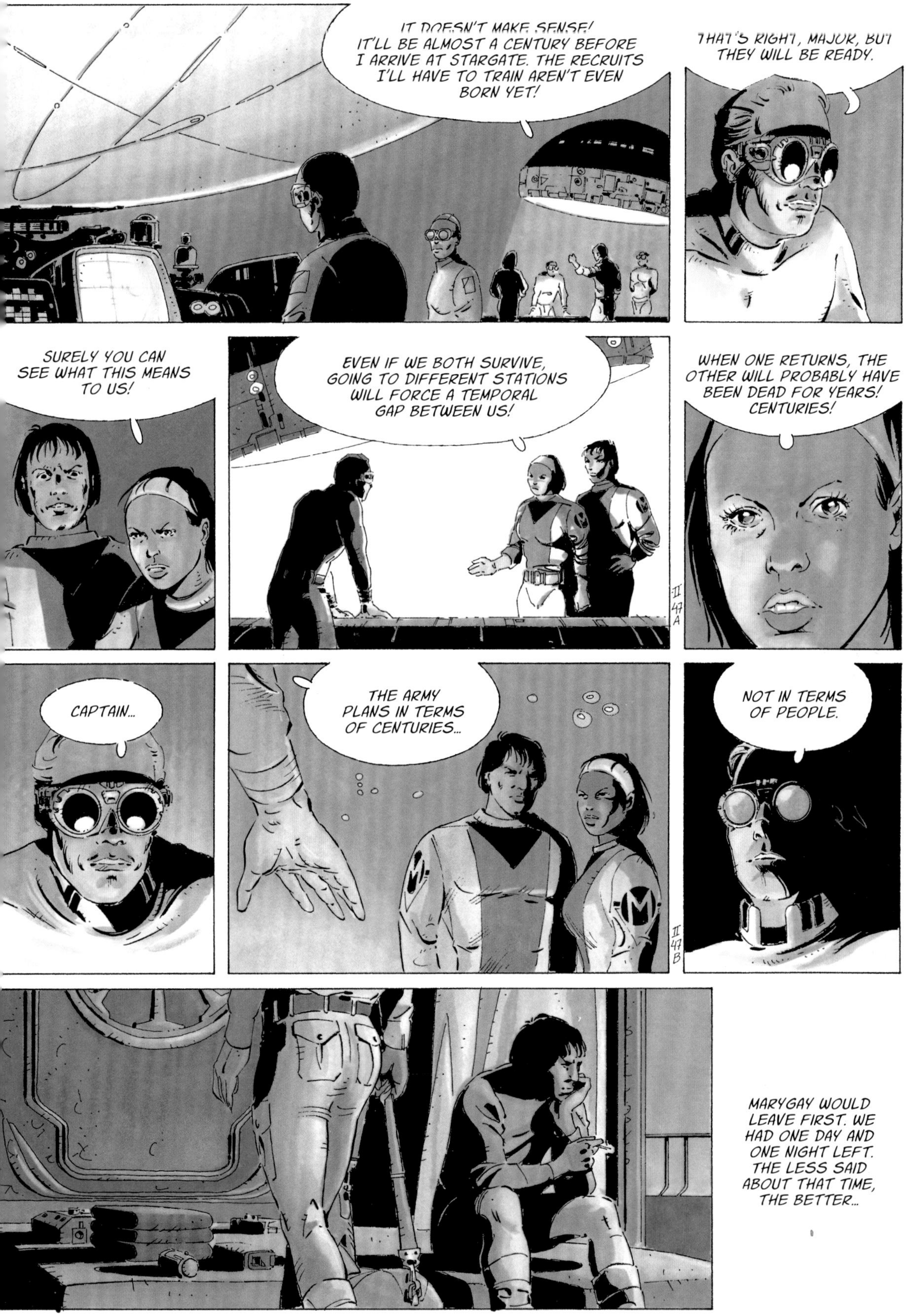
IT DOESN'T MAKE SENSE! IT'LL BE ALMOST A CENTURY BEFORE I ARRIVE AT STARGATE. THE RECRUITS I'LL HAVE TO TRAIN AREN'T EVEN BORN YET!
THAT'S RIGHT, MAJOR, BUT THEY WILL BE READY.
SURELY YOU CAN SEE WHAT THIS MEANS TO US!
EVEN IF WE BOTH SURVIVE, GOING TO DIFFERENT STATIONS WILL FORCE A TEMPORAL GAP BETWEEN US!
WHEN ONE RETURNS, THE OTHER WILL PROBABLY HAVE BEEN DEAD FOR YEARS! CENTURIES!
CAPTAIN...
THE ARMY PLANS IN TERMS OF CENTURIES...
NOT IN TERMS OF PEOPLE.
MARYGAY WOULD LEAVE FIRST. WE HAD ONE DAY AND ONE NIGHT LEFT. THE LESS SAID ABOUT THAT TIME, THE BETTER...

WE WEREN'T JUST
LOSING LOVERS...

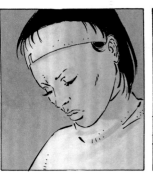

MARYGAY AND I WERE
EACH OTHER'S ONLY LINK
TO REAL LIFE...

TO THAT GOOD OLD EARTH
OF THE 21ST CENTURY...

NOT THE PERVERSE
GROTESQUERIE...

WE WERE SUPPOSEDLY
FIGHTING TO PRESERVE.

THE UGLY, ALIEN
"HOMELAND"...

... AS DISTANT AND
IRRELEVANT TO US...

...AS ANCIENT EGYPT, AS
HOMER'S TROY...

WHEN HER SHUTTLE TOOK OFF IT WAS LIKE A CASKET RATTLING DOWN INTO A GRAVE.

THE COMPUTER
CALCULATED THAT
I COULD SEE HER
STARSHIP LEAVING
ORBIT FROM OUR
CLIFF OVERLOOKING
THE SEA...

I LANDED THE
HELICOPTER AT OUR
USUAL SPOT...

II 49A

II 49B

A NEW
STAR APPEARED,
MARYGAY'S SHIP...
IT FLARED TO
BRILLIANCE, THEN
FADED AS IT
MOVED AWAY.

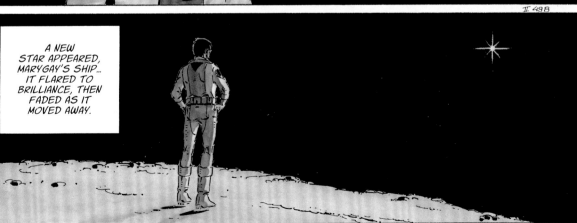

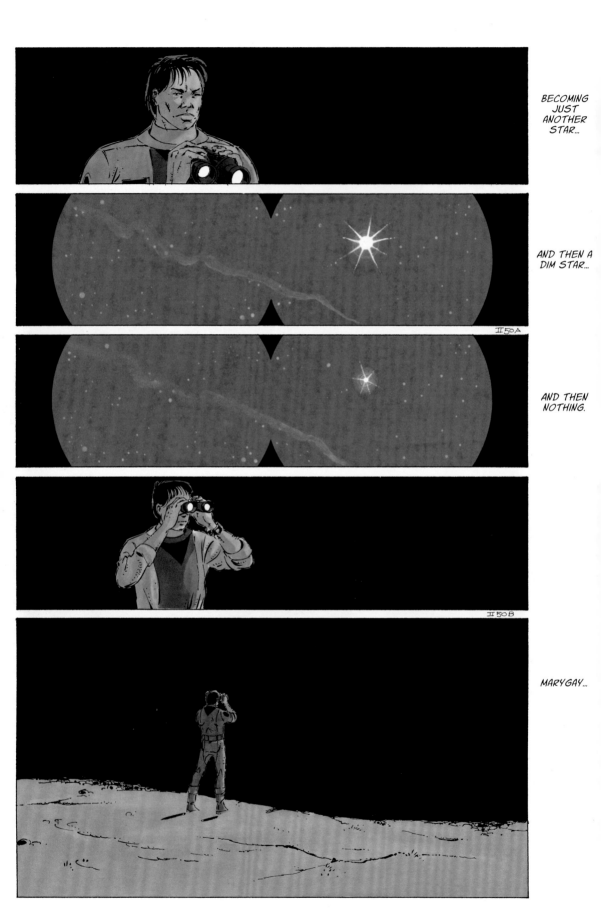

BECOMING JUST ANOTHER STAR...

AND THEN A DIM STAR...

II 50 A

AND THEN NOTHING.

II 50 B

MARYGAY...

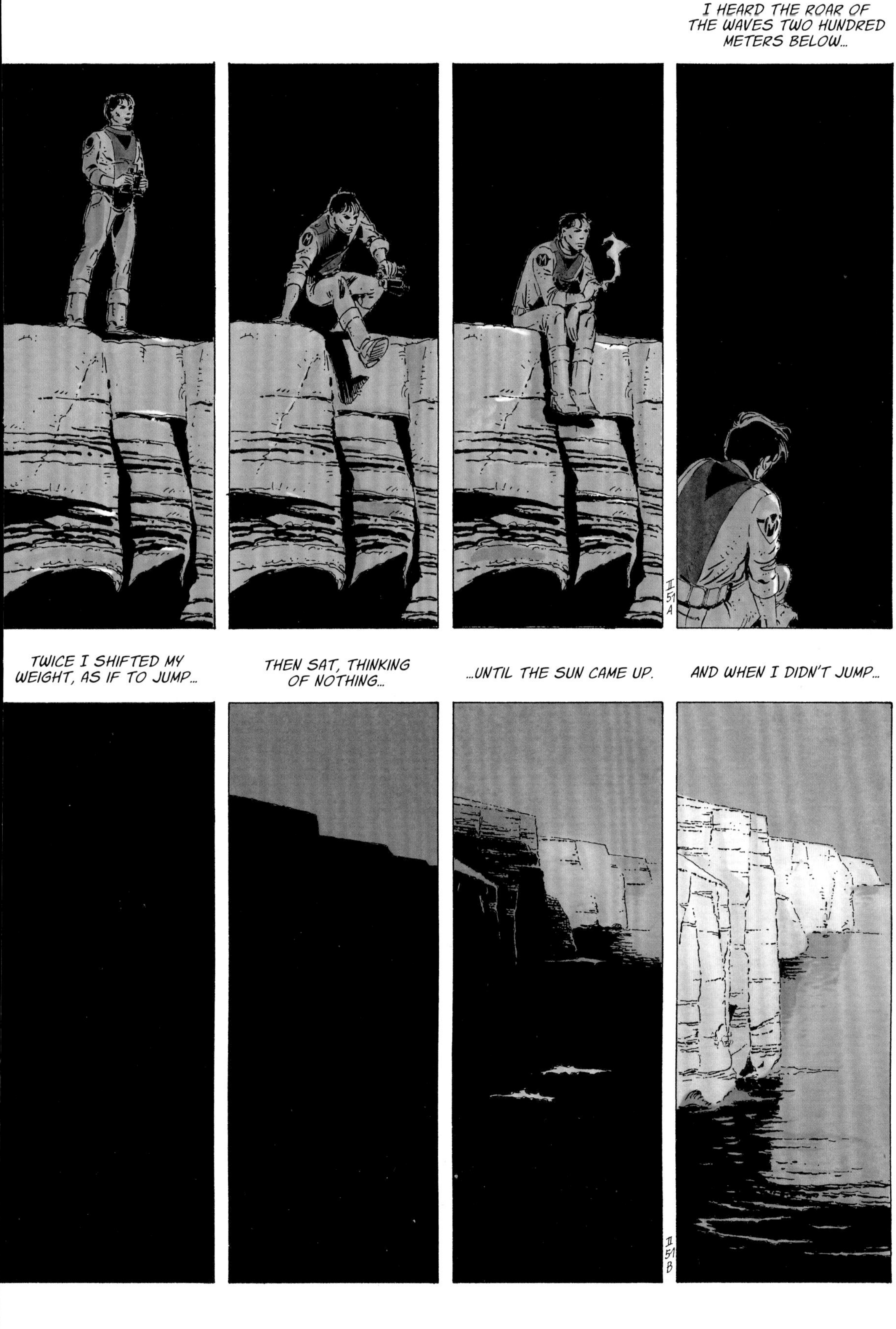
I HEARD THE ROAR OF THE WAVES TWO HUNDRED METERS BELOW...
TWICE I SHIFTED MY WEIGHT, AS IF TO JUMP...
THEN SAT, THINKING OF NOTHING...
...UNTIL THE SUN CAME UP.
AND WHEN I DIDN'T JUMP...

IT WASN'T FEAR OF THE
SPARK OF PAIN, AND THE LOSS
WOULD ONLY BE THE ARMY'S.

IT WOULD BE THEIR
ULTIMATE VICTORY
OVER ME...

HAVING RULED
MY LIFE SO LONG...

TO FORCE
AN END TO IT...

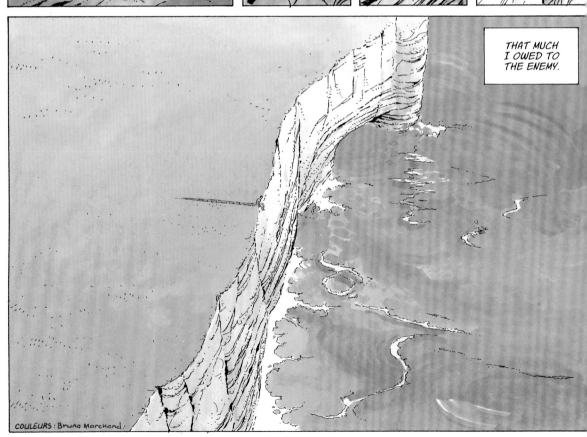

THAT MUCH
I OWED TO
THE ENEMY.

COULEURS : Bruno Marchand.

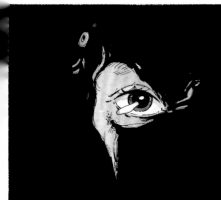

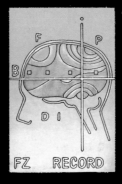

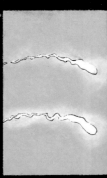

DO YOU KNOW WHO **SCIPIO AEMILIANUS** WAS?

NEITHER DO I...

...BIGGEST OF THE BIG SHOTS OF THE THIRD PUNIC WAR...

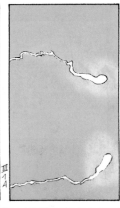

"WAR IS THE PROVINCE OF DANGER, AND THEREFORE COURAGE ABOVE ALL THINGS IS THE FIRST QUALITY OF A WARRIOR."

...HERR VON CLAUSEWITZ MAINTAINED...

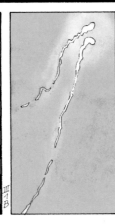

I'LL NEVER FORGET THE POETRY OF: "THE ADVANCE PARTY NORMALLY MOVES IN A COLUMN FORMATION WITH THE PLATOON HEADQUARTERS LEADING, FOLLOWED BY A LASER SQUAD, THE HEAVY WEAPONS SQUAD, AND THE REMAINING LASER SQUAD...

..."THE COLUMN RELIES ON OBSERVATION FOR ITS FLANK SECURITY EXCEPT WHEN..."

LET'S MOVE MAJOR MANDELLA INTO THE ALSC ENVIRONMENT...

..."EXCEPT WHEN TERRAIN AND VISIBILITY DICTATE THE NEED FOR SMALL SECURITY DETACHMENTS TO THE FLANKS IN WHICH THE ADVANCE PARTY COMMANDER WILL DETAIL ONE PLATOON SERGEANT..."

AND SO ON.

DEATHLESS PROSE FROM **STRIKE FORCE COMMAND SMALL UNIT LEADER'S** HANDBOOK.

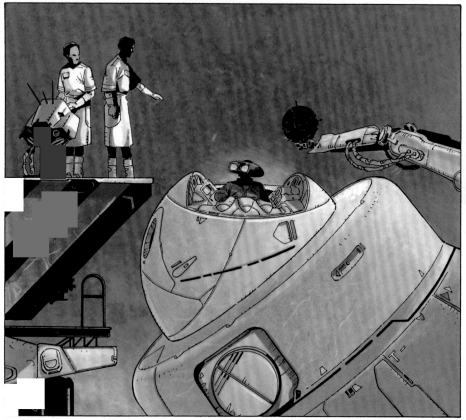

IF YOU WANT TO BECOME A THOROUGHLY ECLECTIC EXPERT ON A SUBJECT THAT DISGUSTS YOU, JOIN U.N.E.F. AND SIGN UP FOR OFFICER TRAINING.

I REMEMBER THAT EXPERIMENT IN HIGH SCHOOL BIOLOGY...

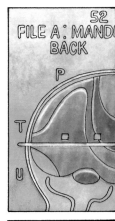

TAKE A FLATWORM AND TEACH IT HOW TO SWIM THROUGH A MAZE.

III 3A

THEN MASH IT UP AND FEED IT TO A STUPID FLATWORM. SURPRISE! THE STUPID FLATWORM WILL BE ABLE TO SWIM THE MAZE, TOO.

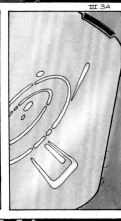

I HAD A BAD TASTE OF MAJOR GENERAL IN MY MOUTH.

ACTUALLY, I WAS JUST IMMERSED IN ALSC, THE ACCELERATED LIFE SITUATION COMPUTER.

THE ALSC TAUGHT ME THE ART (EXCUSE THE EXPRESSION) OF WAR, AS IT HAD BEEN PRACTICED BY HUNDREDS OF GENERATIONS.

NOT JUST INTELLECTUAL. I FELT EVERYTHING.

I FELT THE WEAPONS IN MY HANDS...

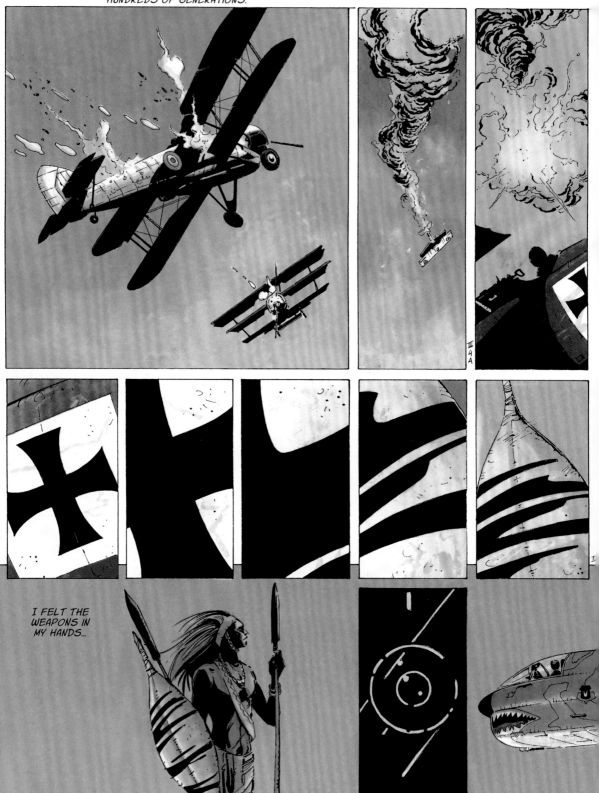

EVERY KIND OF WEAPON, FROM THE SPEAR TO THE NUCLEAR BOMB.

AND I FELT THEIR EFFECTS, TOO.

YOU KNOW AT LEAST A THOUSAND WAYS TO KILL, WILLIAM...

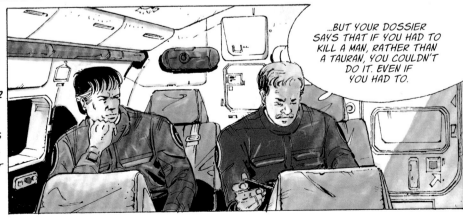

CAPTAIN **CHARLIE MOORE** HAD BEEN ASSIGNED TO ME AS MY EXEC., SECOND IN COMMAND. HE WAS A VETERAN OF THE **AYIN-12** CAMPAIGN. HE'D LOST BOTH LEGS AND MORE, A LOT MORE. BUT YOU COULDN'T TELL. HE WAS ALL RIGHT. WE GOT PAST THE "MAJOR SIR" AND "CAPTAIN" BULLSHIT PRETTY FAST.

...BUT YOUR DOSSIER SAYS THAT IF YOU HAD TO KILL A MAN, RATHER THAN A TAURAN, YOU COULDN'T DO IT. EVEN IF YOU HAD TO.

YOU HAVE ACCESS TO MY DOSSIER, CHARLIE?

JOB PRIVILEGE. AS ORIENTATION AND MORALE OFFICER, I HAVE TO KNOW WHAT MAKES EACH PERSON TICK.

AH! COCKTAILS!

GLAD SOMEBODY DOES.

I WAS A LITTLE CURIOUS. WHAT ANIMAL ISN'T FASCINATED BY A MIRROR?

DOES IT SAY I WON'T MAKE A GOOD OFFICER? I TOLD THEM THAT FROM THE BEGINNING. I'M NOT A LEADER.

YOU HAVE A CERTAIN POTENTIAL. YOUR PSYCHOLOGICAL PROFILE SHOWS THAT YOU WOULD HAVE TO LEAD FROM EMPATHY, COMPASSION. A TEACHER OR A PREACHER. YOU WANT TO IMPOSE YOUR IDEAS ON PEOPLE, NOT YOUR WILL.

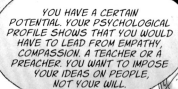

STARGATE MOVED BY BELOW US, WHILE THE MASARYK, OUR SPACE SHIP, ORIENTED ITSELF TOWARD THE GREATER MAGELLANIC CLOUD, WHERE MY UNIT WAS GOING TO DEFEND A CHUNK OF ROCK AGAINST SOME HYPOTHETICAL TAURANS. STARGATE WAS JUST A CHUNK OF ROCK WHEN I WAS DRAFTED INTO THE ARMY. NOW IT WAS A CITY BIGGER THAN NEW YORK.

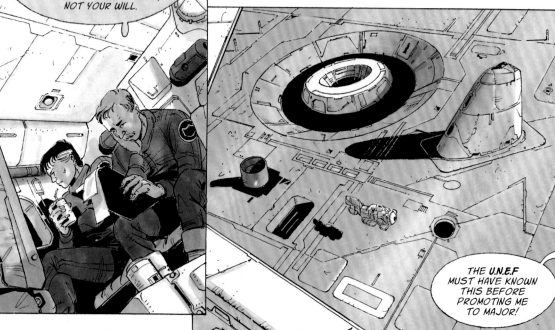

THE U.N.E.F MUST HAVE KNOWN THIS BEFORE PROMOTING ME TO MAJOR!

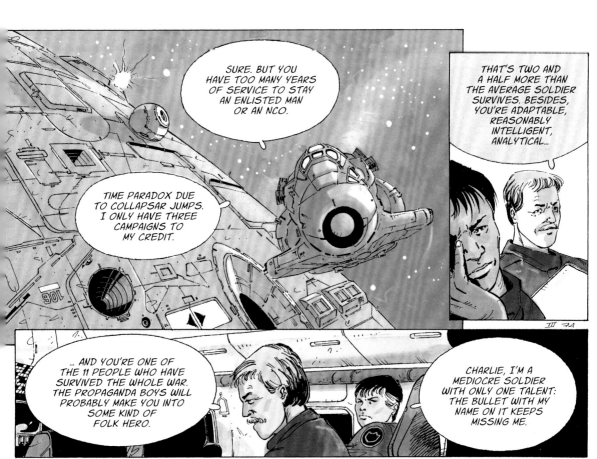

SURE. BUT YOU HAVE TOO MANY YEARS OF SERVICE TO STAY AN ENLISTED MAN OR AN NCO.

TIME PARADOX DUE TO COLLAPSAR JUMPS. I ONLY HAVE THREE CAMPAIGNS TO MY CREDIT.

THAT'S TWO AND A HALF MORE THAN THE AVERAGE SOLDIER SURVIVES. BESIDES, YOU'RE ADAPTABLE, REASONABLY INTELLIGENT, ANALYTICAL...

... AND YOU'RE ONE OF THE 11 PEOPLE WHO HAVE SURVIVED THE WHOLE WAR. THE PROPAGANDA BOYS WILL PROBABLY MAKE YOU INTO SOME KIND OF FOLK HERO.

CHARLIE, I'M A MEDIOCRE SOLDIER WITH ONLY ONE TALENT: THE BULLET WITH MY NAME ON IT KEEPS MISSING ME.

WELL, UM... THAT'S NOT THE ONLY THING THAT'S STRANGE ABOUT YOU, WILLIAM...

YES, I'M 482 YEARS OLD!

THAT'S NOT EXACTLY IT. YOU'RE HETEROSEXUAL!

BIG DEAL. I'M TOLERANT.

YOUR PROFILE SAYS YOU THINK YOU ARE. BUT YOU'VE ALWAYS HAD... OTHERS...

WAIT A MINUTE... YOU MEAN THAT... ON BOARD...

...EVERYONE ON THE SHIP IS HOMOSEXUAL?

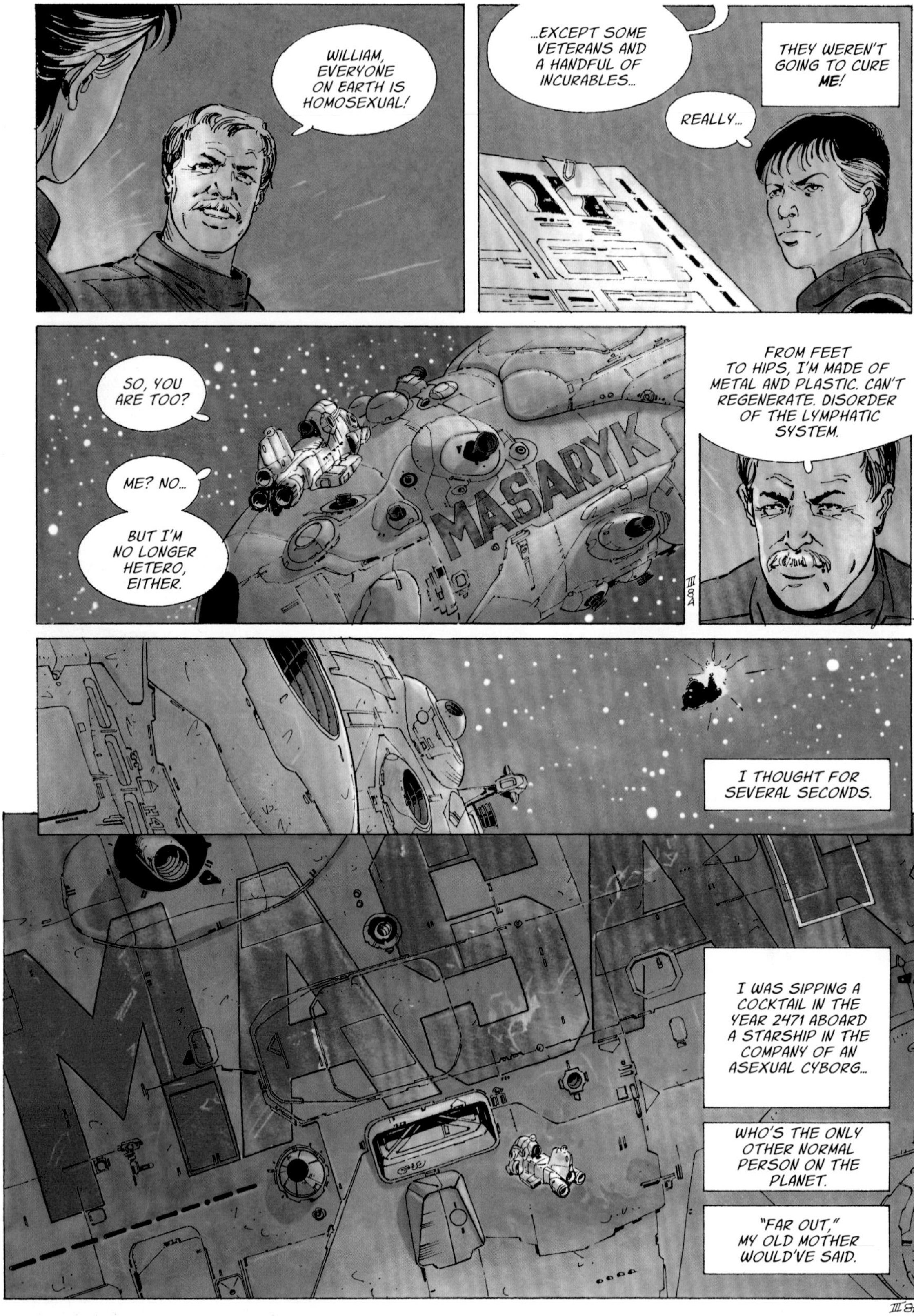
WILLIAM, EVERYONE ON EARTH IS HOMOSEXUAL!
...EXCEPT SOME VETERANS AND A HANDFUL OF INCURABLES...
THEY WEREN'T GOING TO CURE **ME**!
REALLY...
SO, YOU ARE TOO?
ME? NO...
BUT I'M NO LONGER HETERO, EITHER.
MASARYK
FROM FEET TO HIPS, I'M MADE OF METAL AND PLASTIC. CAN'T REGENERATE. DISORDER OF THE LYMPHATIC SYSTEM.
I THOUGHT FOR SEVERAL SECONDS.
I WAS SIPPING A COCKTAIL IN THE YEAR 2471 ABOARD A STARSHIP IN THE COMPANY OF AN ASEXUAL CYBORG...
WHO'S THE ONLY OTHER NORMAL PERSON ON THE PLANET.
"FAR OUT," MY OLD MOTHER WOULD'VE SAID.

III 8B

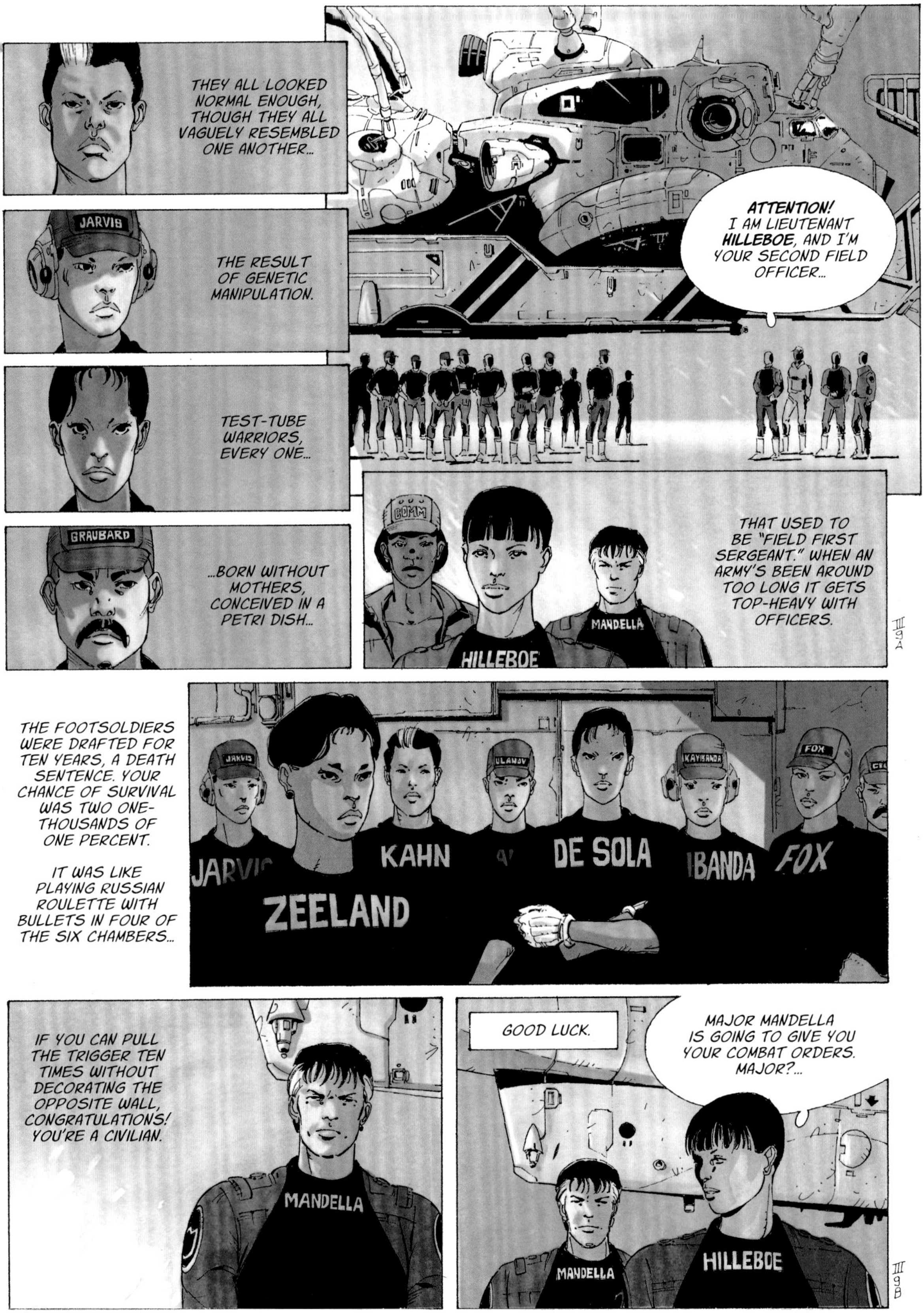
THEY ALL LOOKED NORMAL ENOUGH, THOUGH THEY ALL VAGUELY RESEMBLED ONE ANOTHER...
JARVIS
THE RESULT OF GENETIC MANIPULATION.
TEST-TUBE WARRIORS, EVERY ONE...
GRAUBARD
...BORN WITHOUT MOTHERS, CONCEIVED IN A PETRI DISH...
ATTENTION! I AM LIEUTENANT HILLEBOE, AND I'M YOUR SECOND FIELD OFFICER...
THAT USED TO BE "FIELD FIRST SERGEANT." WHEN AN ARMY'S BEEN AROUND TOO LONG IT GETS TOP-HEAVY WITH OFFICERS.
HILLEBOE
MANDELLA
III 9A
THE FOOTSOLDIERS WERE DRAFTED FOR TEN YEARS, A DEATH SENTENCE. YOUR CHANCE OF SURVIVAL WAS TWO ONE-THOUSANDS OF ONE PERCENT.
IT WAS LIKE PLAYING RUSSIAN ROULETTE WITH BULLETS IN FOUR OF THE SIX CHAMBERS...
ZEELAND
KAHN
DE SOLA
FOX
IF YOU CAN PULL THE TRIGGER TEN TIMES WITHOUT DECORATING THE OPPOSITE WALL, CONGRATULATIONS! YOU'RE A CIVILIAN.
MANDELLA
GOOD LUCK.
MAJOR MANDELLA IS GOING TO GIVE YOU YOUR COMBAT ORDERS. MAJOR?...
MANDELLA
HILLEBOE
III 9B

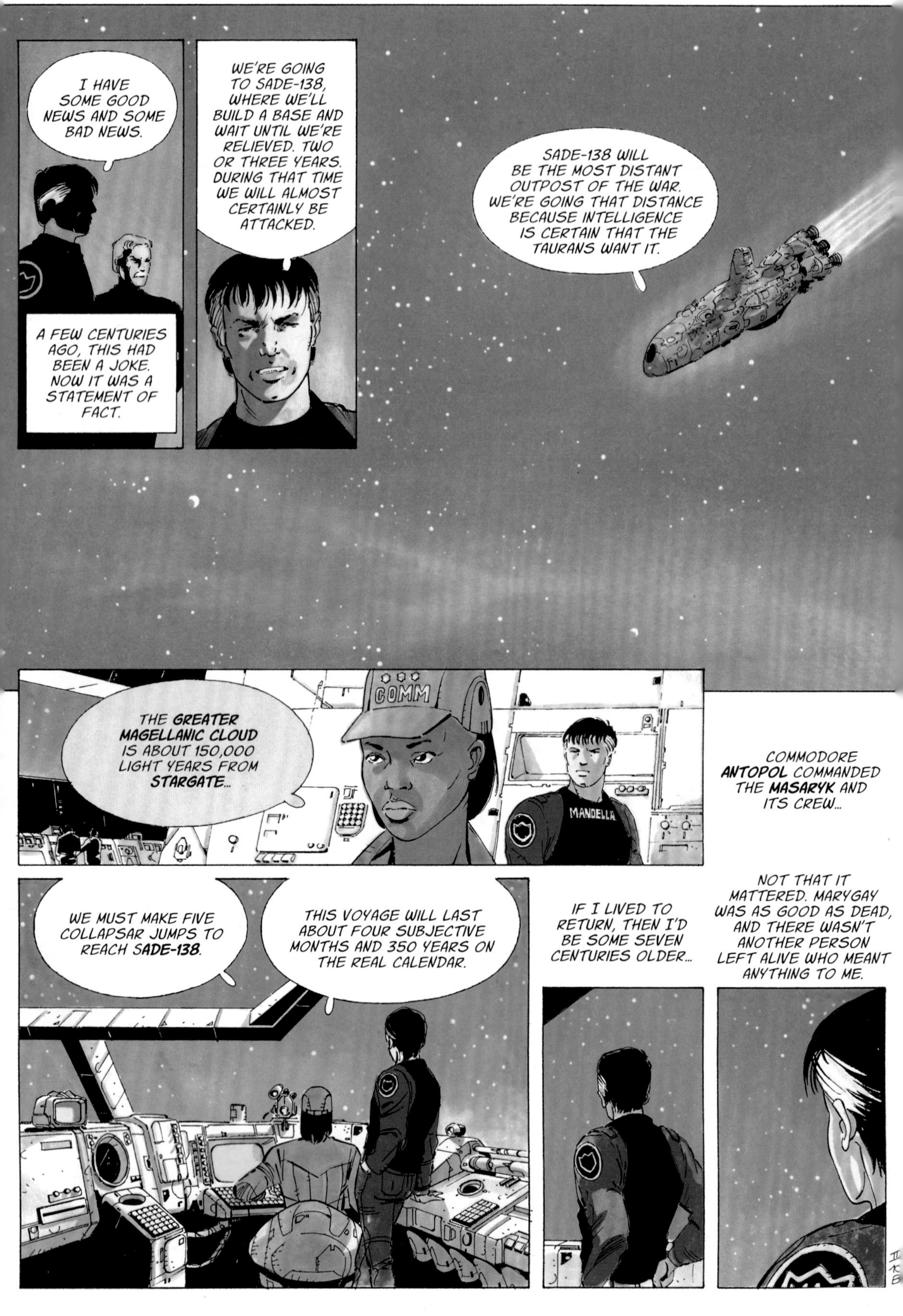
I HAVE SOME GOOD NEWS AND SOME BAD NEWS.
A FEW CENTURIES AGO, THIS HAD BEEN A JOKE. NOW IT WAS A STATEMENT OF FACT.
WE'RE GOING TO SADE-138, WHERE WE'LL BUILD A BASE AND WAIT UNTIL WE'RE RELIEVED. TWO OR THREE YEARS. DURING THAT TIME WE WILL ALMOST CERTAINLY BE ATTACKED.
SADE-138 WILL BE THE MOST DISTANT OUTPOST OF THE WAR. WE'RE GOING THAT DISTANCE BECAUSE INTELLIGENCE IS CERTAIN THAT THE TAURANS WANT IT.
COMM
THE **GREATER MAGELLANIC CLOUD** IS ABOUT 150,000 LIGHT YEARS FROM **STARGATE**...
MANDELLA
COMMODORE **ANTOPOL** COMMANDED THE **MASARYK** AND ITS CREW...
WE MUST MAKE FIVE COLLAPSAR JUMPS TO REACH **SADE-138**.
THIS VOYAGE WILL LAST ABOUT FOUR SUBJECTIVE MONTHS AND 350 YEARS ON THE REAL CALENDAR.
IF I LIVED TO RETURN, THEN I'D BE SOME SEVEN CENTURIES OLDER...
NOT THAT IT MATTERED. MARYGAY WAS AS GOOD AS DEAD, AND THERE WASN'T ANOTHER PERSON LEFT ALIVE WHO MEANT ANYTHING TO ME.

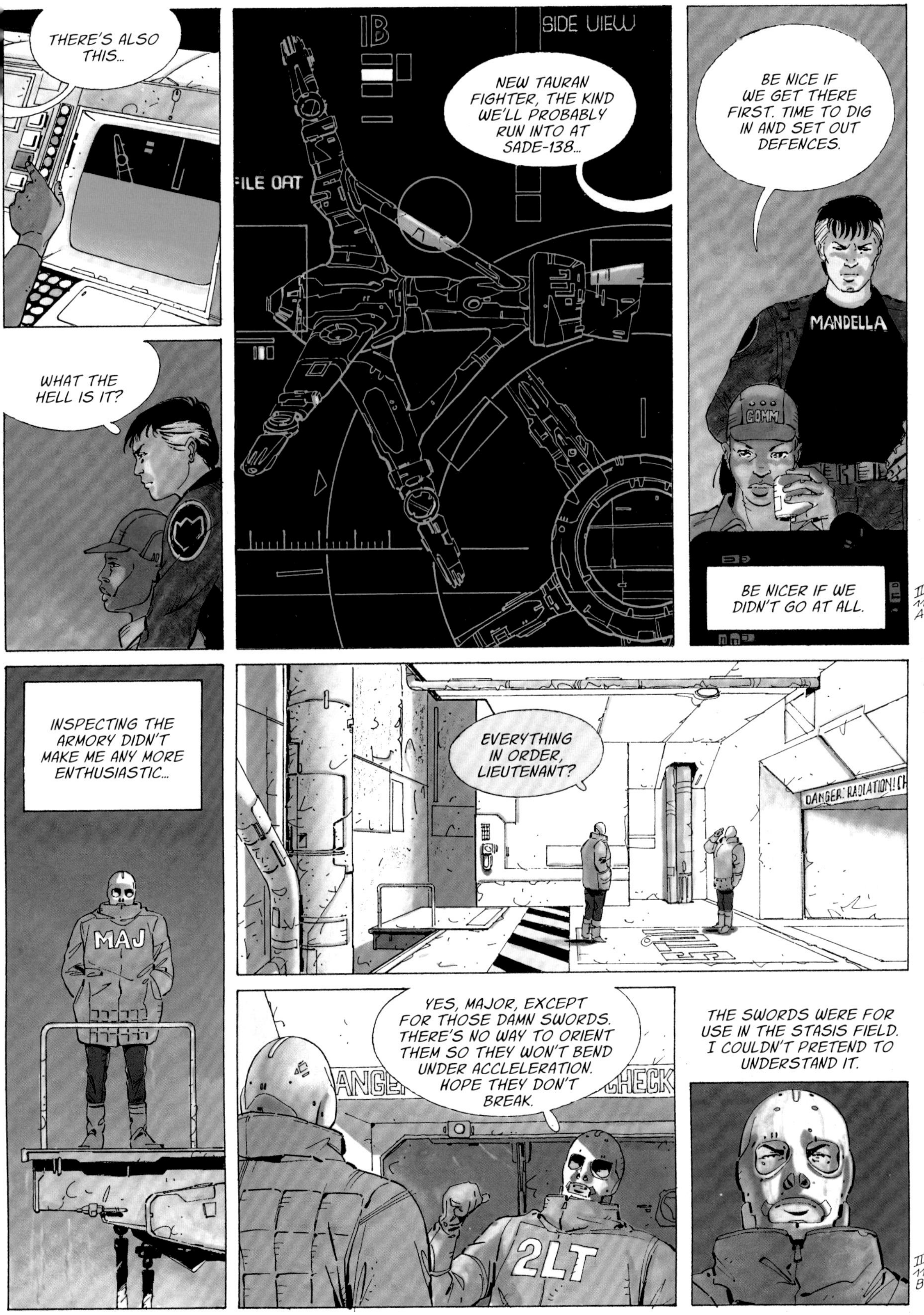
THERE'S ALSO THIS...
WHAT THE HELL IS IT?
IB
SIDE VIEW
FILE DAT
NEW TAURAN FIGHTER, THE KIND WE'LL PROBABLY RUN INTO AT SADE-138...
BE NICE IF WE GET THERE FIRST. TIME TO DIG IN AND SET OUT DEFENCES.
MANDELLA
COMM
BE NICER IF WE DIDN'T GO AT ALL.
II 11 A
INSPECTING THE ARMORY DIDN'T MAKE ME ANY MORE ENTHUSIASTIC...
MAJ
EVERYTHING IN ORDER, LIEUTENANT?
DANGER: RADIATION! CH
YES, MAJOR, EXCEPT FOR THOSE DAMN SWORDS. THERE'S NO WAY TO ORIENT THEM SO THEY WON'T BEND UNDER ACCLELERATION. HOPE THEY DON'T BREAK.
CHECK
2LT
THE SWORDS WERE FOR USE IN THE STASIS FIELD. I COULDN'T PRETEND TO UNDERSTAND IT.
II 11 B

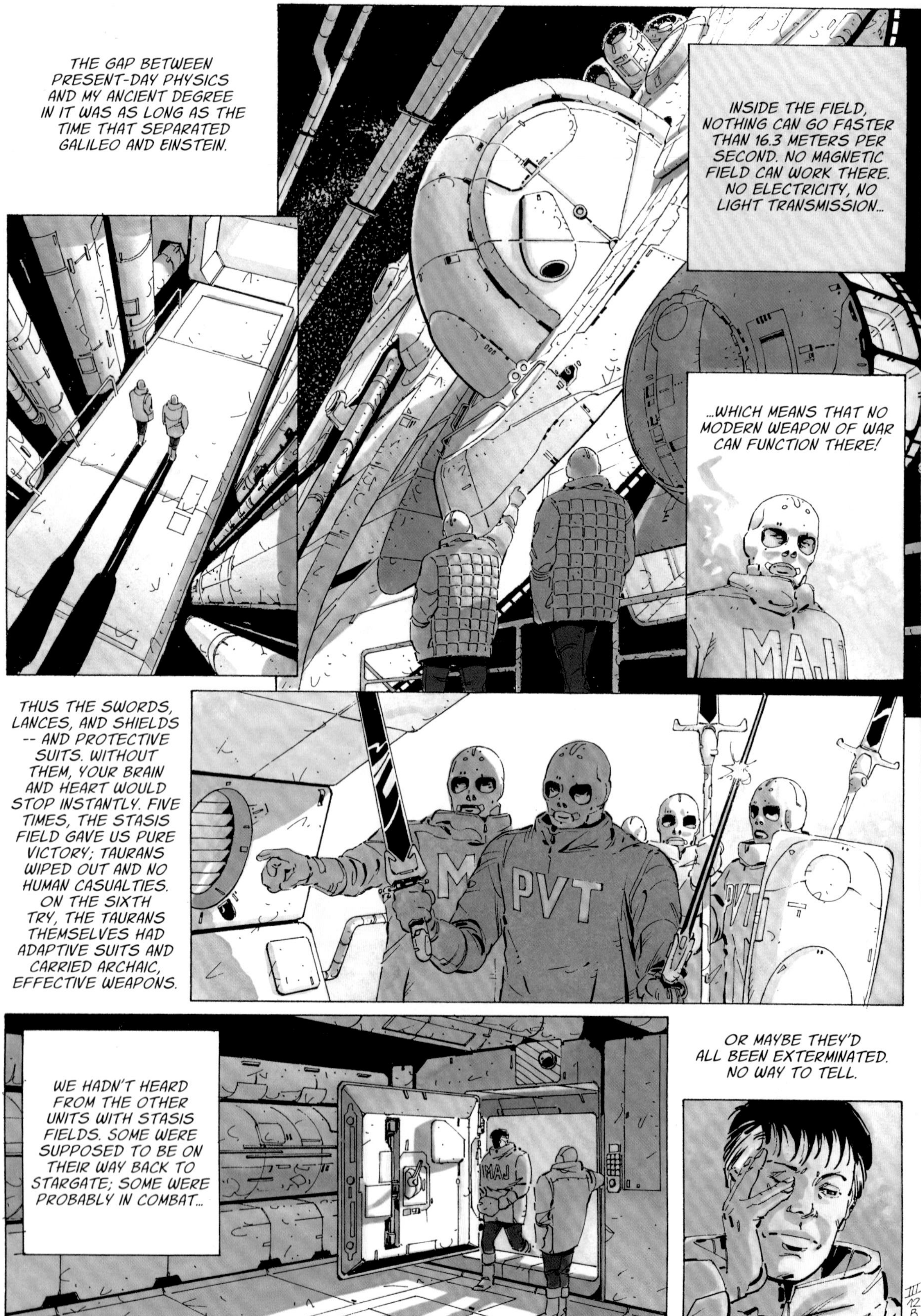
THE GAP BETWEEN PRESENT-DAY PHYSICS AND MY ANCIENT DEGREE IN IT WAS AS LONG AS THE TIME THAT SEPARATED GALILEO AND EINSTEIN.
INSIDE THE FIELD, NOTHING CAN GO FASTER THAN 16.3 METERS PER SECOND. NO MAGNETIC FIELD CAN WORK THERE. NO ELECTRICITY, NO LIGHT TRANSMISSION...
...WHICH MEANS THAT NO MODERN WEAPON OF WAR CAN FUNCTION THERE!
MAJ
THUS THE SWORDS, LANCES, AND SHIELDS -- AND PROTECTIVE SUITS. WITHOUT THEM, YOUR BRAIN AND HEART WOULD STOP INSTANTLY. FIVE TIMES, THE STASIS FIELD GAVE US PURE VICTORY; TAURANS WIPED OUT AND NO HUMAN CASUALTIES. ON THE SIXTH TRY, THE TAURANS THEMSELVES HAD ADAPTIVE SUITS AND CARRIED ARCHAIC, EFFECTIVE WEAPONS.
PVT
WE HADN'T HEARD FROM THE OTHER UNITS WITH STASIS FIELDS. SOME WERE SUPPOSED TO BE ON THEIR WAY BACK TO STARGATE; SOME WERE PROBABLY IN COMBAT...
MAJ
OR MAYBE THEY'D ALL BEEN EXTERMINATED. NO WAY TO TELL.
III 12 B

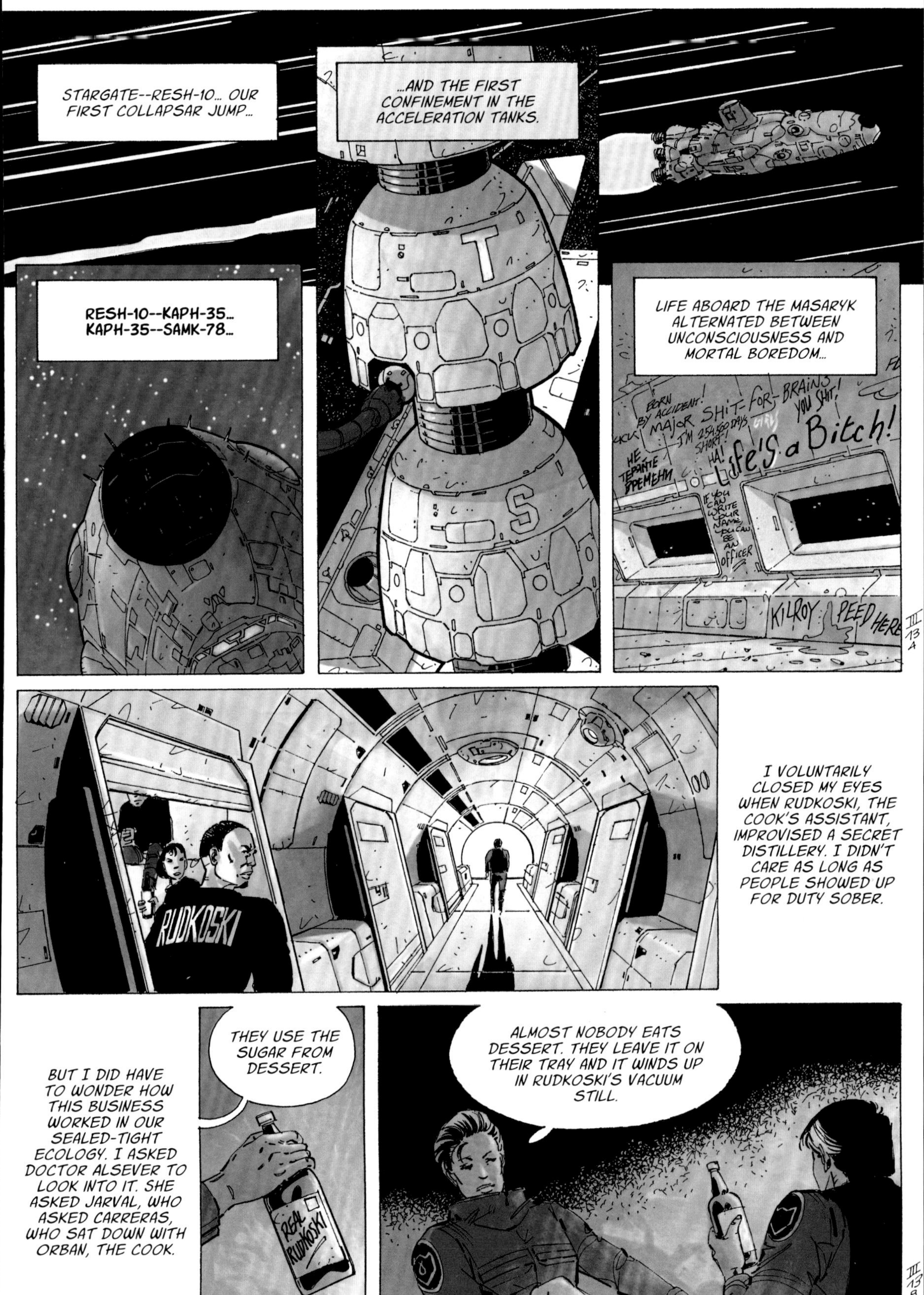
STARGATE--RESH-10... OUR FIRST COLLAPSAR JUMP...
...AND THE FIRST CONFINEMENT IN THE ACCELERATION TANKS.
T
S
RESH-10--KAPH-35... KAPH-35--SAMK-78...
LIFE ABOARD THE MASARYK ALTERNATED BETWEEN UNCONSCIOUSNESS AND MORTAL BOREDOM...
BORN BY ACCIDENT!
MAJOR SHIT-FOR-BRAINS
YOU SHIT!
I'M 254,560 DAYS SHORT! HA!
НЕ ТЕРЯЙТЕ ВРЕМЕНИ
Life's a Bitch!
IF YOU CAN WRITE YOUR NAME, YOU CAN BE AN OFFICER
KILROY PEED HERE
III 13 A
I VOLUNTARILY CLOSED MY EYES WHEN RUDKOSKI, THE COOK'S ASSISTANT, IMPROVISED A SECRET DISTILLERY. I DIDN'T CARE AS LONG AS PEOPLE SHOWED UP FOR DUTY SOBER.
RUDKOSKI
BUT I DID HAVE TO WONDER HOW THIS BUSINESS WORKED IN OUR SEALED-TIGHT ECOLOGY. I ASKED DOCTOR ALSEVER TO LOOK INTO IT. SHE ASKED JARVAL, WHO ASKED CARRERAS, WHO SAT DOWN WITH ORBAN, THE COOK.
THEY USE THE SUGAR FROM DESSERT.
REAL RUDKOSKI
ALMOST NOBODY EATS DESSERT. THEY LEAVE IT ON THEIR TRAY AND IT WINDS UP IN RUDKOSKI'S VACUUM STILL.
III 13 B

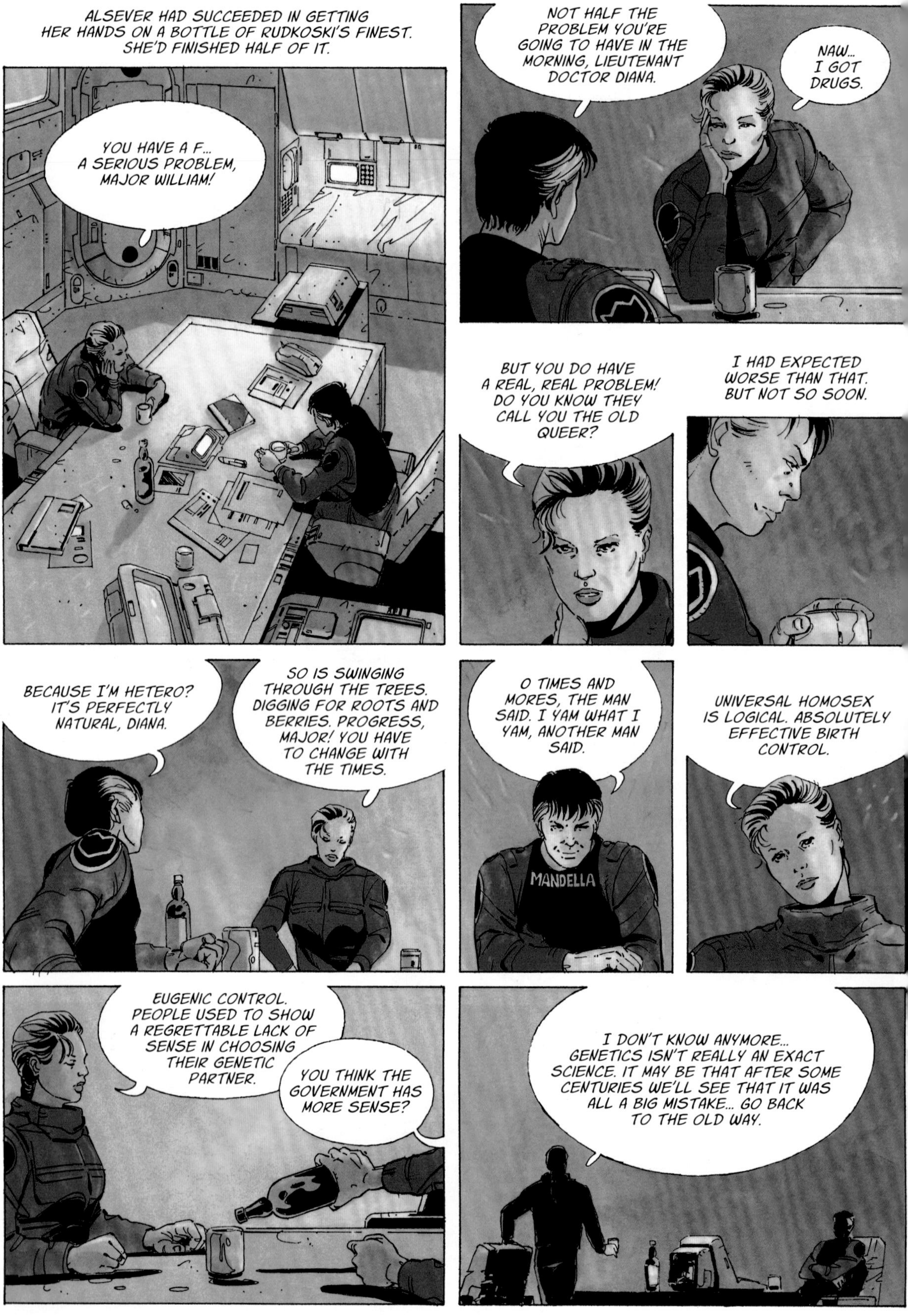
ALSEVER HAD SUCCEEDED IN GETTING HER HANDS ON A BOTTLE OF RUDKOSKI'S FINEST. SHE'D FINISHED HALF OF IT.
YOU HAVE A F... A SERIOUS PROBLEM, MAJOR WILLIAM!
NOT HALF THE PROBLEM YOU'RE GOING TO HAVE IN THE MORNING, LIEUTENANT DOCTOR DIANA.
NAW... I GOT DRUGS.
BUT YOU DO HAVE A REAL, REAL PROBLEM! DO YOU KNOW THEY CALL YOU THE OLD QUEER?
I HAD EXPECTED WORSE THAN THAT. BUT NOT SO SOON.
BECAUSE I'M HETERO? IT'S PERFECTLY NATURAL, DIANA.
SO IS SWINGING THROUGH THE TREES. DIGGING FOR ROOTS AND BERRIES. PROGRESS, MAJOR! YOU HAVE TO CHANGE WITH THE TIMES.
O TIMES AND MORES, THE MAN SAID. I YAM WHAT I YAM, ANOTHER MAN SAID.
MANDELLA
UNIVERSAL HOMOSEX IS LOGICAL. ABSOLUTELY EFFECTIVE BIRTH CONTROL.
EUGENIC CONTROL. PEOPLE USED TO SHOW A REGRETTABLE LACK OF SENSE IN CHOOSING THEIR GENETIC PARTNER.
YOU THINK THE GOVERNMENT HAS MORE SENSE?
I DON'T KNOW ANYMORE... GENETICS ISN'T REALLY AN EXACT SCIENCE. IT MAY BE THAT AFTER SOME CENTURIES WE'LL SEE THAT IT WAS ALL A BIG MISTAKE... GO BACK TO THE OLD WAY.

AS A WOMAN, I HOPE NOT! CHILDBIRTH. HAVING A MAN INSIDE...

SHIT! DRANK TOO MUCH... LIE DOWN... 'FORE I FALL DOWN...

MANDELLA

OKAY, WILLIAM... YOUR ONLY CHANCE...

CHRIST'S SAKE, DIANA. IT WOULDN'T BE FAIR.

MANDELLA

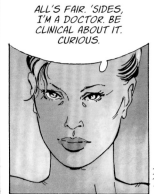

ALL'S FAIR. 'SIDES, I'M A DOCTOR. BE CLINICAL ABOUT IT. CURIOUS.

III 15 A

MAYBE IT WOULDN'T...

...BE SO BAD...

...AT ALL...

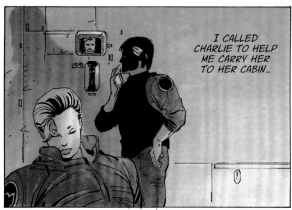

I CALLED CHARLIE TO HELP ME CARRY HER TO HER CABIN...

DEAR SWEET DIANA, LATENT HETEROSEXUAL... I'LL BUY YOU A GOOD SCOTCH NEXT TIME WE COME INTO PORT...

SIX OR SEVEN CENTURIES FROM NOW...

GOOD GRIEF! WHAT IS IT? VARNISH? YOU GUYS REALLY DRANK THAT STUFF?!

CAREFUL WITH THAT BOTTLE, CHARLIE... IT MIGHT EXPLODE IF YOU SHAKE IT UP TOO MUCH!

III 15 B

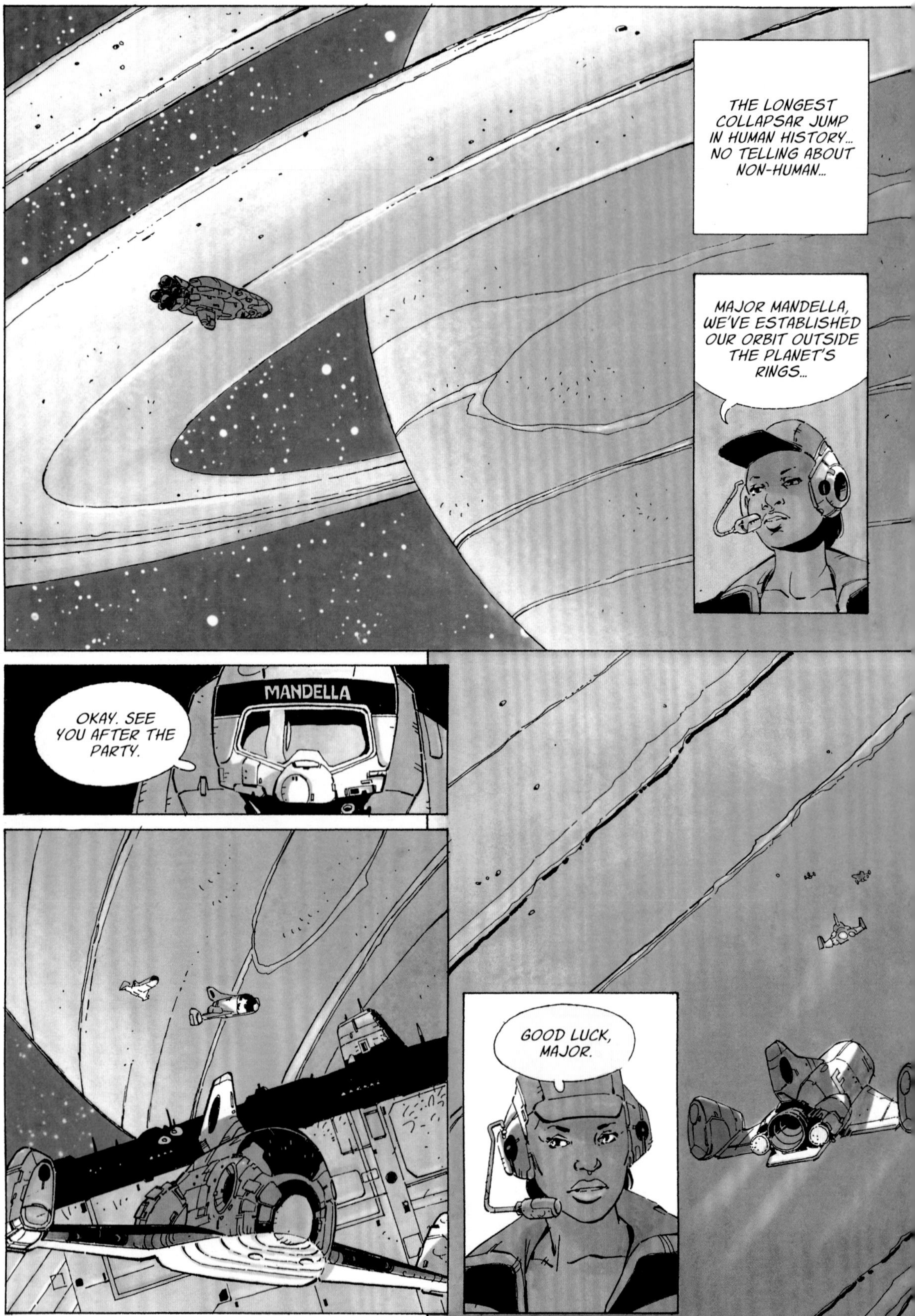
THE LONGEST COLLAPSAR JUMP IN HUMAN HISTORY... NO TELLING ABOUT NON-HUMAN...
MAJOR MANDELLA, WE'VE ESTABLISHED OUR ORBIT OUTSIDE THE PLANET'S RINGS...
MANDELLA
OKAY. SEE YOU AFTER THE PARTY.
GOOD LUCK, MAJOR.

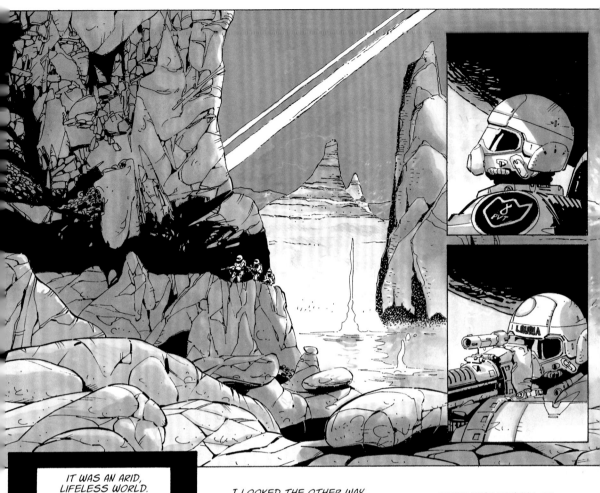

PVT
LOURIA
IT WAS AN ARID, LIFELESS WORLD. BUT NO TAURANS.
I LOOKED THE OTHER WAY WHEN RUDKOSKI REASSEMBLED HIS STILL ON THE NEW BASE...BUT BOREDOM AND STRESS BEGAN TO AFFECT THE TROOPS...
AFTER FIVE MONTHS OF RELATIVELY COMFORTABLE ROUTINE A CERTAIN PRIVATE GRAUBARD ACTED UP...
MP
GRAUBARD
MP

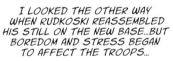

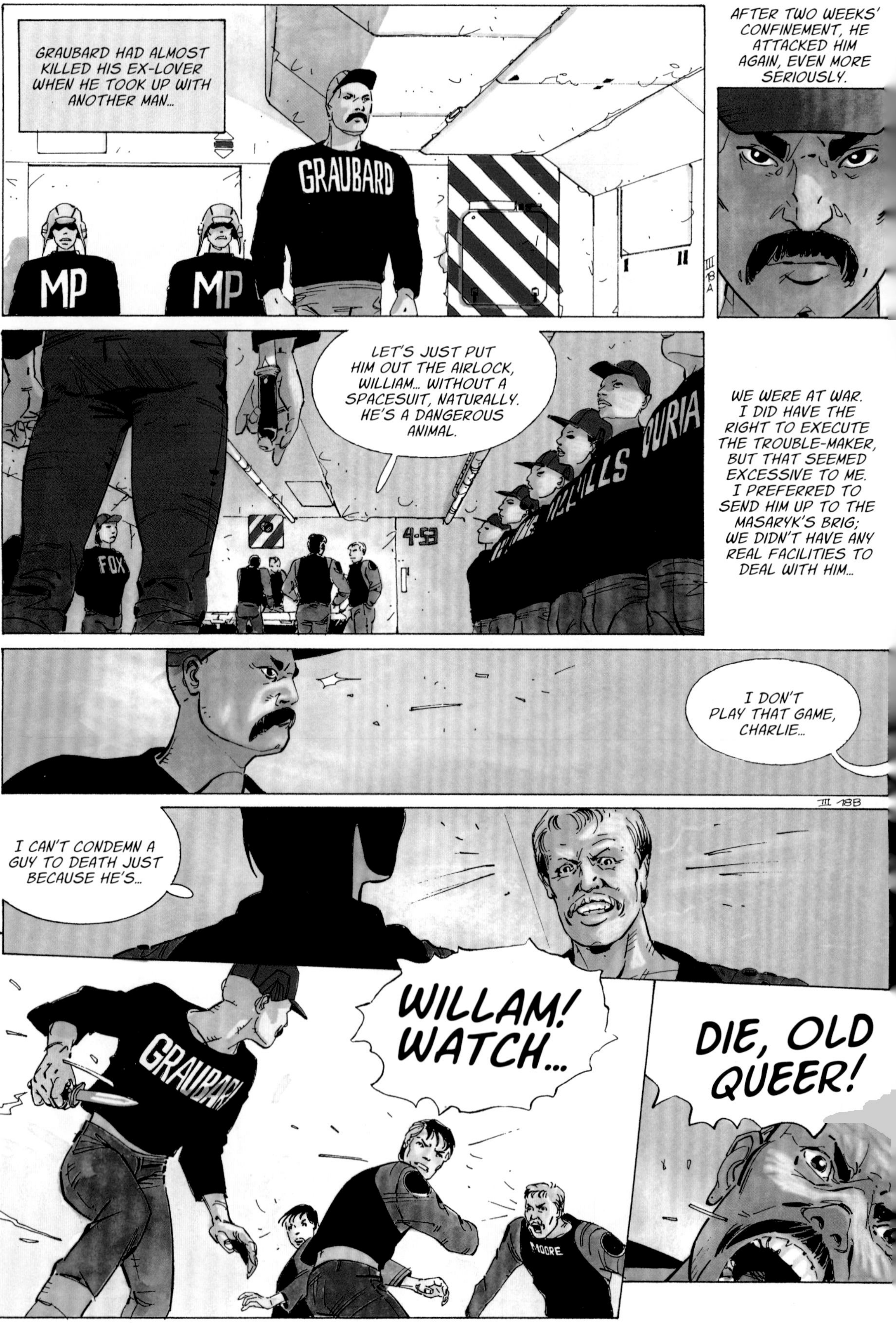
GRAUBARD HAD ALMOST KILLED HIS EX-LOVER WHEN HE TOOK UP WITH ANOTHER MAN...
GRAUBARD
MP
MP
AFTER TWO WEEKS' CONFINEMENT, HE ATTACKED HIM AGAIN, EVEN MORE SERIOUSLY.
LET'S JUST PUT HIM OUT THE AIRLOCK, WILLIAM... WITHOUT A SPACESUIT, NATURALLY. HE'S A DANGEROUS ANIMAL.
FOX
4-53
WE WERE AT WAR. I DID HAVE THE RIGHT TO EXECUTE THE TROUBLE-MAKER, BUT THAT SEEMED EXCESSIVE TO ME. I PREFERRED TO SEND HIM UP TO THE MASARYK'S BRIG; WE DIDN'T HAVE ANY REAL FACILITIES TO DEAL WITH HIM...
I DON'T PLAY THAT GAME, CHARLIE...
III 18B
I CAN'T CONDEMN A GUY TO DEATH JUST BECAUSE HE'S...
WILLAM! WATCH...
DIE, OLD QUEER!

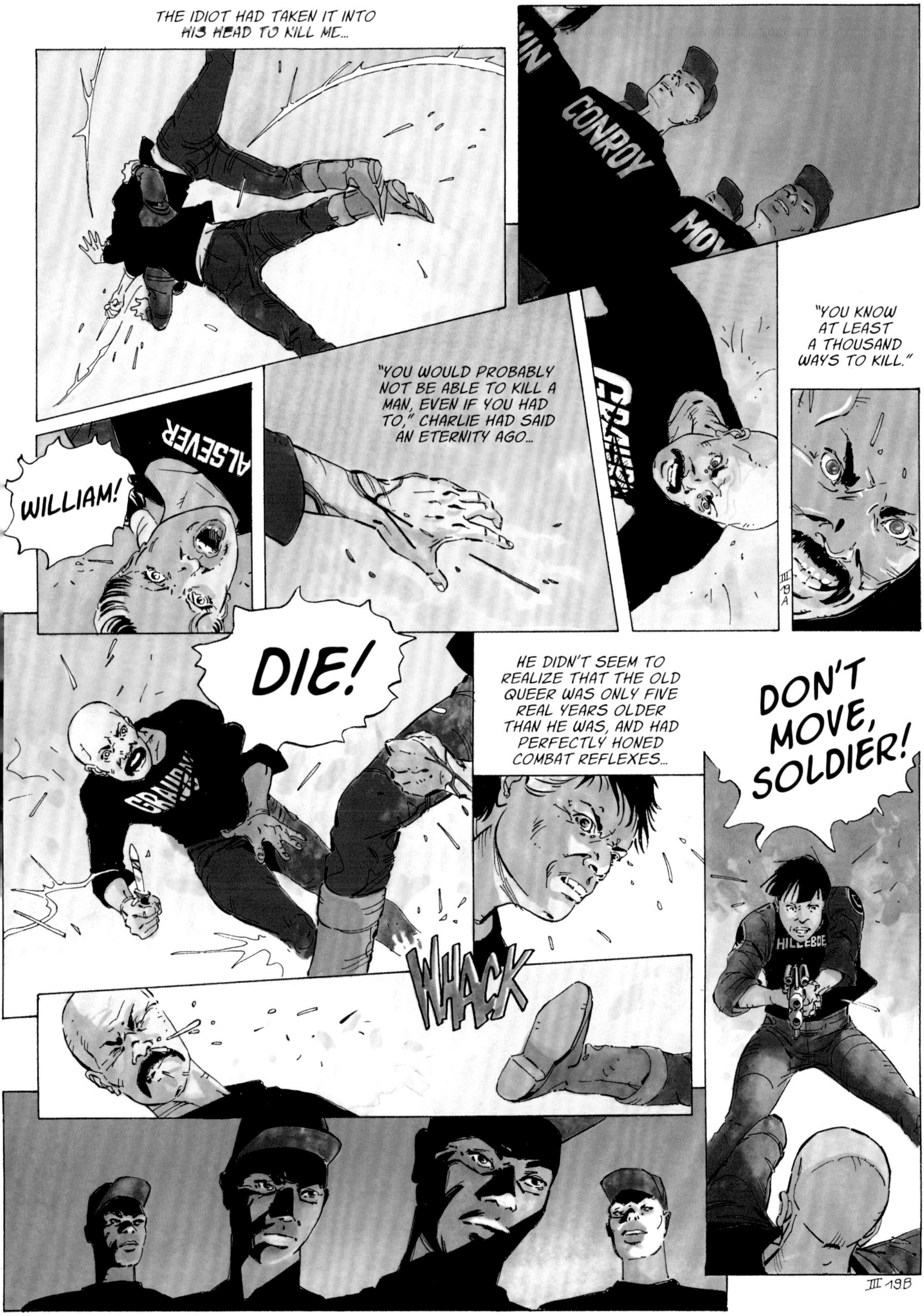

THE IDIOT HAD TAKEN IT INTO HIS HEAD TO KILL ME...
CONROY
"YOU WOULD PROBABLY NOT BE ABLE TO KILL A MAN, EVEN IF YOU HAD TO," CHARLIE HAD SAID AN ETERNITY AGO...
ALSEVER
WILLIAM!
"YOU KNOW AT LEAST A THOUSAND WAYS TO KILL."
III 19 A
DIE!
HE DIDN'T SEEM TO REALIZE THAT THE OLD QUEER WAS ONLY FIVE REAL YEARS OLDER THAN HE WAS, AND HAD PERFECTLY HONED COMBAT REFLEXES...
WHACK
DON'T MOVE, SOLDIER!
III 19B

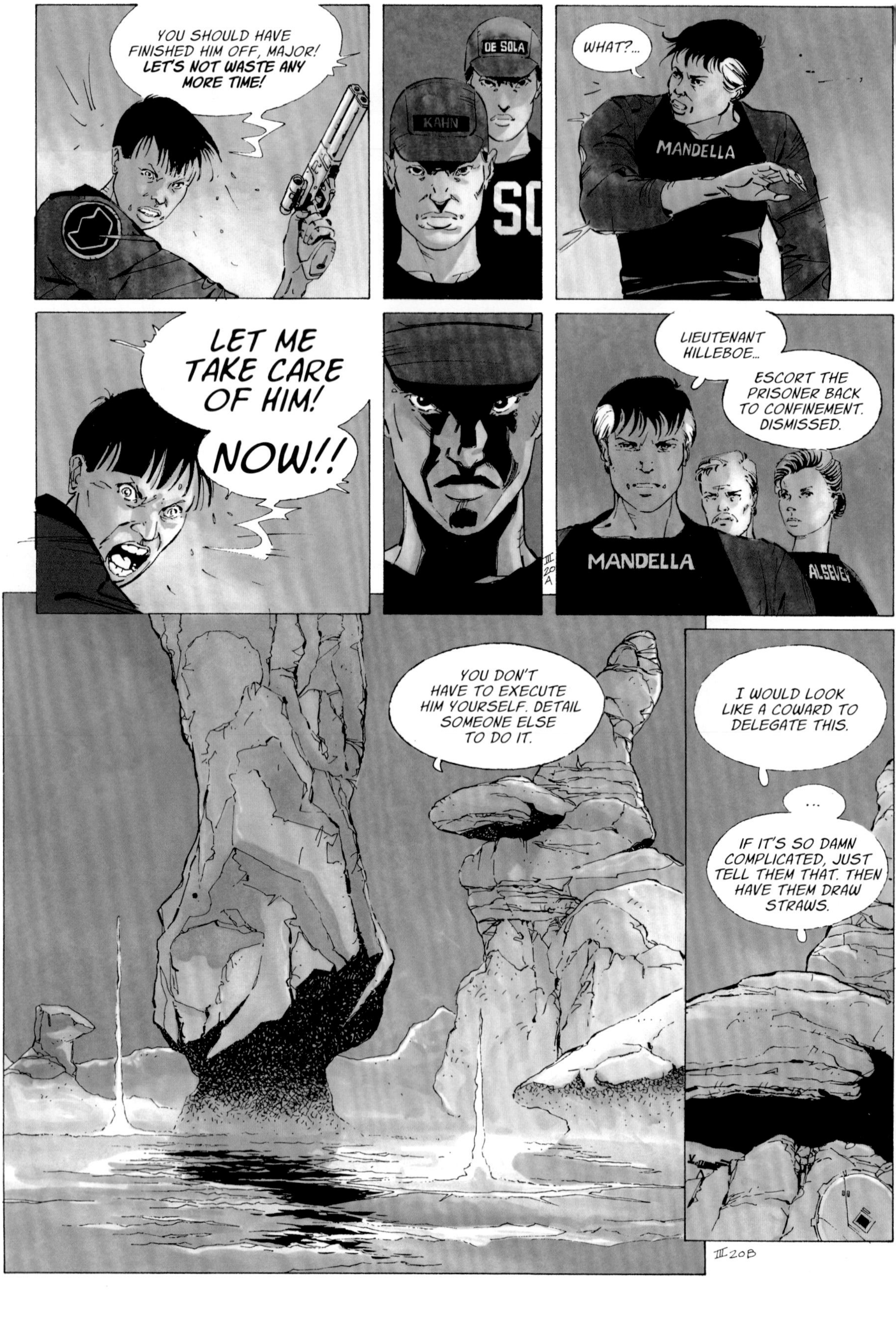
YOU SHOULD HAVE FINISHED HIM OFF, MAJOR! **LET'S NOT WASTE ANY MORE TIME!**
DE SOLA
KAHN
SO
WHAT?...
MANDELLA
LET ME TAKE CARE OF HIM!
NOW!!
LIEUTENANT HILLEBOE...
ESCORT THE PRISONER BACK TO CONFINEMENT. DISMISSED.
MANDELLA
ALSEVER
YOU DON'T HAVE TO EXECUTE HIM YOURSELF. DETAIL SOMEONE ELSE TO DO IT.
I WOULD LOOK LIKE A COWARD TO DELEGATE THIS.
...
IF IT'S SO DAMN COMPLICATED, JUST TELL THEM THAT. THEN HAVE THEM DRAW STRAWS.

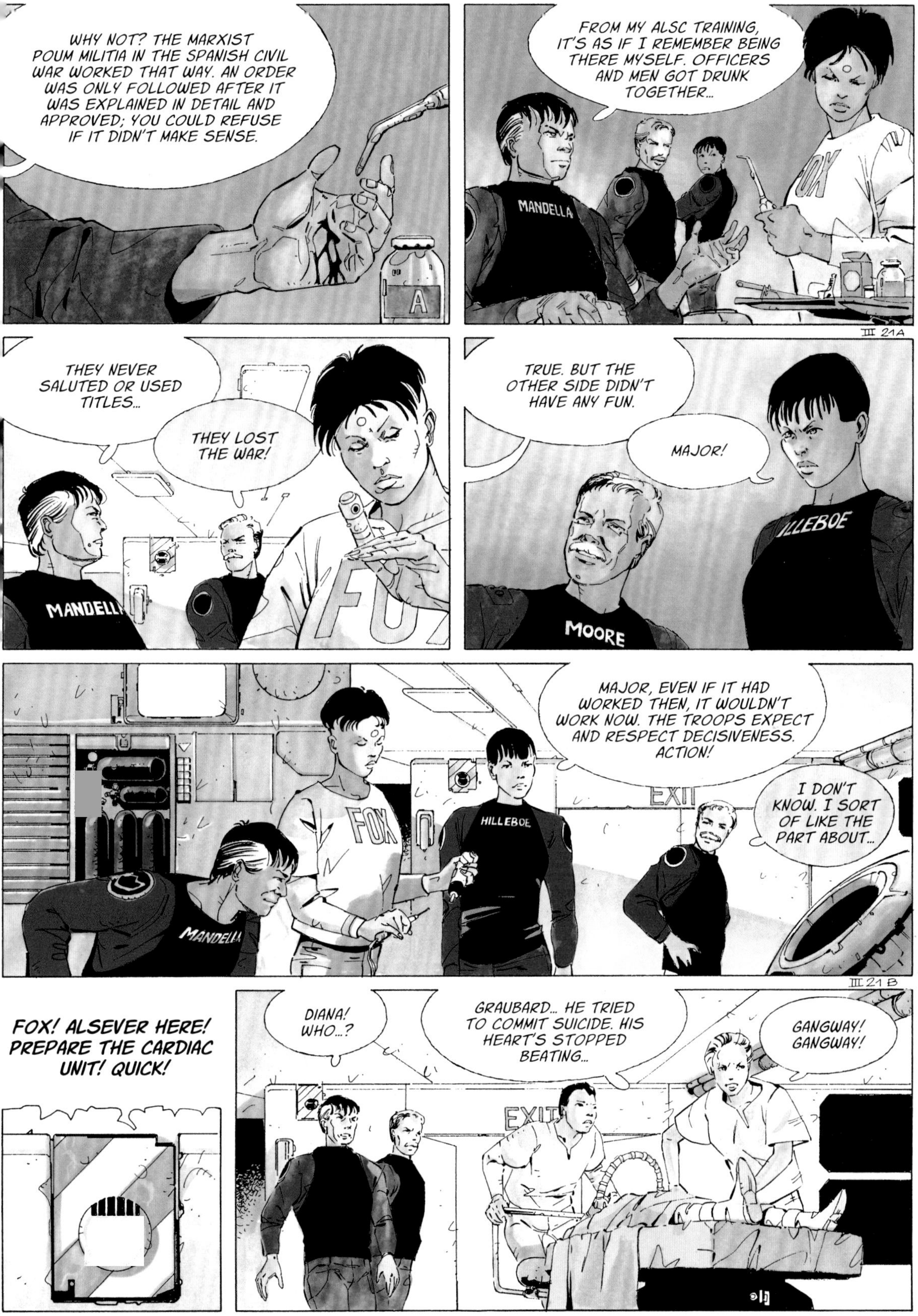
WHY NOT? THE MARXIST POUM MILITIA IN THE SPANISH CIVIL WAR WORKED THAT WAY. AN ORDER WAS ONLY FOLLOWED AFTER IT WAS EXPLAINED IN DETAIL AND APPROVED; YOU COULD REFUSE IF IT DIDN'T MAKE SENSE.
A
FROM MY ALSC TRAINING, IT'S AS IF I REMEMBER BEING THERE MYSELF. OFFICERS AND MEN GOT DRUNK TOGETHER...
MANDELLA
FOX
III 21A
THEY NEVER SALUTED OR USED TITLES...
THEY LOST THE WAR!
MANDELLA
FOX
TRUE. BUT THE OTHER SIDE DIDN'T HAVE ANY FUN.
MAJOR!
MOORE
ILLEBOE
MAJOR, EVEN IF IT HAD WORKED THEN, IT WOULDN'T WORK NOW. THE TROOPS EXPECT AND RESPECT DECISIVENESS. ACTION!
I DON'T KNOW. I SORT OF LIKE THE PART ABOUT...
FOX
HILLEBOE
EXIT
MANDELLA
III 21 B
FOX! ALSEVER HERE! PREPARE THE CARDIAC UNIT! QUICK!
DIANA! WHO...?
GRAUBARD... HE TRIED TO COMMIT SUICIDE. HIS HEART'S STOPPED BEATING...
GANGWAY! GANGWAY!
EXIT

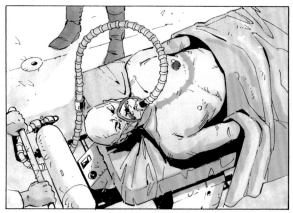

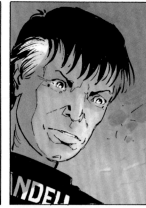

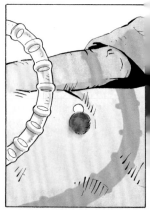

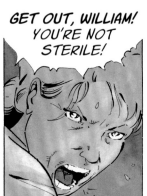

GET OUT, WILLIAM! YOU'RE NOT STERILE!
OKAY, FOX. LET'S CRACK THE CHEST.
MOORE
MANDELLA
16:32:20
16:32:28
17:05:04
17:05:18
3B
HE'S DEAD.
WHAT HAPPENED?
HE HANGED HIMSELF WITH HIS BELT.
MANDELLA

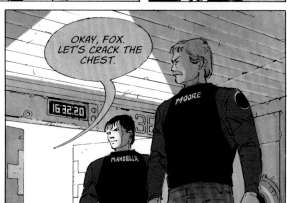

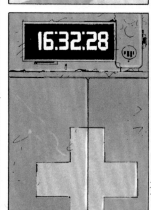

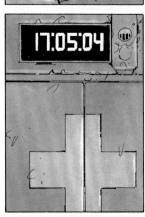

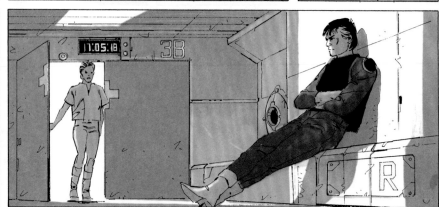

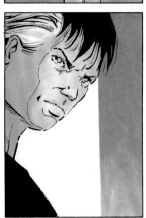

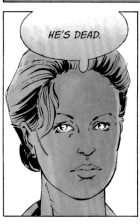

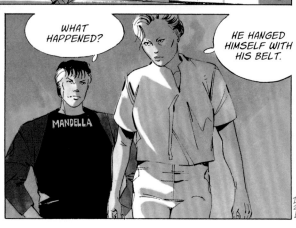

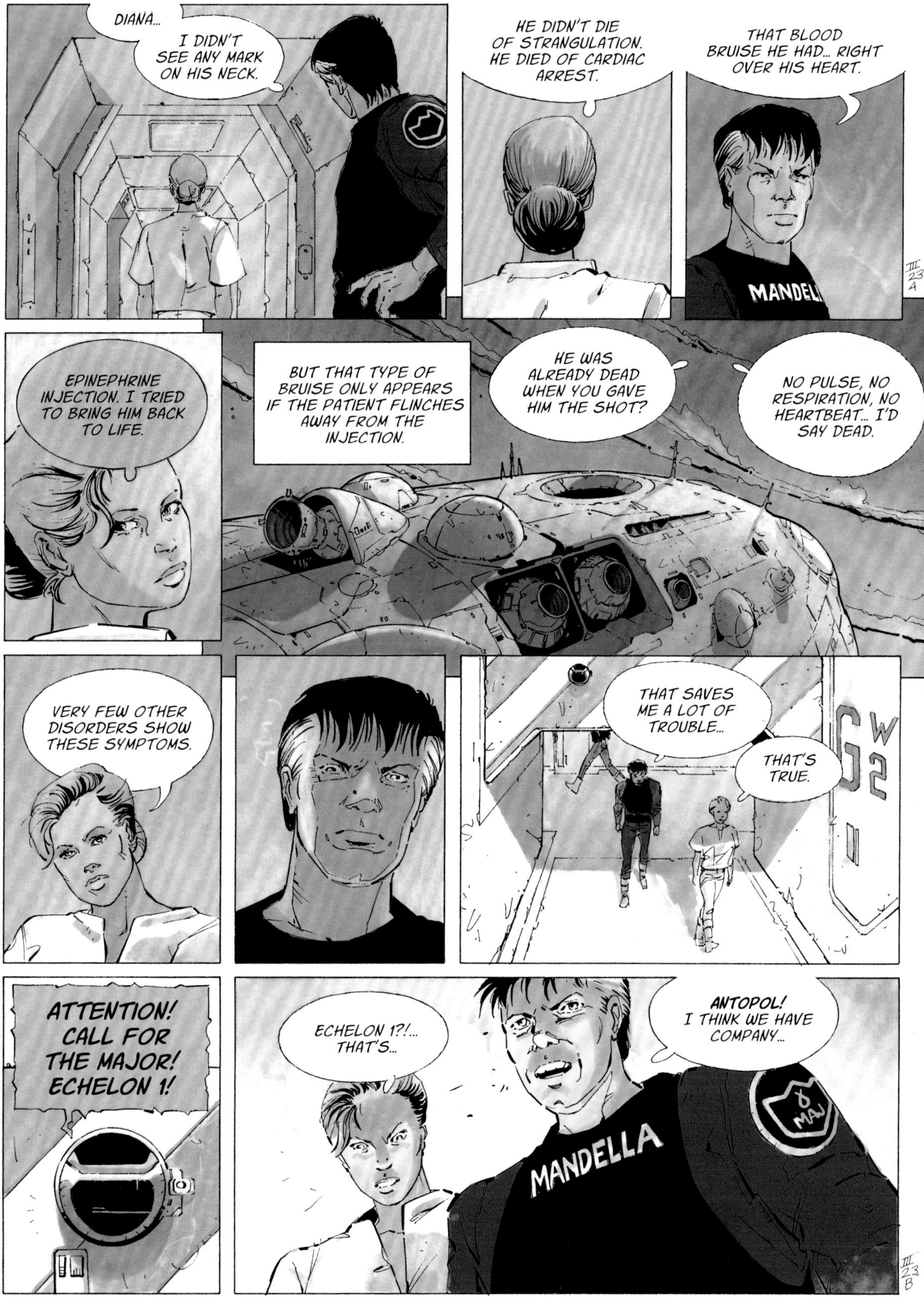
DIANA...
I DIDN'T SEE ANY MARK ON HIS NECK.
HE DIDN'T DIE OF STRANGULATION. HE DIED OF CARDIAC ARREST.
THAT BLOOD BRUISE HE HAD... RIGHT OVER HIS HEART.
MANDELL
III 23 A
EPINEPHRINE INJECTION. I TRIED TO BRING HIM BACK TO LIFE.
BUT THAT TYPE OF BRUISE ONLY APPEARS IF THE PATIENT FLINCHES AWAY FROM THE INJECTION.
HE WAS ALREADY DEAD WHEN YOU GAVE HIM THE SHOT?
NO PULSE, NO RESPIRATION, NO HEARTBEAT... I'D SAY DEAD.
VERY FEW OTHER DISORDERS SHOW THESE SYMPTOMS.
THAT SAVES ME A LOT OF TROUBLE...
THAT'S TRUE.
GW2
ATTENTION! CALL FOR THE MAJOR! ECHELON 1!
ECHELON 1?!... THAT'S...
ANTOPOL! I THINK WE HAVE COMPANY...
MANDELLA
III 23 B

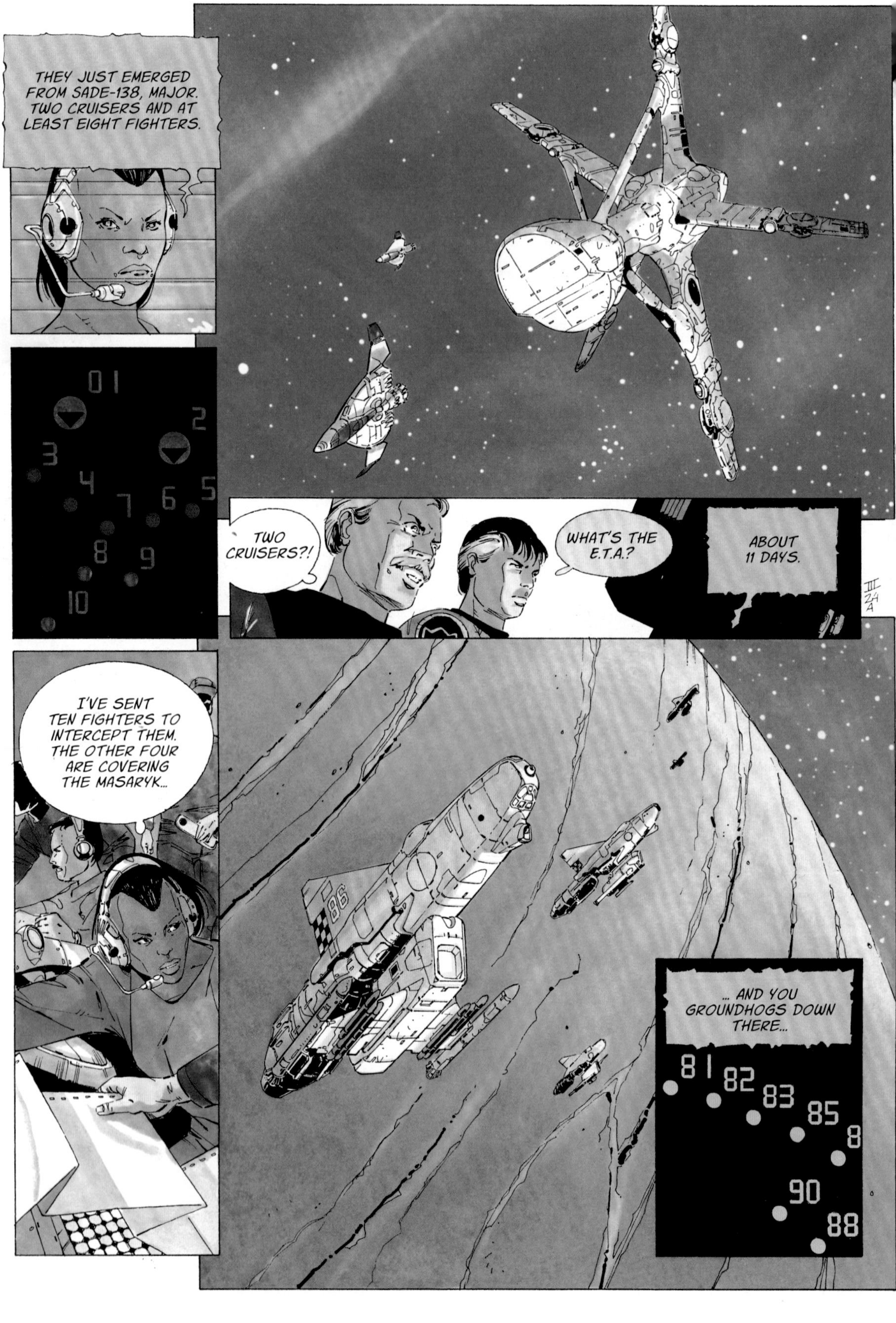
THEY JUST EMERGED FROM SADE-138, MAJOR. TWO CRUISERS AND AT LEAST EIGHT FIGHTERS.
01 2 3 4 5 6 7 8 9 10
TWO CRUISERS?!
WHAT'S THE E.T.A.?
ABOUT 11 DAYS.
I'VE SENT TEN FIGHTERS TO INTERCEPT THEM. THE OTHER FOUR ARE COVERING THE MASARYK...
... AND YOU GROUNDHOGS DOWN THERE...
81 82 83 85 8 90 88

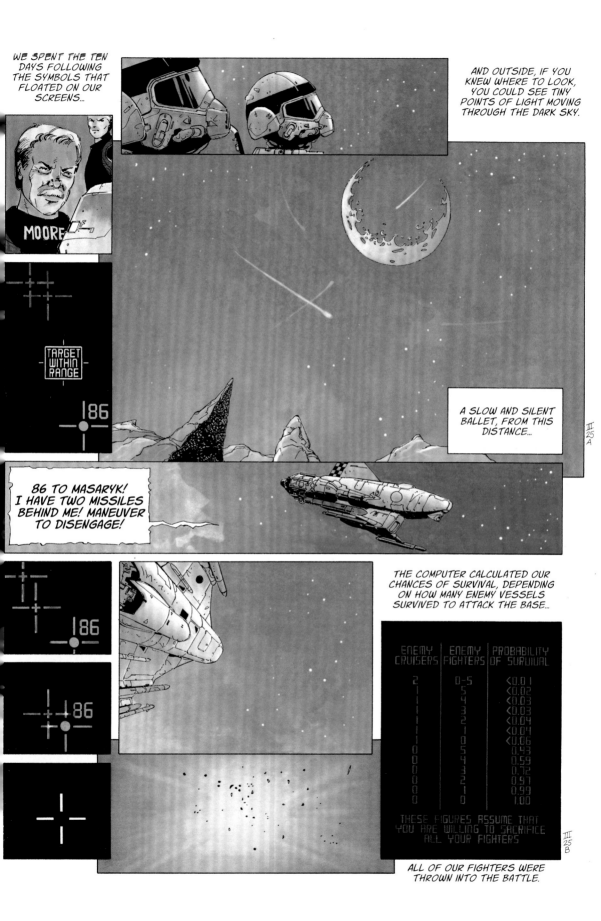

WE SPENT THE TEN DAYS FOLLOWING THE SYMBOLS THAT FLOATED ON OUR SCREENS...

MOORE

TARGET WITHIN RANGE

86

AND OUTSIDE, IF YOU KNEW WHERE TO LOOK, YOU COULD SEE TINY POINTS OF LIGHT MOVING THROUGH THE DARK SKY.

A SLOW AND SILENT BALLET, FROM THIS DISTANCE...

III 25 A

86 TO MASARYK! I HAVE TWO MISSILES BEHIND ME! MANEUVER TO DISENGAGE!

86

86

THE COMPUTER CALCULATED OUR CHANCES OF SURVIVAL, DEPENDING ON HOW MANY ENEMY VESSELS SURVIVED TO ATTACK THE BASE...

ENEMY CRUISERS	ENEMY FIGHTERS	PROBABILITY OF SURVIVAL
2	0-5	<0.01
1	5	<0.02
1	4	<0.03
1	3	<0.03
1	2	<0.04
1	1	<0.04
1	0	<0.06
0	5	0.43
0	4	0.59
0	3	0.72
0	2	0.97
0	1	0.99
0	0	1.00

THESE FIGURES ASSUME THAT YOU ARE WILLING TO SACRIFICE ALL YOUR FIGHTERS

III 25 B

ALL OF OUR FIGHTERS WERE THROWN INTO THE BATTLE.

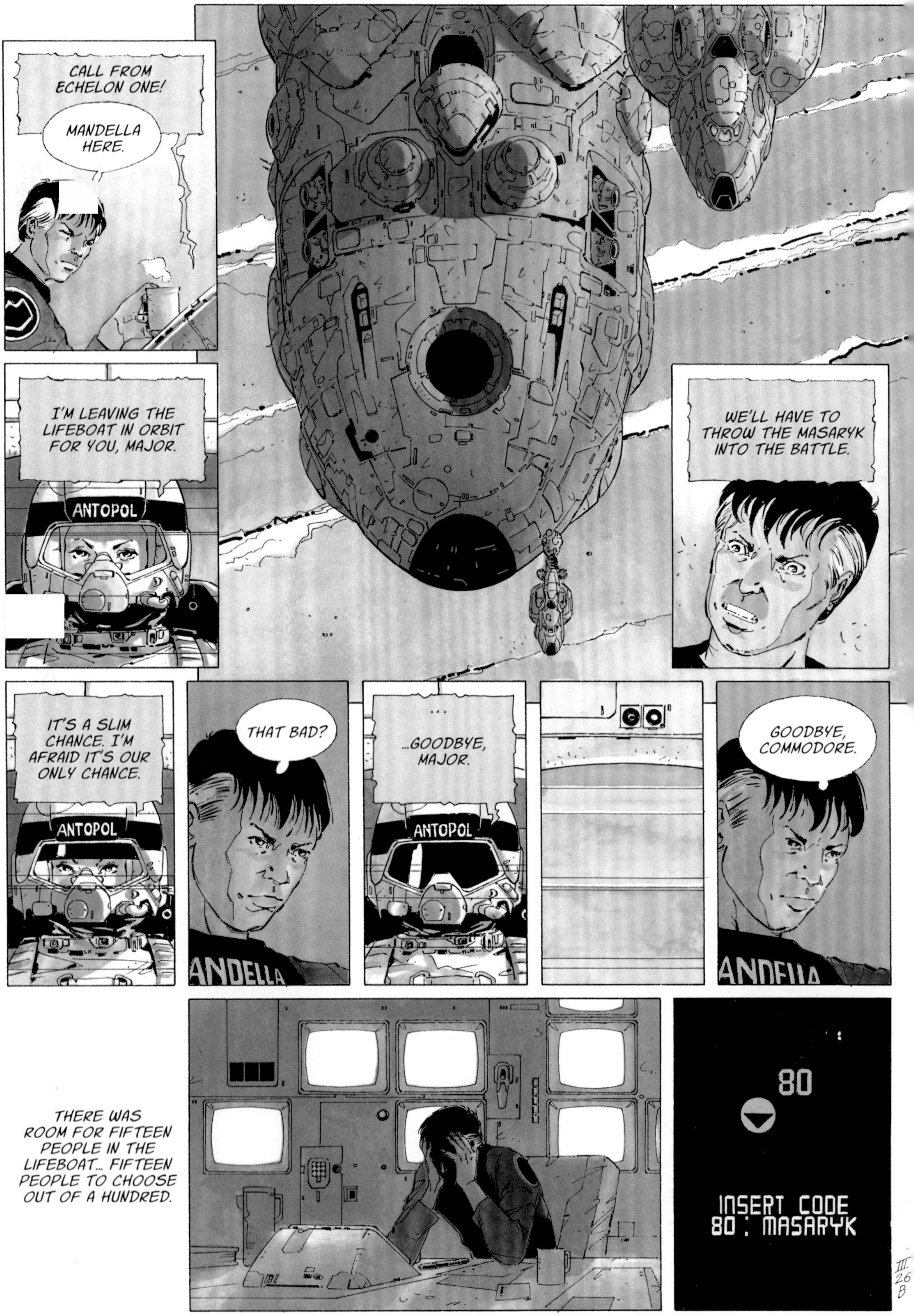
CALL FROM ECHELON ONE!
MANDELLA HERE.
I'M LEAVING THE LIFEBOAT IN ORBIT FOR YOU, MAJOR.
ANTOPOL
WE'LL HAVE TO THROW THE MASARYK INTO THE BATTLE.
IT'S A SLIM CHANCE. I'M AFRAID IT'S OUR ONLY CHANCE.
ANTOPOL
THAT BAD?
ANDELLA
...
...GOODBYE, MAJOR.
ANTOPOL
GOODBYE, COMMODORE.
ANDELLA
THERE WAS ROOM FOR FIFTEEN PEOPLE IN THE LIFEBOAT... FIFTEEN PEOPLE TO CHOOSE OUT OF A HUNDRED.
80
INSERT CODE
80 : MASARYK

III. 26 B

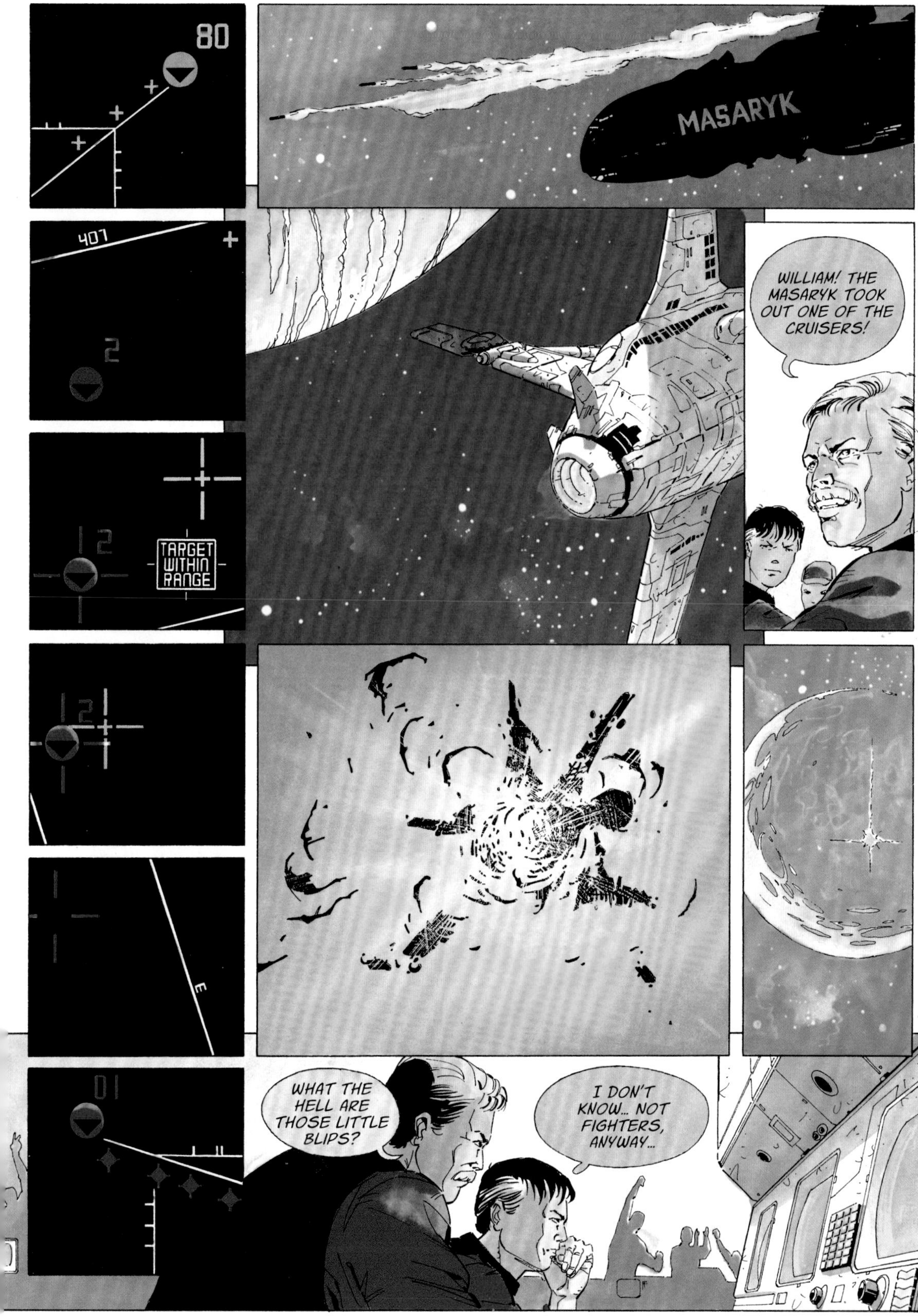
80
MASARYK
407
2
WILLIAM! THE MASARYK TOOK OUT ONE OF THE CRUISERS!
2
TARGET WITHIN RANGE
III 27 A
2
E
01
WHAT THE HELL ARE THOSE LITTLE BLIPS?
I DON'T KNOW... NOT FIGHTERS, ANYWAY...

III 27 B

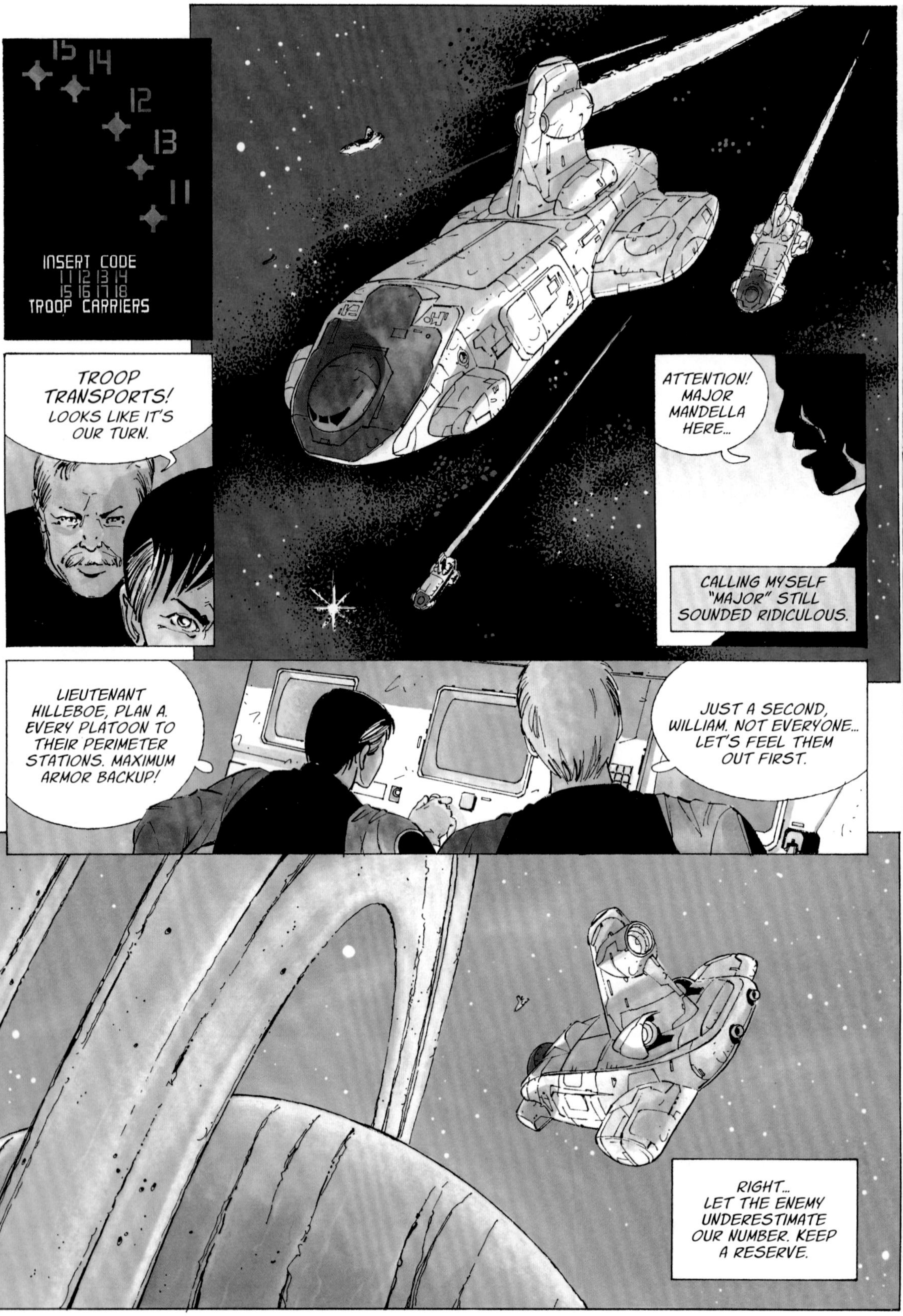
15 14 12 13 11
INSERT CODE
11 12 13 14
15 16 17 18
TROOP CARRIERS
TROOP TRANSPORTS! LOOKS LIKE IT'S OUR TURN.
ATTENTION! MAJOR MANDELLA HERE...
CALLING MYSELF "MAJOR" STILL SOUNDED RIDICULOUS.
LIEUTENANT HILLEBOE, PLAN A. EVERY PLATOON TO THEIR PERIMETER STATIONS. MAXIMUM ARMOR BACKUP!
JUST A SECOND, WILLIAM. NOT EVERYONE... LET'S FEEL THEM OUT FIRST.
RIGHT... LET THE ENEMY UNDERESTIMATE OUR NUMBER. KEEP A RESERVE.

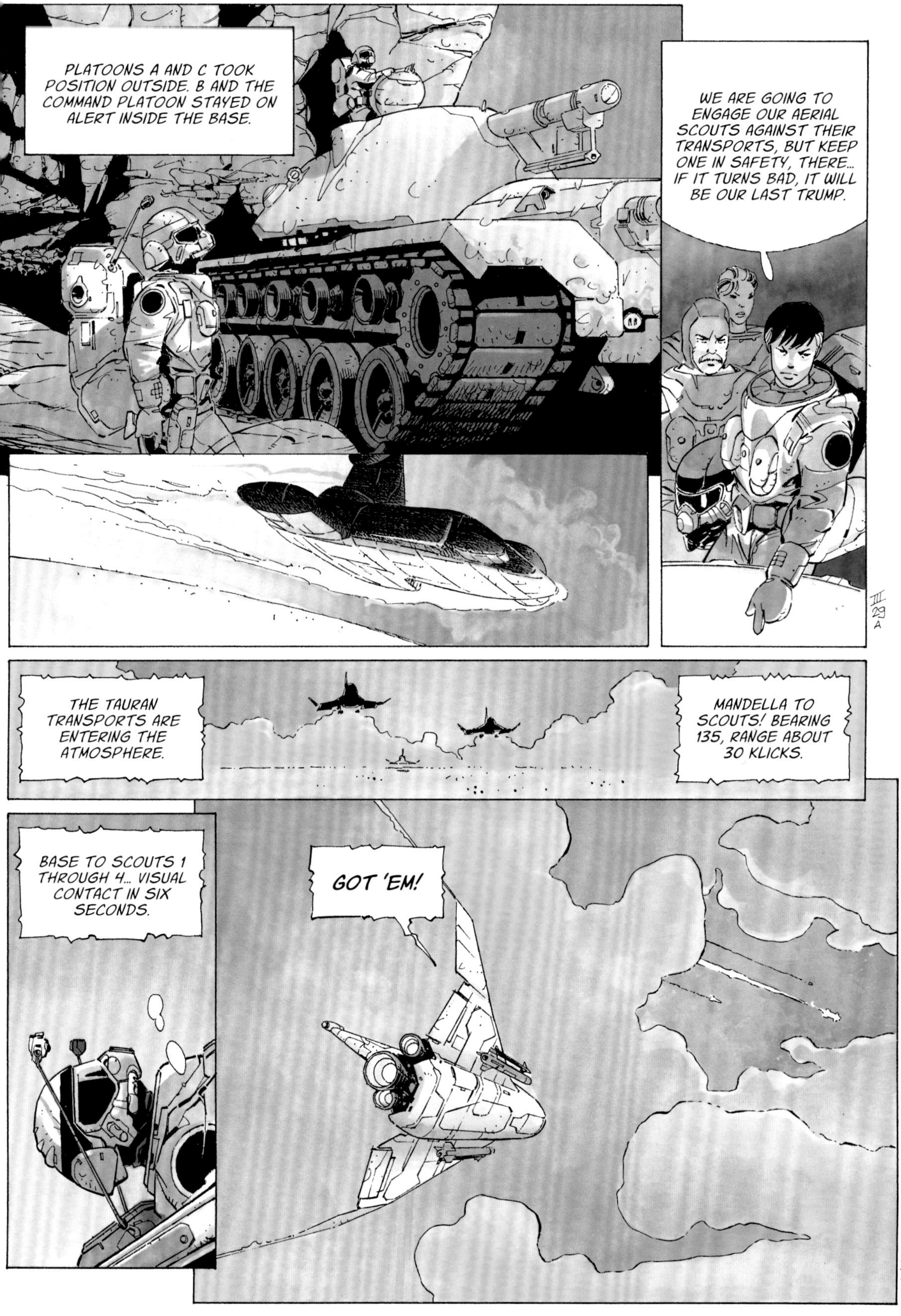
PLATOONS A AND C TOOK POSITION OUTSIDE. B AND THE COMMAND PLATOON STAYED ON ALERT INSIDE THE BASE.
WE ARE GOING TO ENGAGE OUR AERIAL SCOUTS AGAINST THEIR TRANSPORTS, BUT KEEP ONE IN SAFETY, THERE... IF IT TURNS BAD, IT WILL BE OUR LAST TRUMP.
III 29 A
THE TAURAN TRANSPORTS ARE ENTERING THE ATMOSPHERE.
MANDELLA TO SCOUTS! BEARING 135, RANGE ABOUT 30 KLICKS.
BASE TO SCOUTS 1 THROUGH 4... VISUAL CONTACT IN SIX SECONDS.
GOT 'EM!
III 29 B

SCOUT 4 REPORTING. ONE TRANSPORT ELIMINATED.

FIGHTER ESCORT COMING AROUND! SCOUT 4, YOU HAVE ONE OF THEM BEHIND YOU!

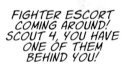

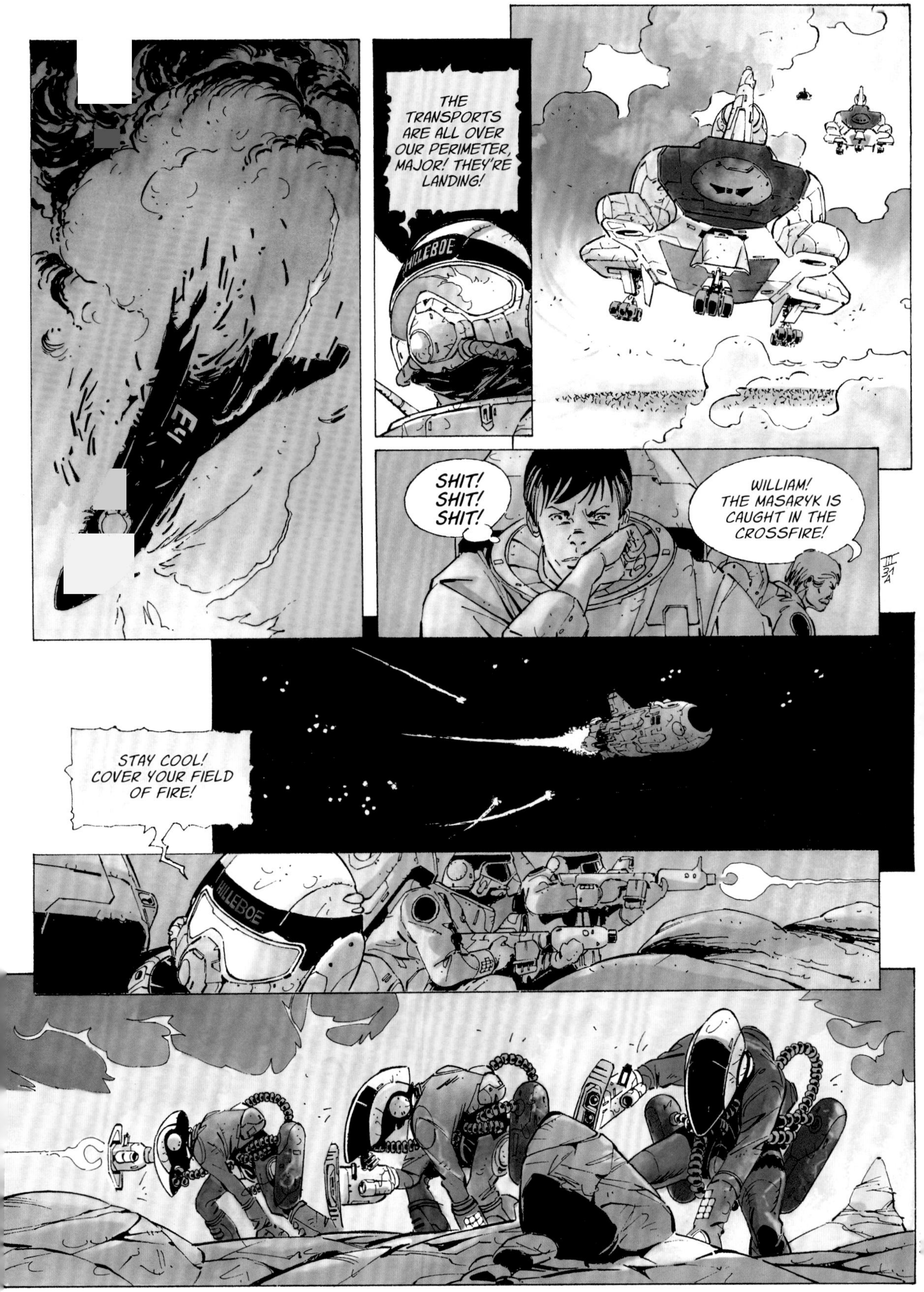
THE TRANSPORTS ARE ALL OVER OUR PERIMETER, MAJOR! THEY'RE LANDING!
HILLEBOE
SHIT! SHIT! SHIT!
WILLIAM! THE MASARYK IS CAUGHT IN THE CROSSFIRE!
STAY COOL! COVER YOUR FIELD OF FIRE!
HILLEBOE

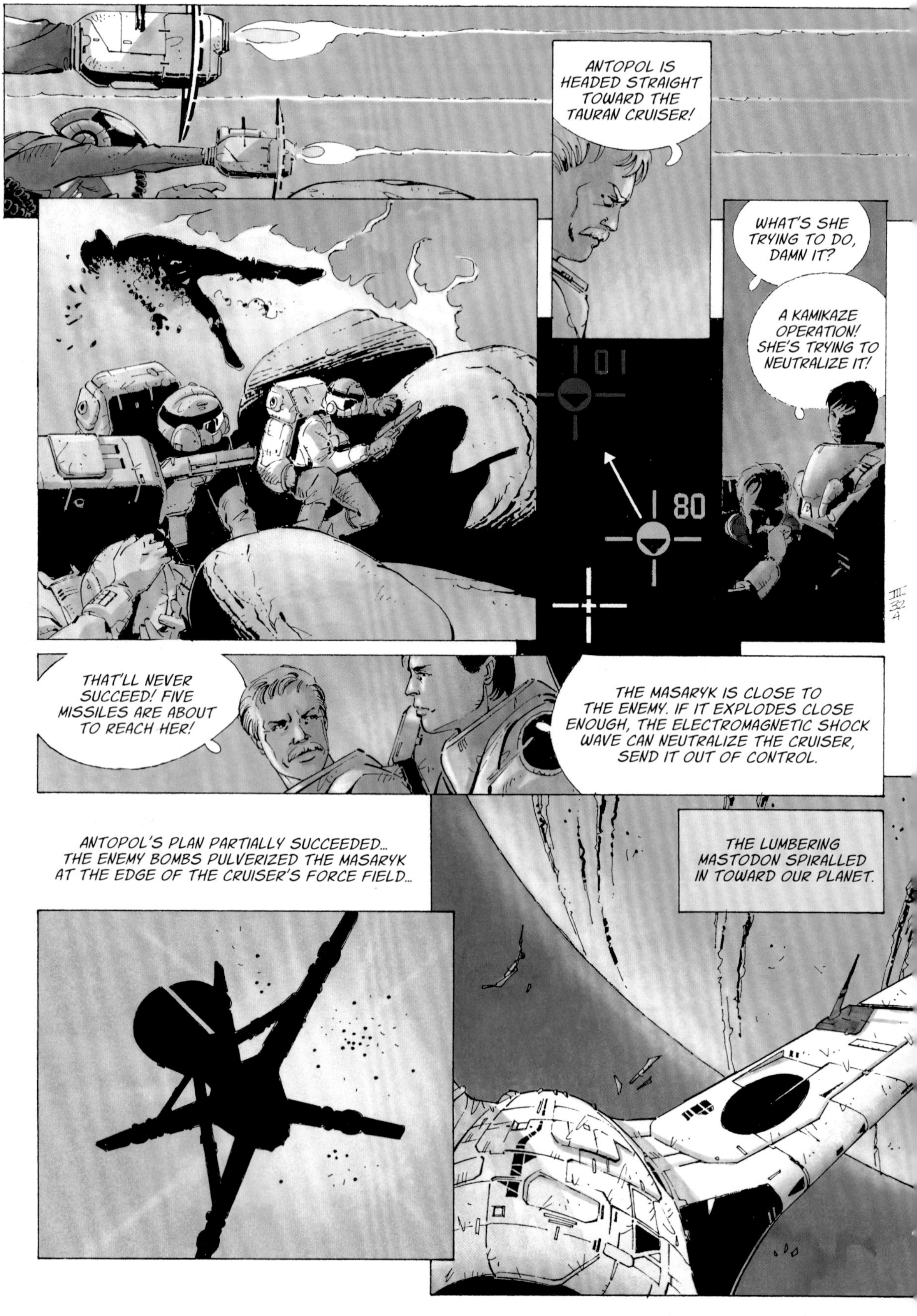
ANTOPOL IS HEADED STRAIGHT TOWARD THE TAURAN CRUISER!
WHAT'S SHE TRYING TO DO, DAMN IT?
A KAMIKAZE OPERATION! SHE'S TRYING TO NEUTRALIZE IT!
01
80
THAT'LL NEVER SUCCEED! FIVE MISSILES ARE ABOUT TO REACH HER!
THE MASARYK IS CLOSE TO THE ENEMY. IF IT EXPLODES CLOSE ENOUGH, THE ELECTROMAGNETIC SHOCK WAVE CAN NEUTRALIZE THE CRUISER, SEND IT OUT OF CONTROL.
ANTOPOL'S PLAN PARTIALLY SUCCEEDED... THE ENEMY BOMBS PULVERIZED THE MASARYK AT THE EDGE OF THE CRUISER'S FORCE FIELD...
THE LUMBERING MASTODON SPIRALLED IN TOWARD OUR PLANET.

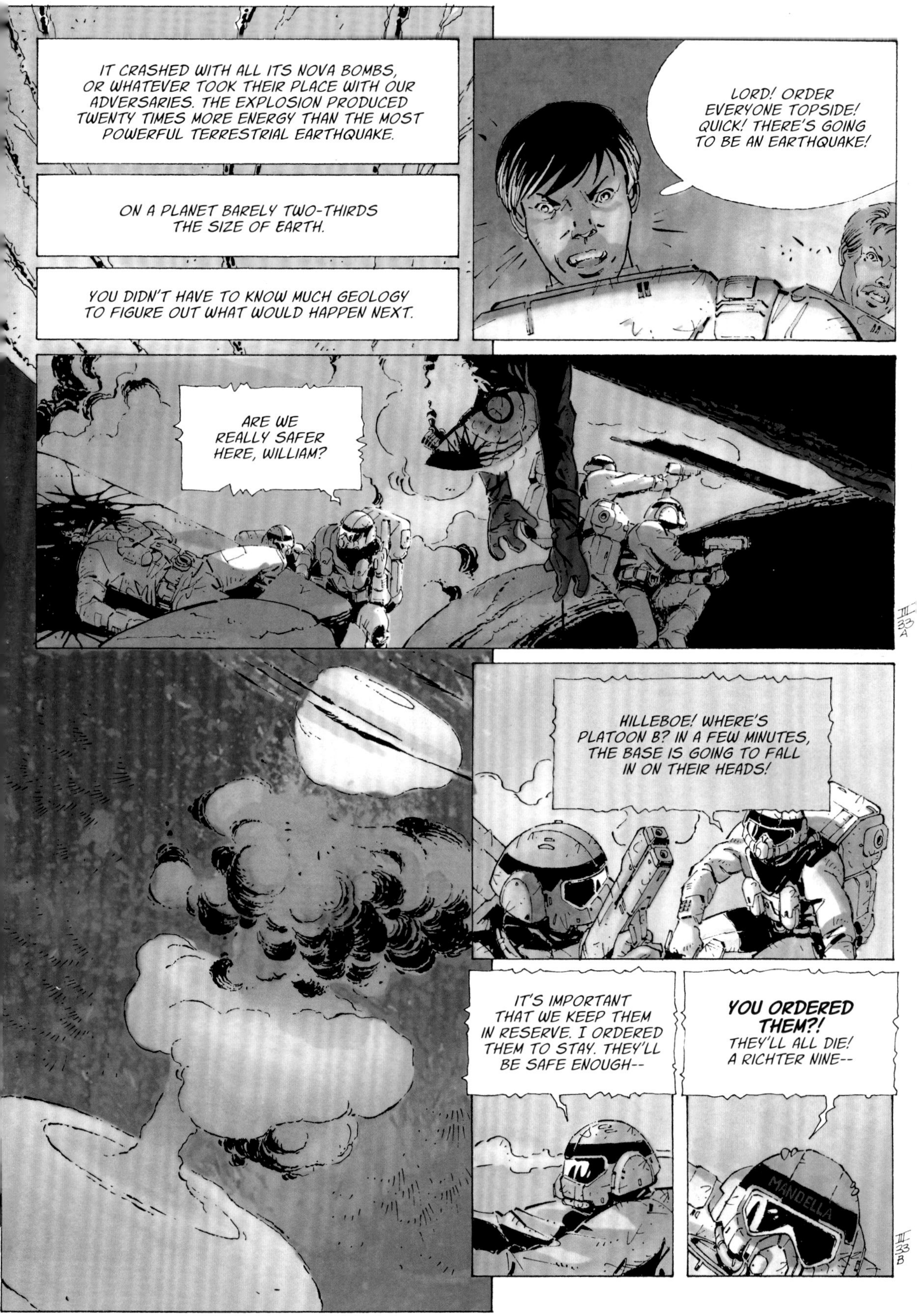
IT CRASHED WITH ALL ITS NOVA BOMBS, OR WHATEVER TOOK THEIR PLACE WITH OUR ADVERSARIES. THE EXPLOSION PRODUCED TWENTY TIMES MORE ENERGY THAN THE MOST POWERFUL TERRESTRIAL EARTHQUAKE.
ON A PLANET BARELY TWO-THIRDS THE SIZE OF EARTH.
YOU DIDN'T HAVE TO KNOW MUCH GEOLOGY TO FIGURE OUT WHAT WOULD HAPPEN NEXT.
LORD! ORDER EVERYONE TOPSIDE! QUICK! THERE'S GOING TO BE AN EARTHQUAKE!
ARE WE REALLY SAFER HERE, WILLIAM?
III 33 A
HILLEBOE! WHERE'S PLATOON B? IN A FEW MINUTES, THE BASE IS GOING TO FALL IN ON THEIR HEADS!
IT'S IMPORTANT THAT WE KEEP THEM IN RESERVE. I ORDERED THEM TO STAY. THEY'LL BE SAFE ENOUGH--
YOU ORDERED THEM?! THEY'LL ALL DIE! A RICHTER NINE--
MANDELLA
III 33 B

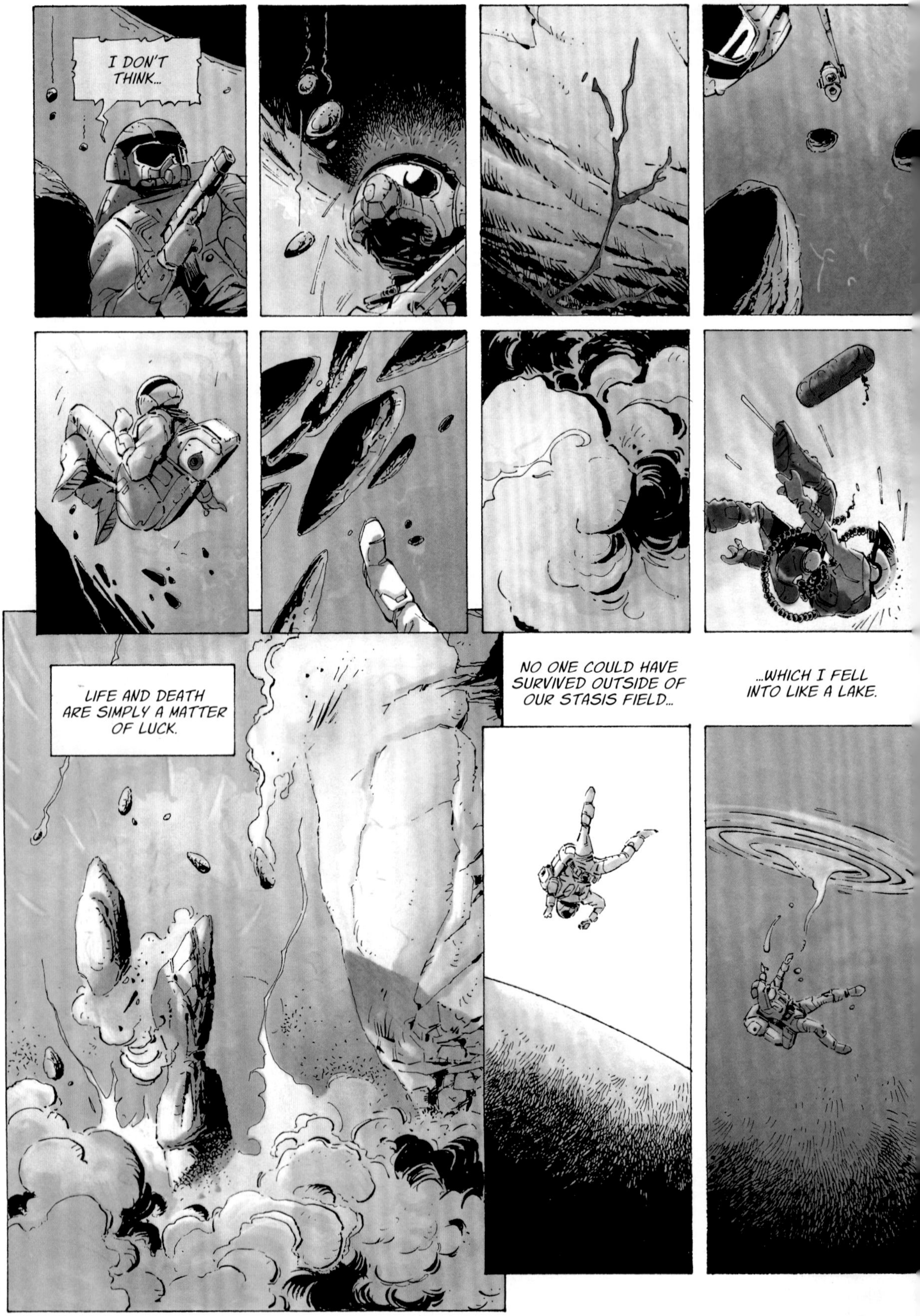
I DON'T THINK...
LIFE AND DEATH ARE SIMPLY A MATTER OF LUCK.
NO ONE COULD HAVE SURVIVED OUTSIDE OF OUR STASIS FIELD...
...WHICH I FELL INTO LIKE A LAKE.

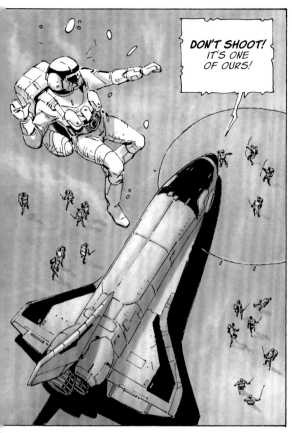

DON'T SHOOT! IT'S ONE OF OURS!

OTHERS HAD ALREADY FOUND REFUGE THERE...

CHARLIE? DIANA?

WILLIAM?!

OUR TRANSPORT HAD BEEN IN THE AIR. IF THERE WAS ANYONE ALIVE OUTSIDE, THEY WERE TAURANS.

FOX! DESOLA! KAYIBANDA! TAKE THE NOVA BOMB AWAY FROM THE SCOUT AND CARRY IT OUT TO THE EDGES OF THE STASIS FIELD!

AND THEN, WILLIAM?

WE TRIGGER THE BOMB. IT CAN'T DETONATE IN HERE. THEN WE ROLL IT OUT AND IT VAPORIZES EVERYTHING FOR KILOMETERS.

THE TAURANS!

THEY COULDN'T HAVE TIMED IT BETTER.

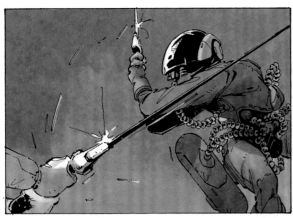

I THOUGHT OF A PROPHECY OF EINSTEIN'S...

"I DON'T KNOW WHAT WEAPONS WILL BE USED IN THE THIRD WORLD WAR, BUT THE FOURTH WILL SEE THE SURVIVORS..."

"...ARMED WITH CLUBS!"

THEY WEREN'T AS GOOD AS WE WERE WITH CLUBS AND SWORDS. WE CUT THE FIRST WAVE TO PIECES... BUT WE DIDN'T KNOW HOW MANY WERE STILL WAITING FOR US OUTSIDE...

WE POINTED OUR BOMB TOWARD THE EXTERIOR...

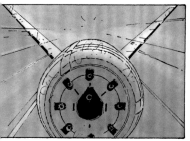

AND WE PUSHED IT FORWARD...

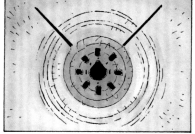

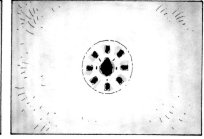

SOME SECONDS LATER, THE TEMPERATURE OUTSIDE WAS AS HOT AS THE INSIDE OF A STAR. WE FELT THE STASIS FIELD SETTLE TO THE BOTTOM OF THE CRATER CAUSED BY THE EXPLOSION.

IT TOOK SIX DAYS FOR THE SURROUNDING RADIATION TO REACH A REASONABLE LEVEL. WE SCATTERED OURSELVES AROUND THE PERIMETER AND CUT OFF THE STASIS FIELD GENERATOR.

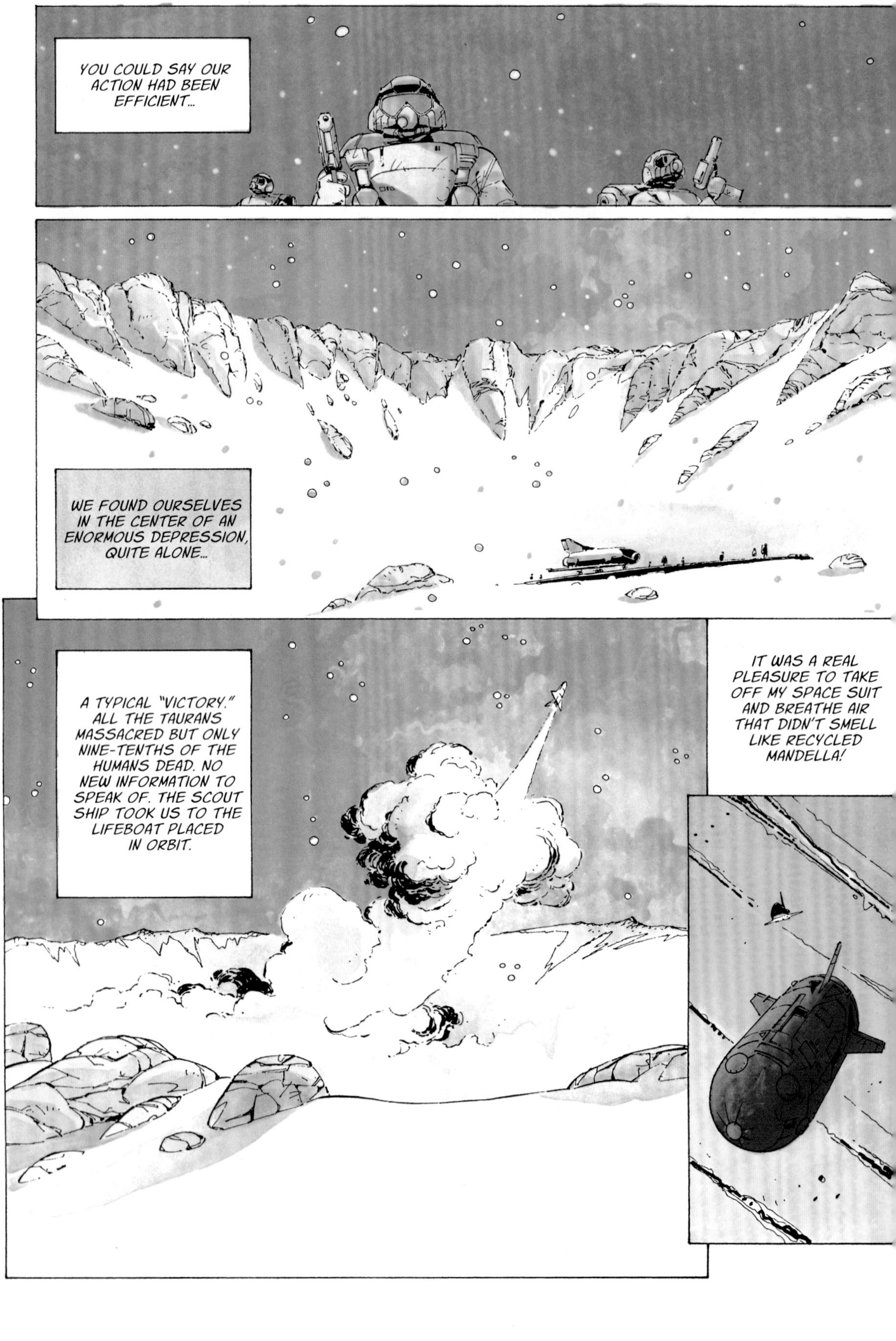
YOU COULD SAY OUR ACTION HAD BEEN EFFICIENT...
WE FOUND OURSELVES IN THE CENTER OF AN ENORMOUS DEPRESSION, QUITE ALONE...
A TYPICAL "VICTORY." ALL THE TAURANS MASSACRED BUT ONLY NINE-TENTHS OF THE HUMANS DEAD. NO NEW INFORMATION TO SPEAK OF. THE SCOUT SHIP TOOK US TO THE LIFEBOAT PLACED IN ORBIT.
IT WAS A REAL PLEASURE TO TAKE OFF MY SPACE SUIT AND BREATHE AIR THAT DIDN'T SMELL LIKE RECYCLED MANDELLA!

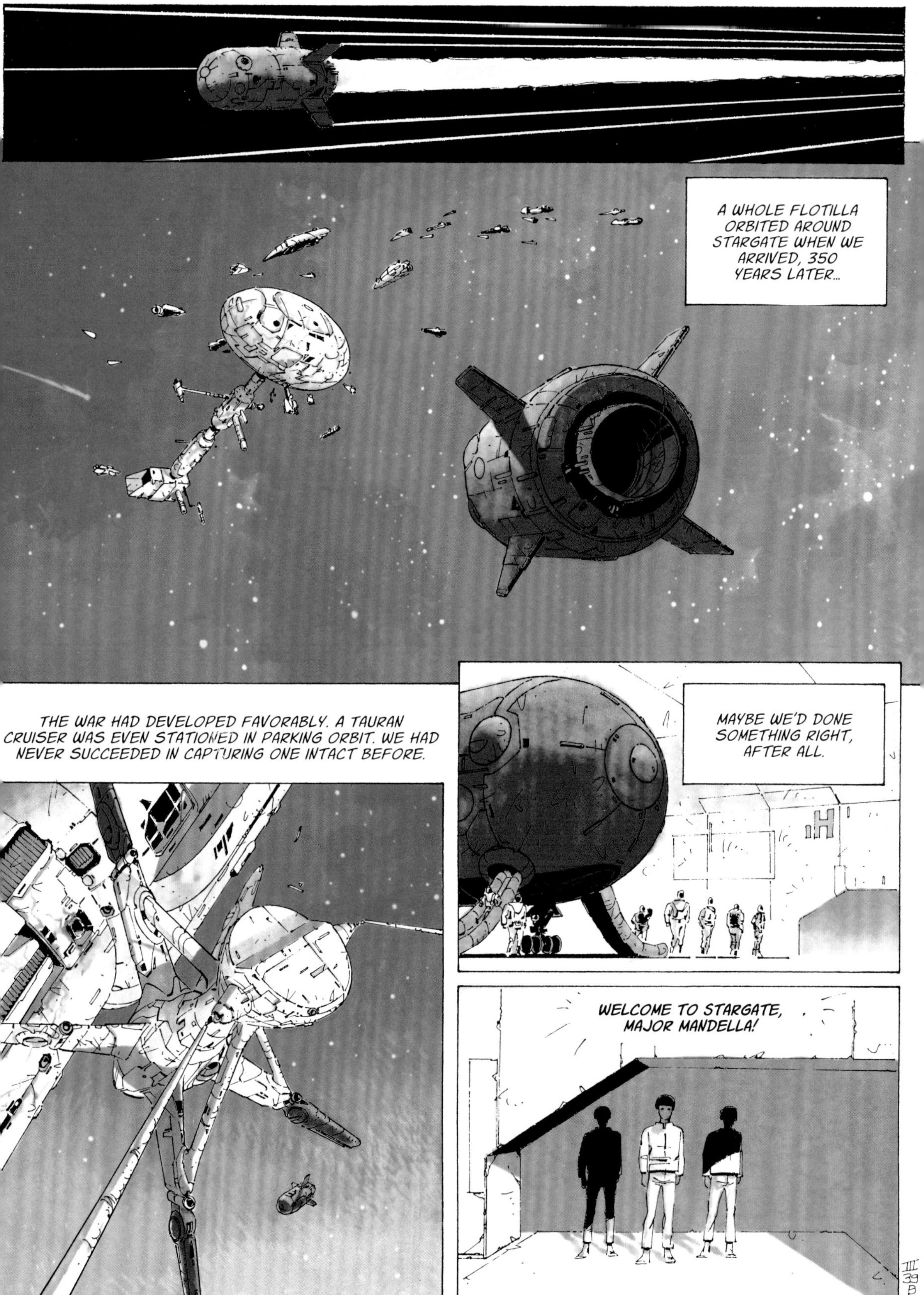
A WHOLE FLOTILLA ORBITED AROUND STARGATE WHEN WE ARRIVED, 350 YEARS LATER...
THE WAR HAD DEVELOPED FAVORABLY. A TAURAN CRUISER WAS EVEN STATIONED IN PARKING ORBIT. WE HAD NEVER SUCCEEDED IN CAPTURING ONE INTACT BEFORE.
MAYBE WE'D DONE SOMETHING RIGHT, AFTER ALL.
WELCOME TO STARGATE, MAJOR MANDELLA!
III 39 B

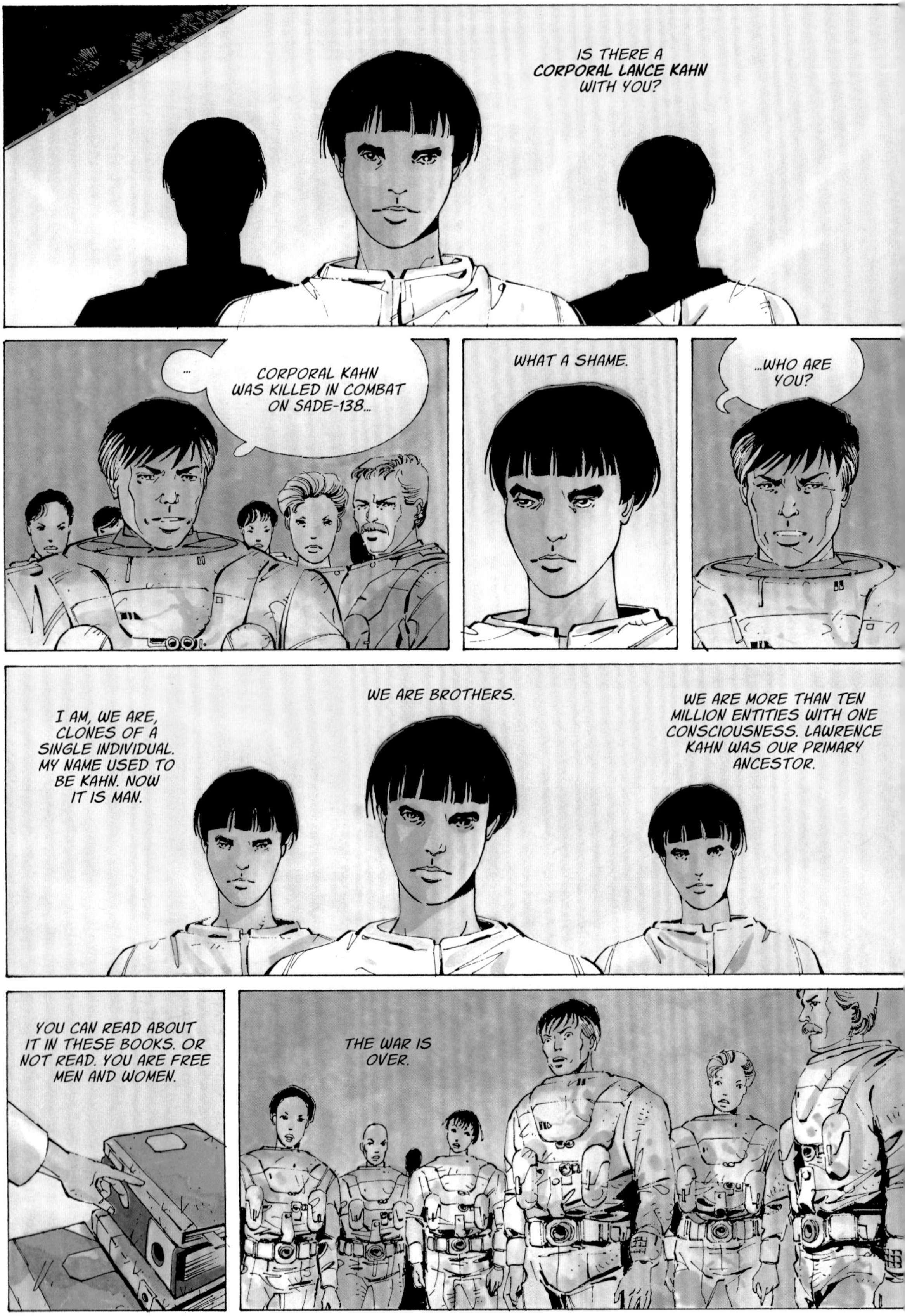
IS THERE A CORPORAL LANCE KAHN WITH YOU?
...
CORPORAL KAHN WAS KILLED IN COMBAT ON SADE-138...
WHAT A SHAME.
...WHO ARE YOU?
WE ARE BROTHERS.
I AM, WE ARE, CLONES OF A SINGLE INDIVIDUAL. MY NAME USED TO BE KAHN. NOW IT IS MAN.
WE ARE MORE THAN TEN MILLION ENTITIES WITH ONE CONSCIOUSNESS. LAWRENCE KAHN WAS OUR PRIMARY ANCESTOR.
YOU CAN READ ABOUT IT IN THESE BOOKS. OR NOT READ. YOU ARE FREE MEN AND WOMEN.
THE WAR IS OVER.

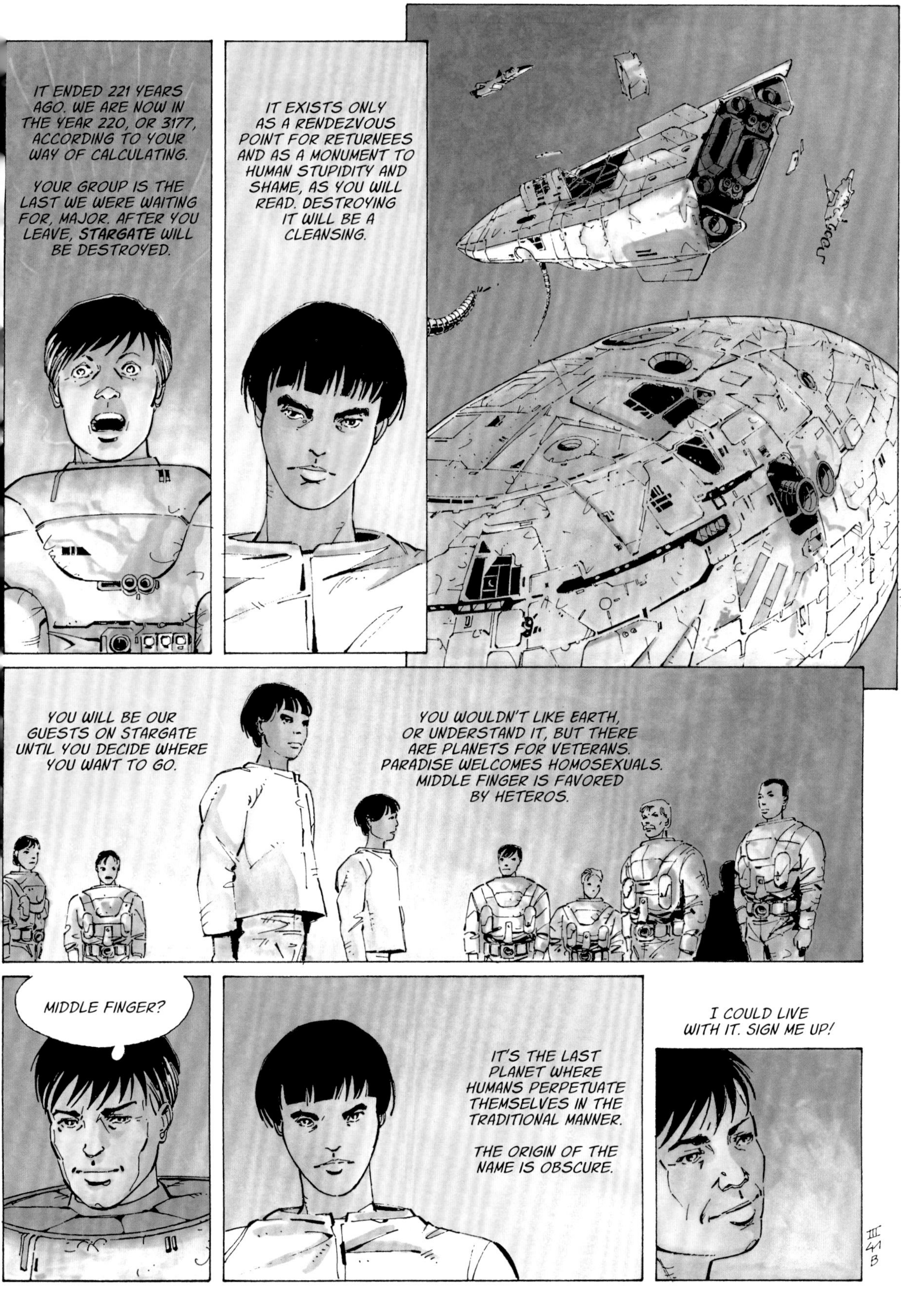

IT ENDED 221 YEARS AGO. WE ARE NOW IN THE YEAR 220, OR 3177, ACCORDING TO YOUR WAY OF CALCULATING.
YOUR GROUP IS THE LAST WE WERE WAITING FOR, MAJOR. AFTER YOU LEAVE, STARGATE WILL BE DESTROYED.
IT EXISTS ONLY AS A RENDEZVOUS POINT FOR RETURNEES AND AS A MONUMENT TO HUMAN STUPIDITY AND SHAME, AS YOU WILL READ. DESTROYING IT WILL BE A CLEANSING.
III 42
YOU WILL BE OUR GUESTS ON STARGATE UNTIL YOU DECIDE WHERE YOU WANT TO GO.
YOU WOULDN'T LIKE EARTH, OR UNDERSTAND IT, BUT THERE ARE PLANETS FOR VETERANS. PARADISE WELCOMES HOMOSEXUALS. MIDDLE FINGER IS FAVORED BY HETEROS.
MIDDLE FINGER?
IT'S THE LAST PLANET WHERE HUMANS PERPETUATE THEMSELVES IN THE TRADITIONAL MANNER.
THE ORIGIN OF THE NAME IS OBSCURE.
I COULD LIVE WITH IT. SIGN ME UP!
III 41 B

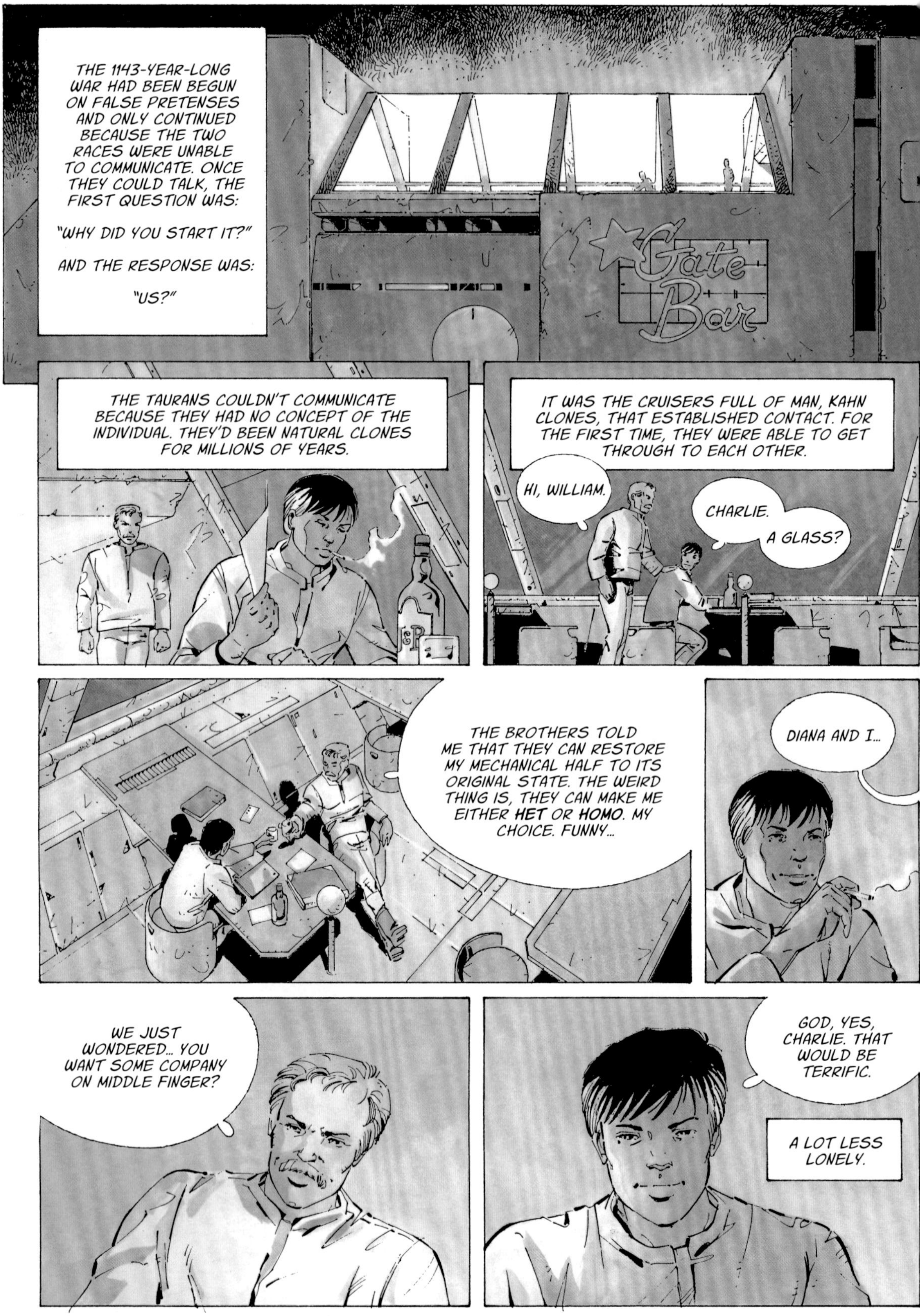
THE 1143-YEAR-LONG WAR HAD BEEN BEGUN ON FALSE PRETENSES AND ONLY CONTINUED BECAUSE THE TWO RACES WERE UNABLE TO COMMUNICATE. ONCE THEY COULD TALK, THE FIRST QUESTION WAS:
"WHY DID YOU START IT?"
AND THE RESPONSE WAS:
"US?"
Gate Bar
THE TAURANS COULDN'T COMMUNICATE BECAUSE THEY HAD NO CONCEPT OF THE INDIVIDUAL. THEY'D BEEN NATURAL CLONES FOR MILLIONS OF YEARS.
IT WAS THE CRUISERS FULL OF MAN, KAHN CLONES, THAT ESTABLISHED CONTACT. FOR THE FIRST TIME, THEY WERE ABLE TO GET THROUGH TO EACH OTHER.
HI, WILLIAM.
CHARLIE.
A GLASS?
THE BROTHERS TOLD ME THAT THEY CAN RESTORE MY MECHANICAL HALF TO ITS ORIGINAL STATE. THE WEIRD THING IS, THEY CAN MAKE ME EITHER **HET** OR **HOMO**. MY CHOICE. FUNNY...
DIANA AND I...
WE JUST WONDERED... YOU WANT SOME COMPANY ON MIDDLE FINGER?
GOD, YES, CHARLIE. THAT WOULD BE TERRIFIC.
A LOT LESS LONELY.

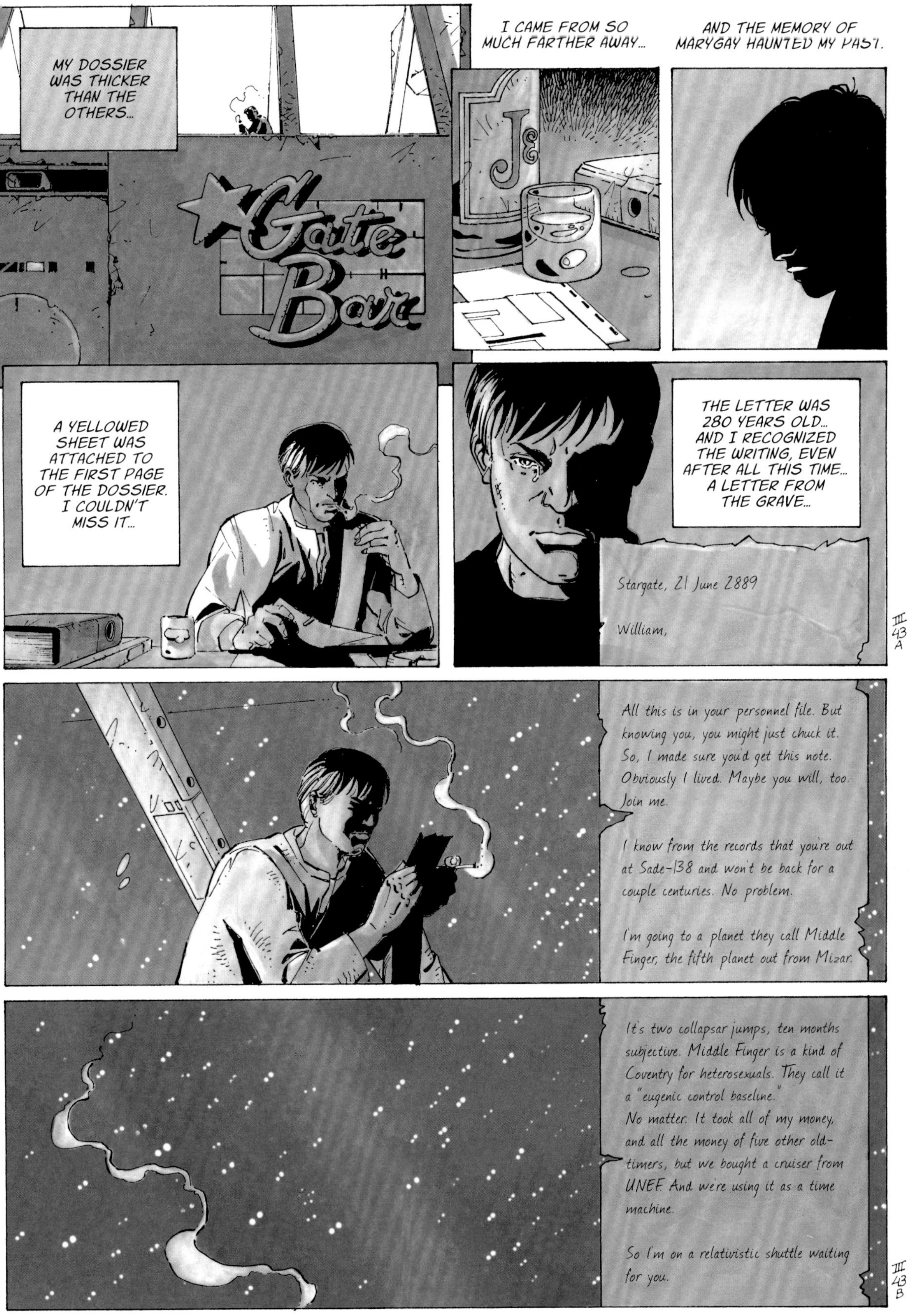
MY DOSSIER WAS THICKER THAN THE OTHERS...
Gate Bar
I CAME FROM SO MUCH FARTHER AWAY...
AND THE MEMORY OF MARYGAY HAUNTED MY PAST.
A YELLOWED SHEET WAS ATTACHED TO THE FIRST PAGE OF THE DOSSIER. I COULDN'T MISS IT...
THE LETTER WAS 280 YEARS OLD... AND I RECOGNIZED THE WRITING, EVEN AFTER ALL THIS TIME... A LETTER FROM THE GRAVE...
Stargate, 21 June 2889
William,
III 43 A
All this is in your personnel file. But knowing you, you might just chuck it. So, I made sure you'd get this note. Obviously I lived. Maybe you will, too. Join me.
I know from the records that you're out at Sade-138 and won't be back for a couple centuries. No problem.
I'm going to a planet they call Middle Finger, the fifth planet out from Mizar.
It's two collapsar jumps, ten months subjective. Middle Finger is a kind of Coventry for heterosexuals. They call it a "eugenic control baseline."
No matter. It took all of my money, and all the money of five other old-timers, but we bought a cruiser from UNEF. And we're using it as a time machine.
So I'm on a relativistic shuttle waiting for you.
III 43 B

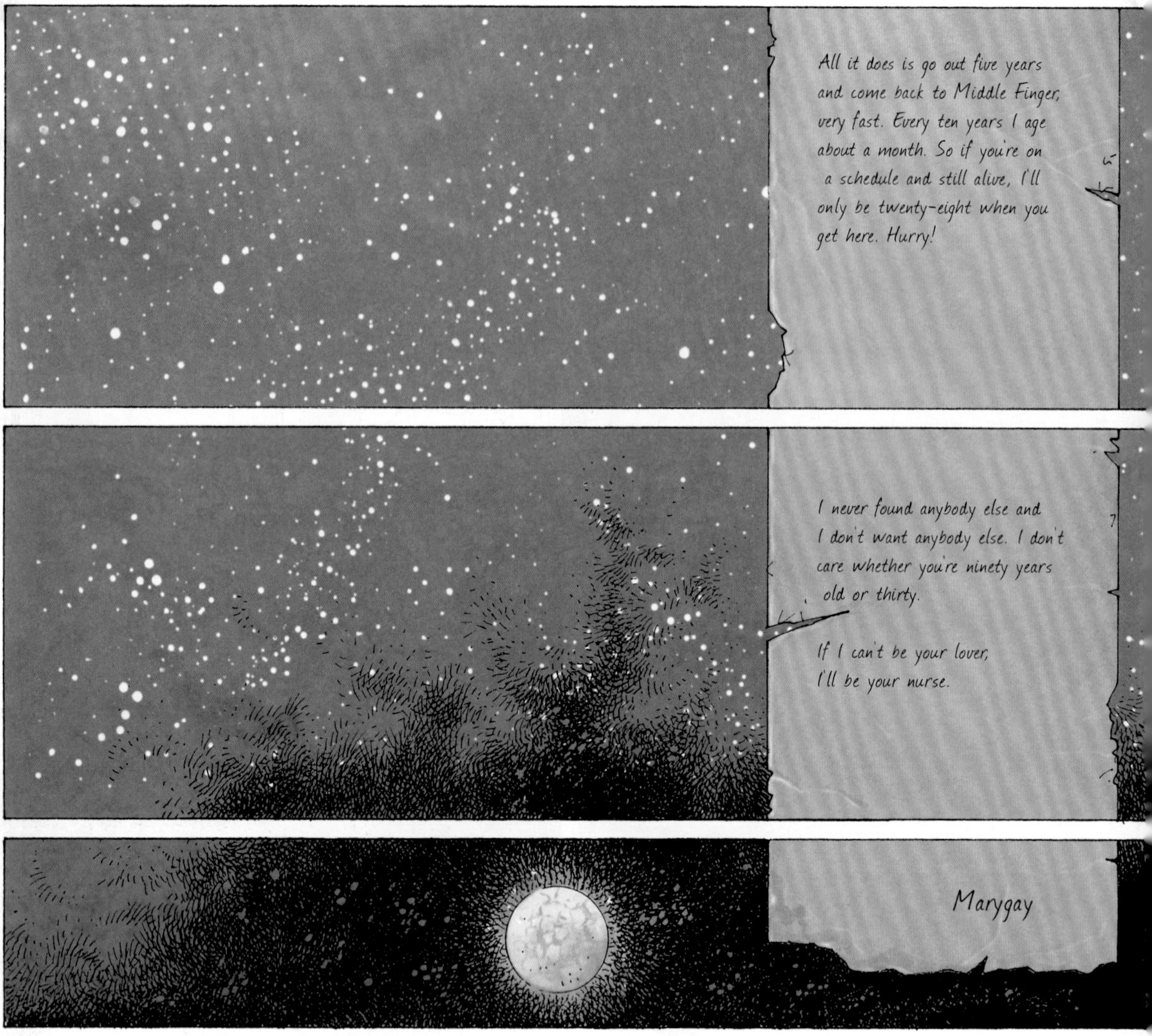
All it does is go out five years and come back to Middle Finger, very fast. Every ten years I age about a month. So if you're on a schedule and still alive, I'll only be twenty-eight when you get here. Hurry!
I never found anybody else and I don't want anybody else. I don't care whether you're ninety years old or thirty.
If I can't be your lover, I'll be your nurse.
Marygay

OLD-TIMER HAS FIRST BOY

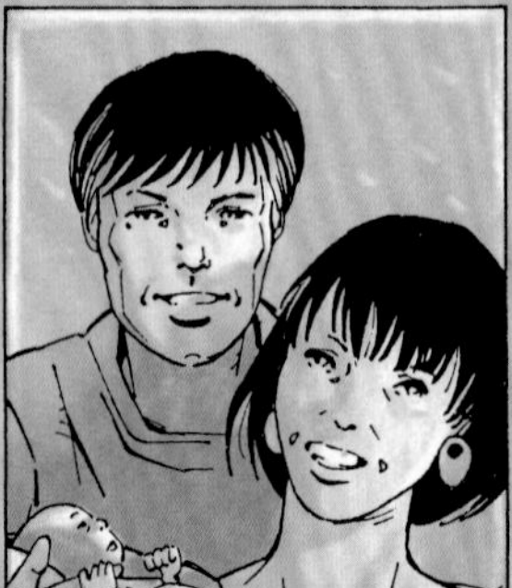

Marygay Potter-Mandella (24 Post Road, Paxton) gave birth on 25 August 3183 to a fine baby boy, 3.1 kilos.

Marygay lays claim to being the second-"oldest" resident of Middle Finger, having been born in 1990. She fought through most of the Forever War and then waited for her mate on the time shuttle for 286 years.

The baby, not yet named, was delivered at home with the help of a friend of the family, Dr. Diana Alsever-Moore.

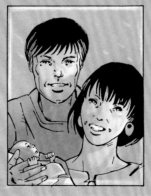

MARVANO / Joe W. Haldeman
SUMMER '89

COLOUR: BRUNO MARCHAND

COVER GALLERY

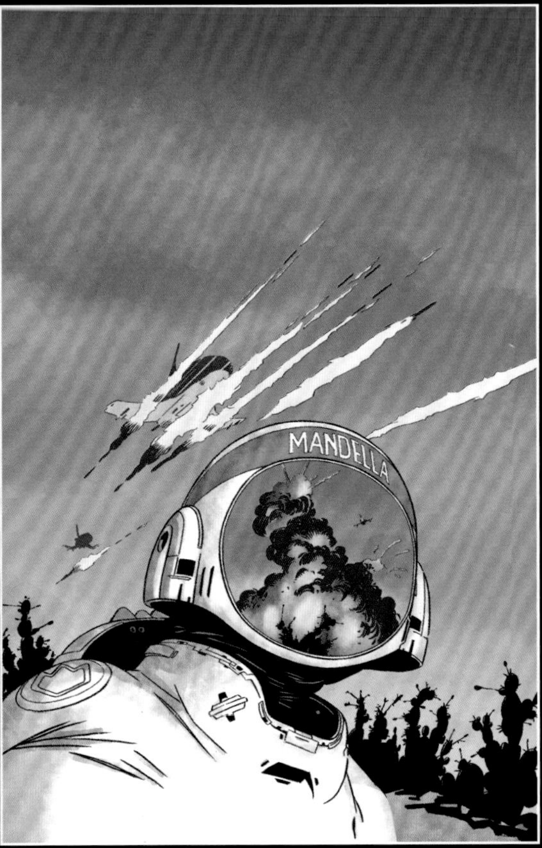
MANDELLA

#1 COVER A **MARVANO & JASON WORDIE**

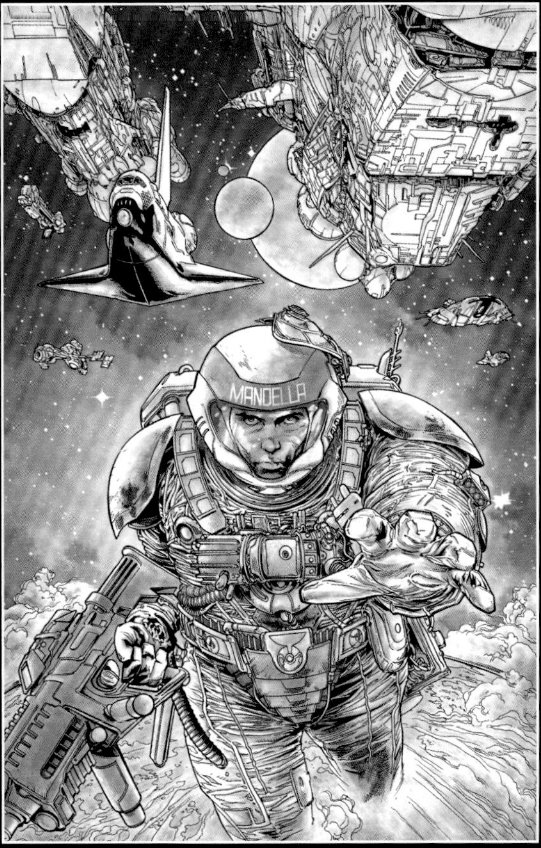
MANDELLA

#1 COVER B **STEVE KURTH**

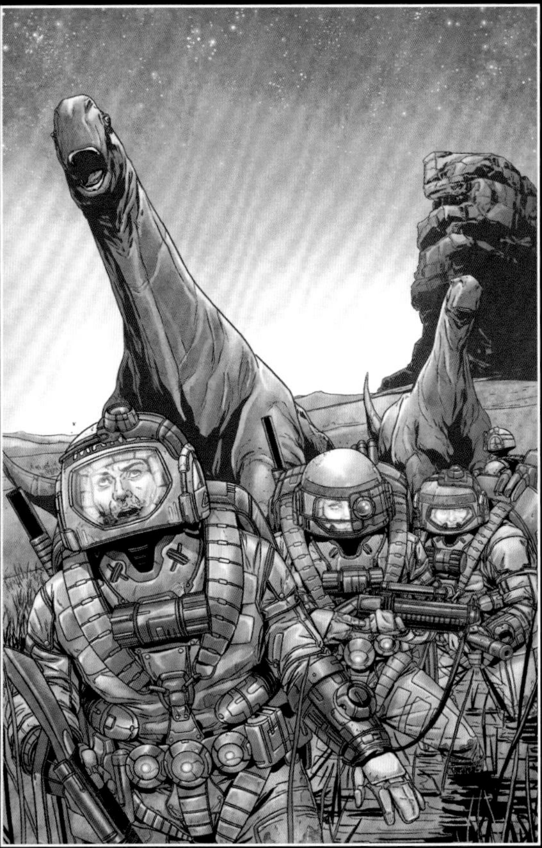

#1 COVER C **MARC LAMING & DYLAN TEAGUE**

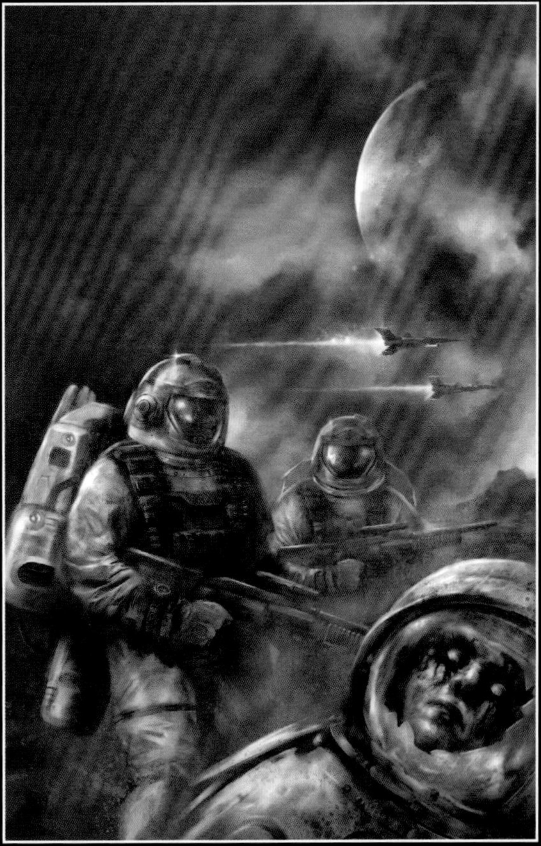

#1 COVER D **NICK PERCIVAL**

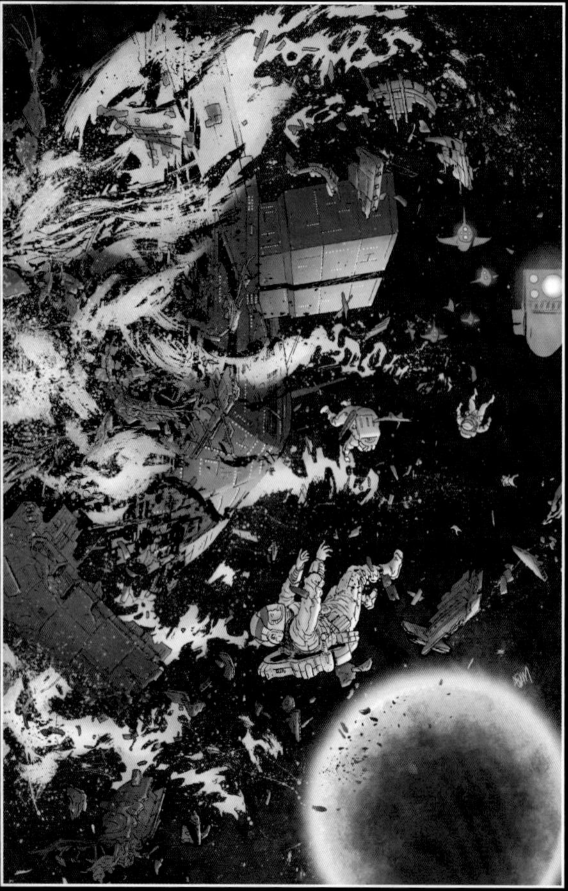

#1 COVER E **DAM GORHAM & DEE CUNLIFFE**

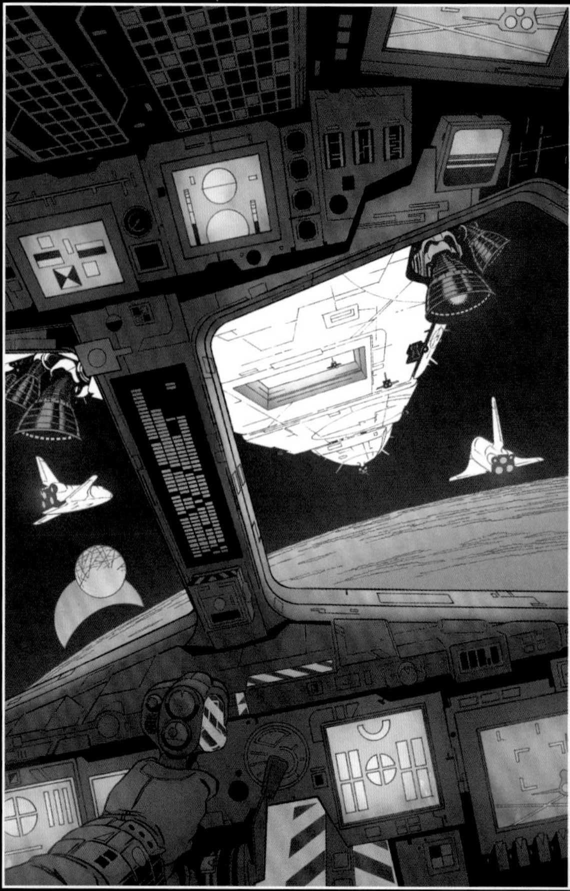

#2 COVER A **MARVANO**

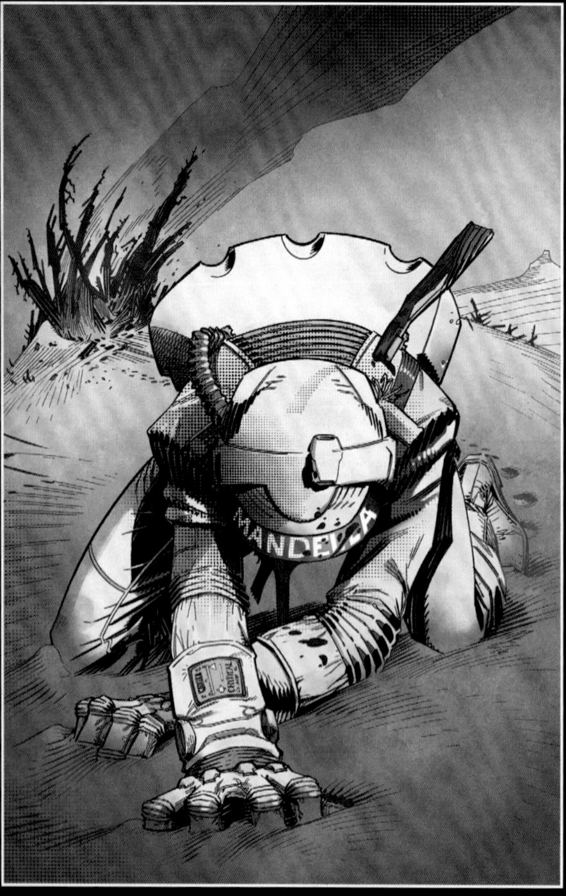

#2 COVER B **JOHN MCCREA & MIKE SPICER**

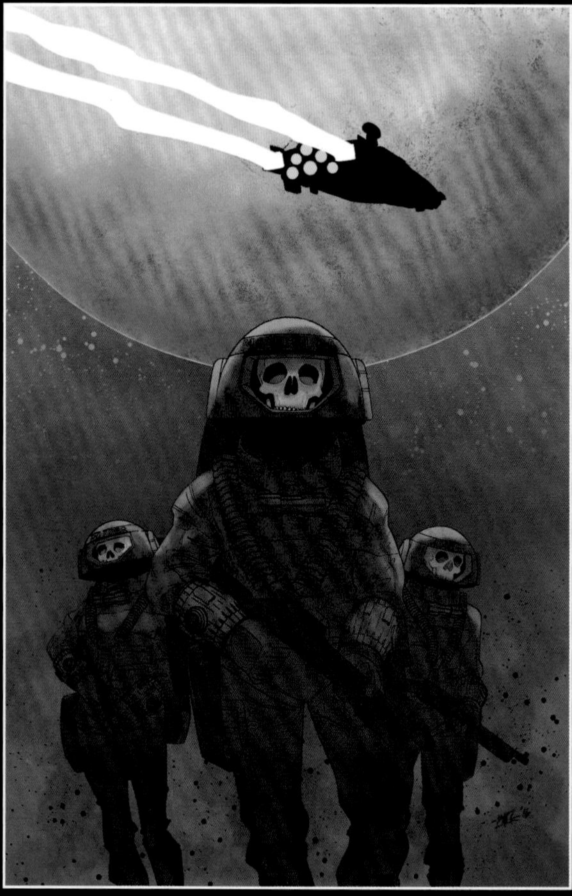

#2 COVER C **I.N.J. CULBARD**

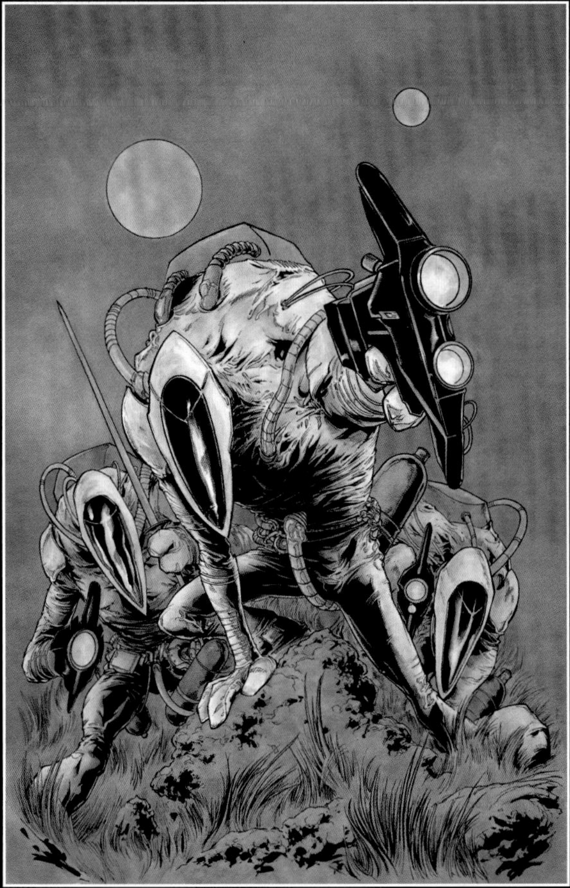

#2 COVER D **STEVE KURTH**

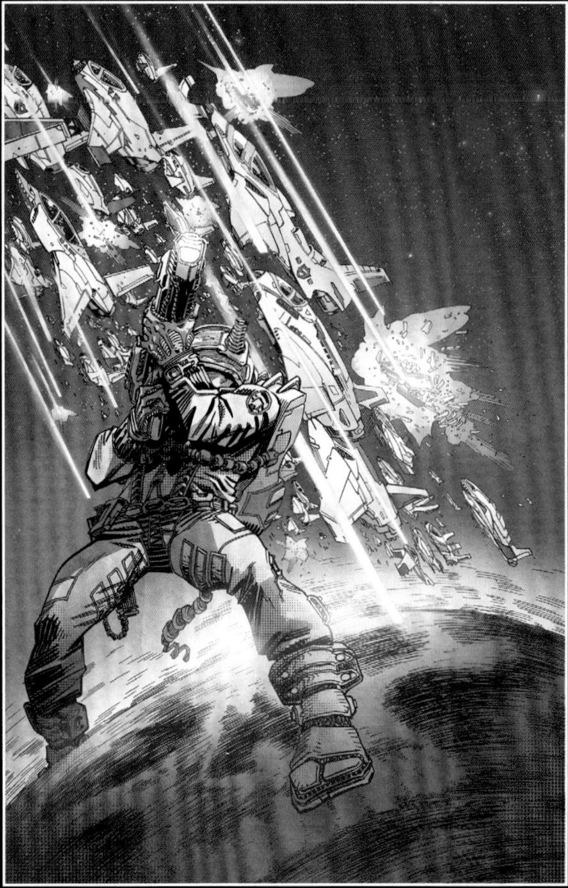

#3 COVER A **JOHN MCCREA & MIKE SPICER**

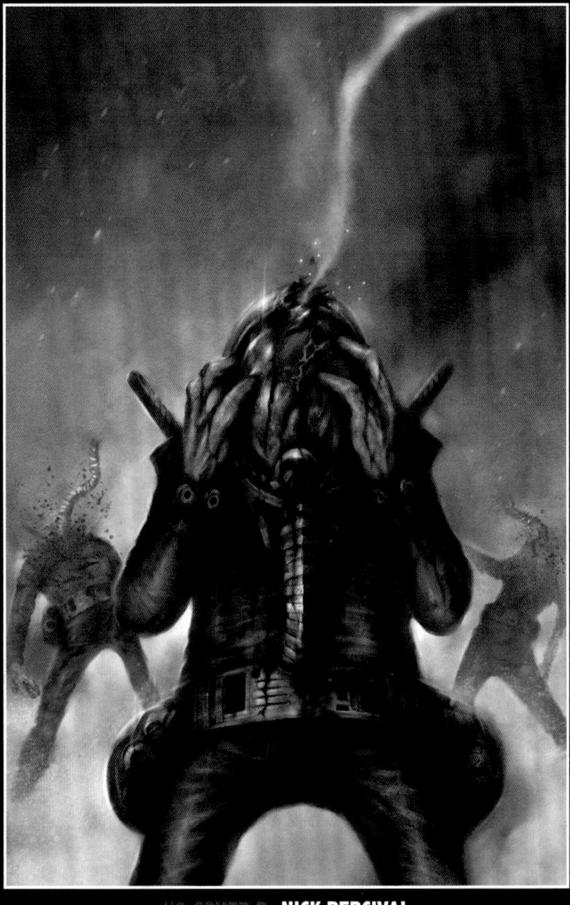

#3 COVER B **NICK PERCIVAL**

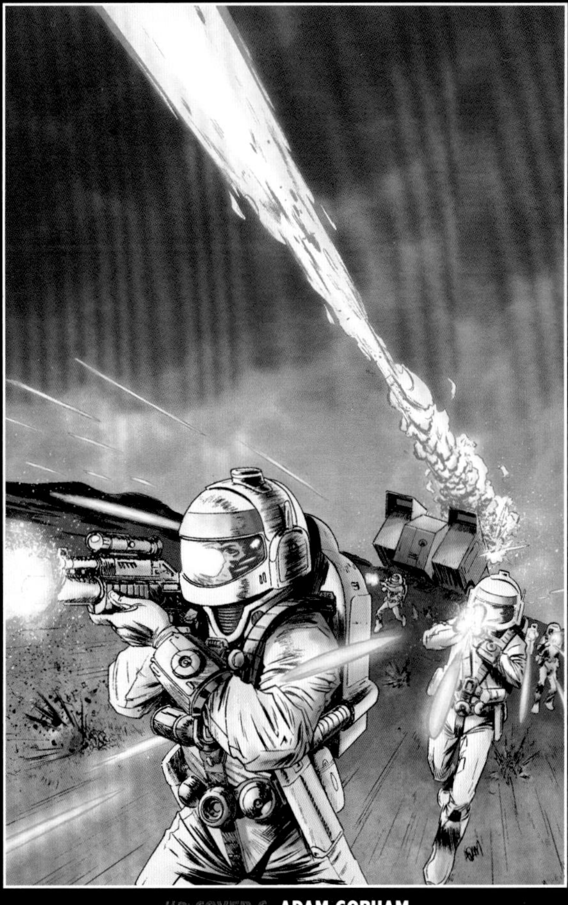

#3 COVER C **ADAM GORHAM**

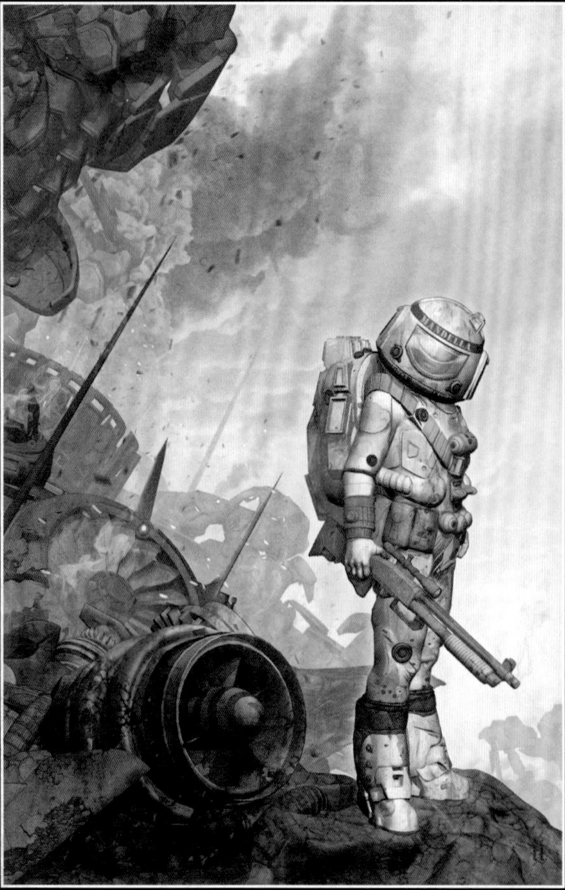

#4 COVER A **FABIO LISTRANI**

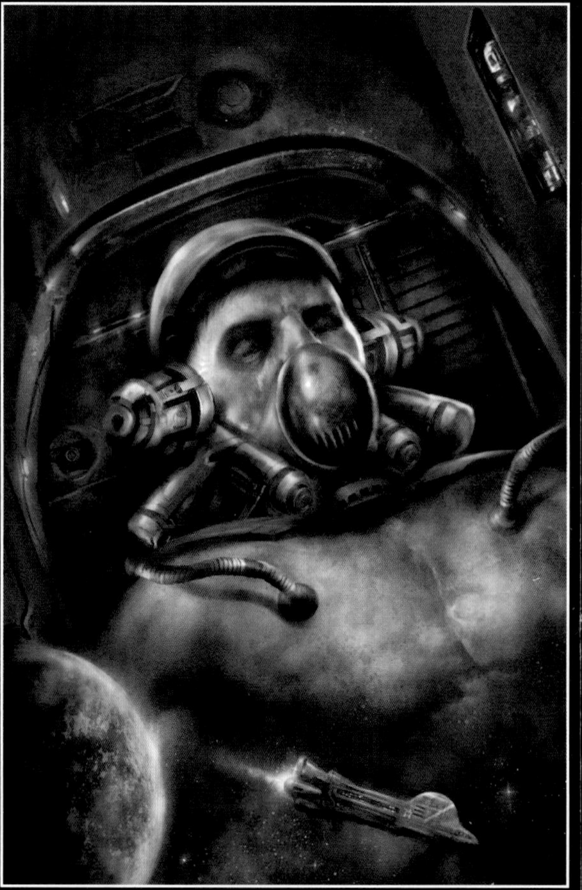

#4 COVER B **NICK PERCIVAL**

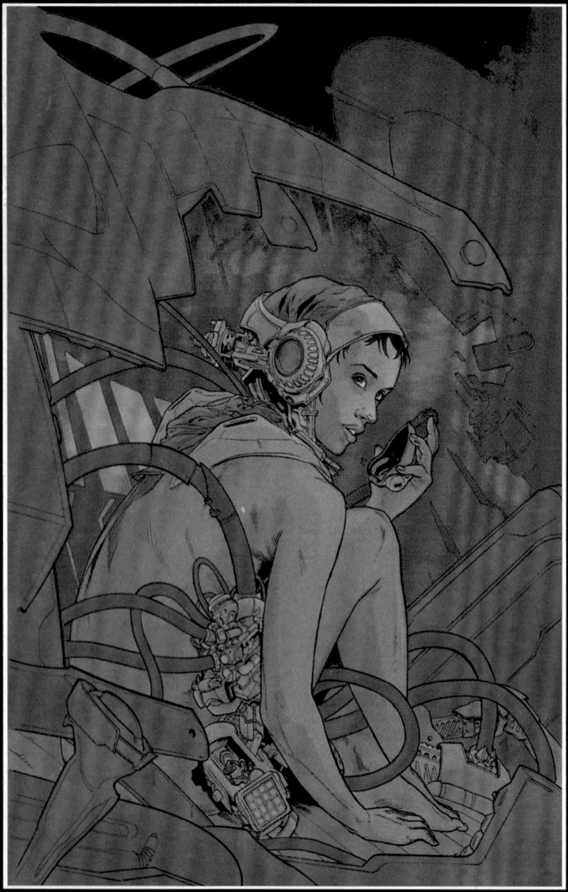

#4 COVER C **STEVE KURTH**

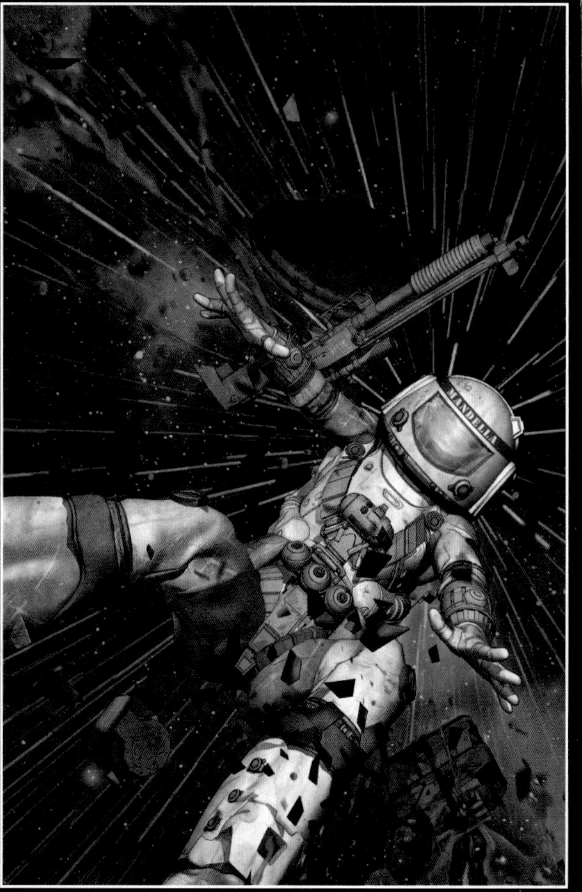
MANDELLA

#5 COVER A **FABIO LISTRANI**

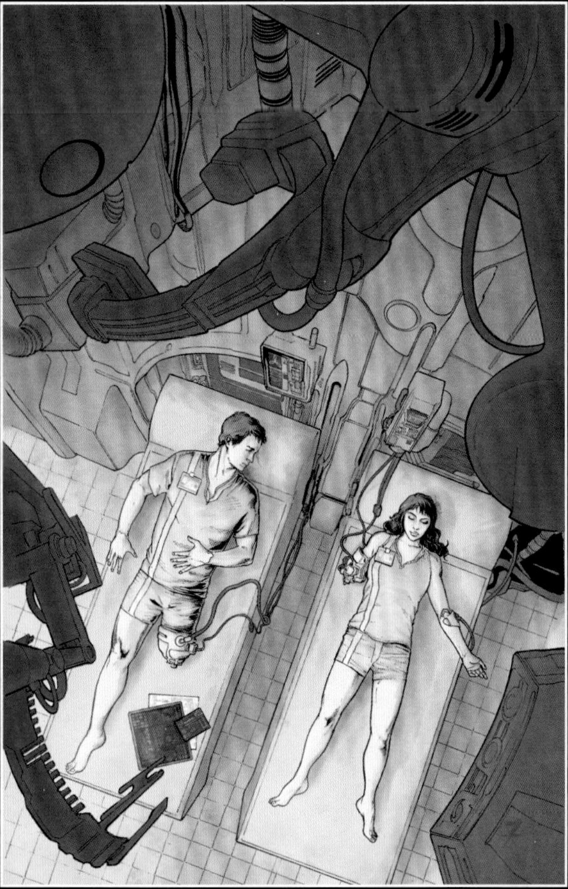

#5 COVER B **STEVE KURTH**

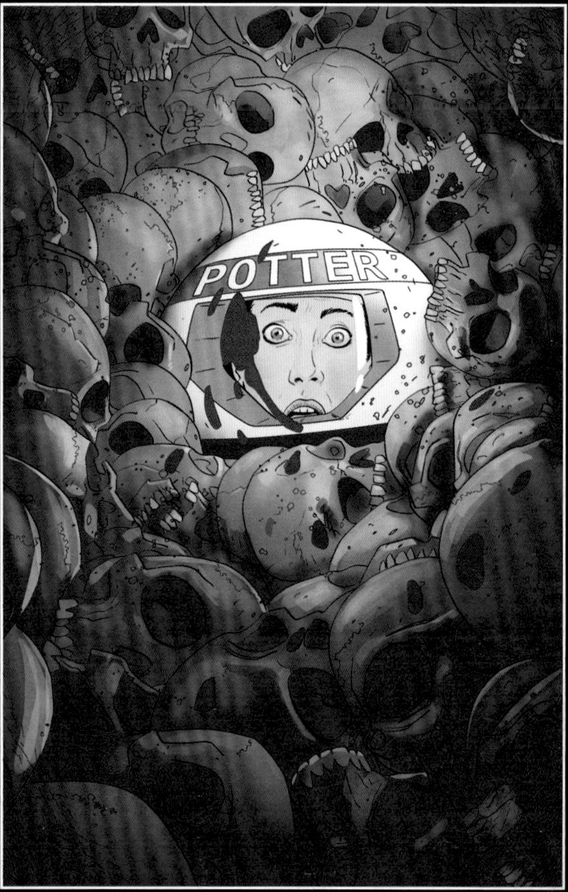
POTTER

#5 COVER C **I.N.J. CULBARD**

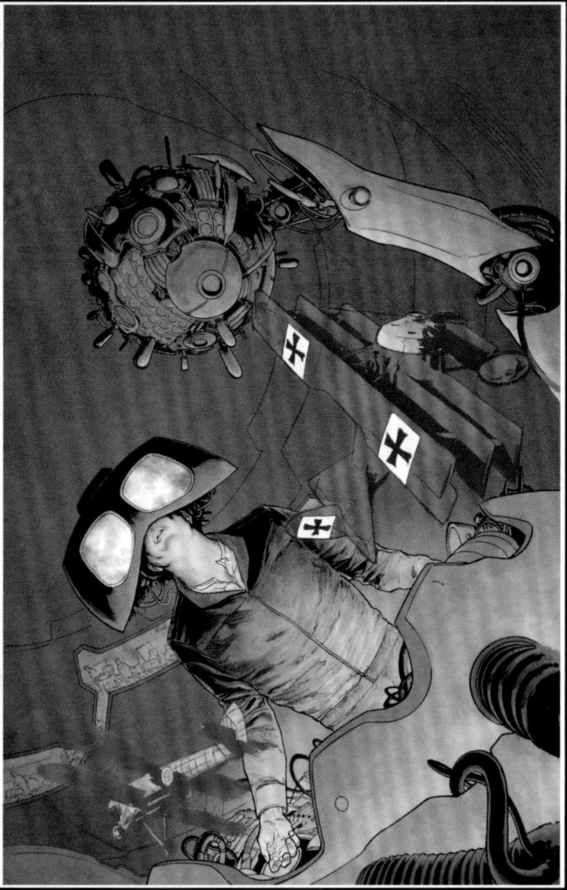

#6 COVER A **STEVE KURTH**

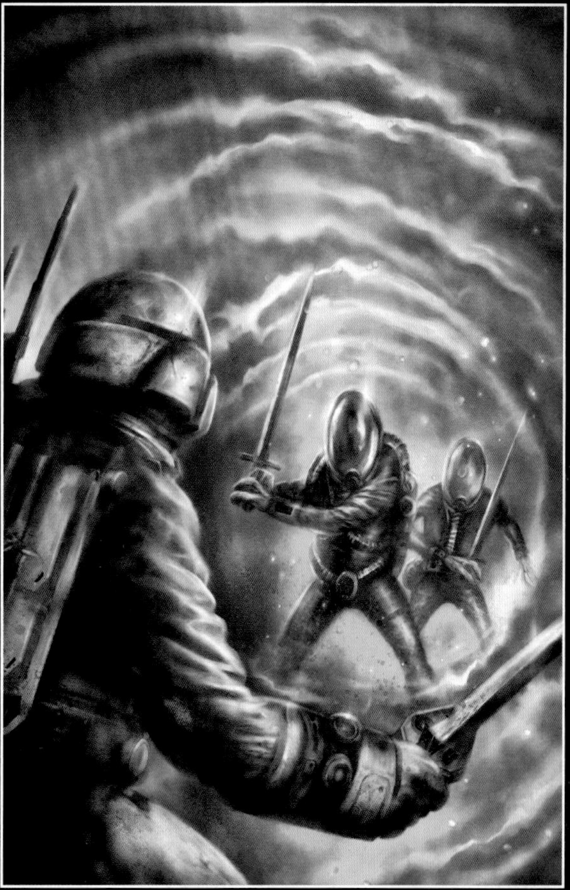

#6 COVER B **NICK PERCIVAL**

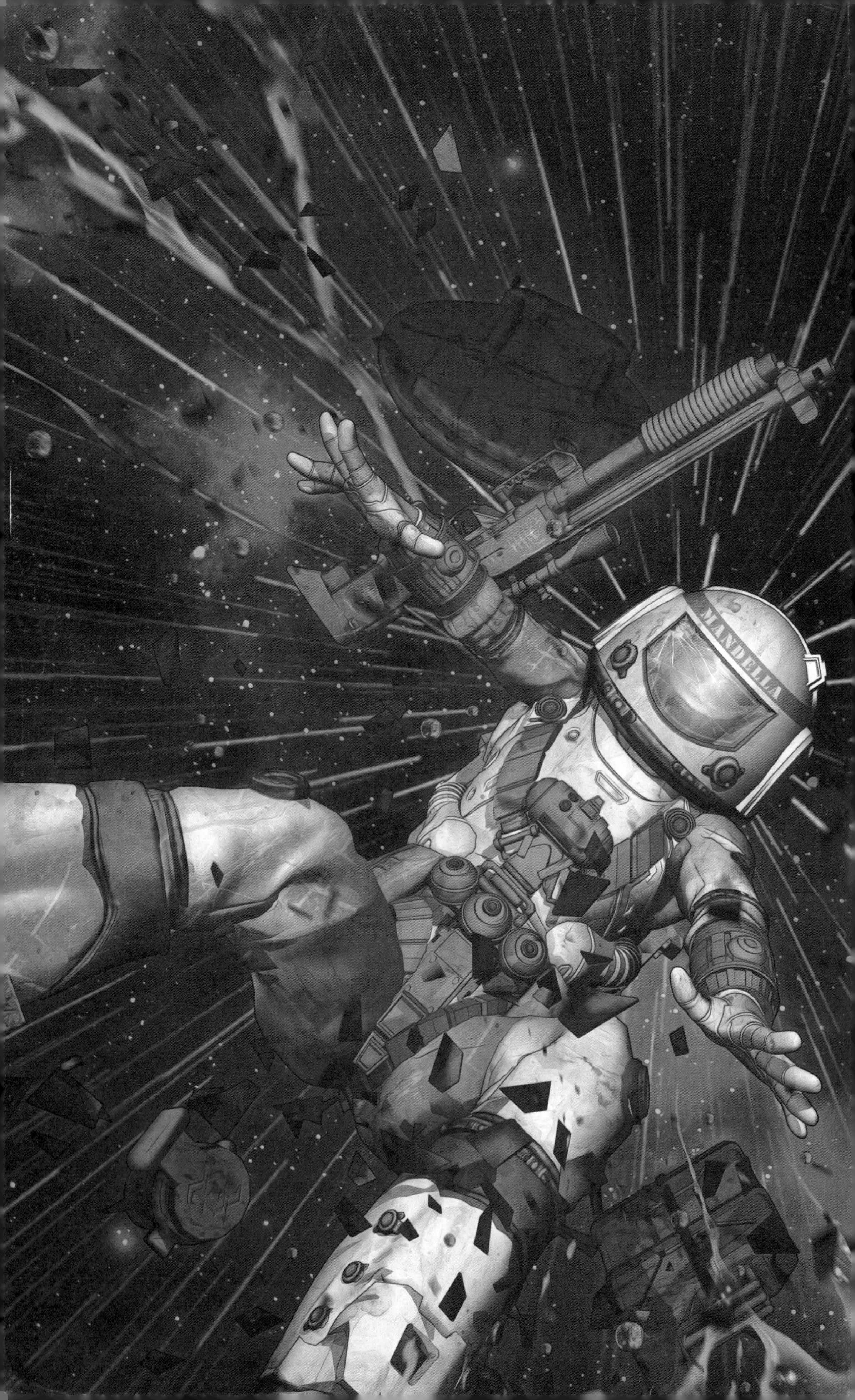
MANDELLA